Studies in Russia and East Europe

This series includes books on general, political, historical, economic and cultural themes relating to Russia and East Europe written or edited by members of the School of Slavonic and East European Studies, University College London, or by authors working in association with the School.

Titles include:

Roger Bartlett and Karen Schönwälder (*editors*)
THE GERMAN LANDS AND EASTERN EUROPE

John Channon (*editor*)
POLITICS, SOCIETY AND STALINISM IN THE USSR

Stanislaw Eile
LITERATURE AND NATIONALISM IN PARTITIONED POLAND, 1795–1918

Rebecca Haynes
ROMANIAN POLICY TOWARDS GERMANY, 1936–40

Geoffrey Hosking and Robert Service (*editors*)
RUSSIAN NATIONALISM, PAST AND PRESENT

Lindsey Hughes (*editor*)
PETER THE GREAT AND THE WEST
New Perspectives

Krystyna Iglicka and Keith Sword (*editors*)
THE CHALLENGE OF EAST–WEST MIGRATION FOR POLAND

Andres Kasekamp
THE RADICAL RIGHT IN INTERWAR ESTONIA

Stephen Lovell
THE RUSSIAN READING REVOLUTION

Marja Nissinen
LATVIA'S TRANSITION TO A MARKET ECONOMY

Danuta Paszyn
THE SOVIET ATTITUDE TO POLITICAL AND SOCIAL CHANGE IN CENTRAL AMERICA, 1979–90

Vesna Popovski
NATIONAL MINORITIES AND CITIZENSHIP RIGHTS IN LITHUANIA, 1988–93

Alan Smith
THE RETURN TO EUROPE
The Reintegration of Eastern Europe into the European Economy

Jeremy Smith
THE BOLSHEVIKS AND THE NATIONAL QUESTION, 1917–23

Jeanne Sutherland
SCHOOLING IN THE NEW RUSSIA

Kieran Williams and Dennis Deletant
SECURITY INTELLIGENCE SERVICES IN NEW DEMOCRACIES
The Czech Republic, Slovakia and Romania

Studies in Russia and East Europe
Series Standing Order ISBN 0–333–71018-5
(*outside North America only*)

You can receive future titles in this series as they are published by placing a standing order. Please contact your bookseller or, in case of difficulty, write to us at the address below with your name and address, the title of the series and the ISBN quoted above.

Customer Services Department, Macmillan Distribution Ltd, Houndmills, Basingstoke, Hampshire RG21 6XS, England

Peter the Great and the West

New Perspectives

Edited by

Lindsey Hughes
Professor of Russian History
School of Slavonic and East European Studies
University College London

in association with
School of Slavonic and East European Studies,
University College London, and
National Maritime Museum, Greenwich

palgrave

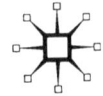

© School of Slavonic and East European Studies, University College London and National Maritime Museum 2001

All rights reserved. No reproduction, copy or transmission of this publication may be made without written permission.

No paragraph of this publication may be reproduced, copied or transmitted save with written permission or in accordance with the provisions of the Copyright, Designs and Patents Act 1988, or under the terms of any licence permitting limited copying issued by the Copyright Licensing Agency, 90 Tottenham Court Road, London W1P 0LP.

Any person who does any unauthorised act in relation to this publication may be liable to criminal prosecution and civil claims for damages.

The authors have asserted their rights to be identified as the authors of this work in accordance with the Copyright, Designs and Patents Act 1988.

First published 2001 by
PALGRAVE
Houndmills, Basingstoke, Hampshire RG21 6XS and
175 Fifth Avenue, New York, N.Y. 10010
Companies and representatives throughout the world

PALGRAVE is the new global academic imprint of
St. Martin's Press LLC Scholarly and Reference Division and
Palgrave Publishers Ltd (formerly Macmillan Press Ltd).

ISBN 0–333–92009–0

This book is printed on paper suitable for recycling and made from fully managed and sustained forest sources.

A catalogue record for this book is available from the British Library.

Library of Congress Cataloging-in-Publication Data
Peter the Great and the West : new perspectives / edited by Lindsey Hughes.
    p. cm. — (Studies in Russia and East Europe)
Includes bibliographical references and index.
ISBN 0–333–92009–0
    1. Russia—History—Peter I, 1689–1725. 2. Peter I, Emperor of Russia, 1672–1725. I. Hughes, Lindsey, 1949– II. University of London. School of Slavonic and East European Studies. III. National Maritime Museum (Great Britain) IV. Series.
DK133 .P444 2000
947'.05—dc21

                                                        00–052441

10 9 8 7 6 5 4 3 2 1
10 09 08 07 06 05 04 03 02 01

Text prepared and typeset by Martin Mellor Publishing Services, Edinburgh

Printed in Great Britain by Antony Rowe Ltd, Chippenham, Wiltshire

Contents

List of Plates	vii
List of Tables	viii
List of Abbreviations	ix
Note on Transliteration and Proper Names	x
List of Contributors	xi
Foreword	xvi
Introduction	xvii

Part I	Opening Address	1
1	The Old Man from Cambridge, Mrs Cross, and Other Anglo-Petrine Matters of Due Weight and Substance *Anthony Cross*	3
Part II	The Reforms in Context	27
2	The Petrine Reforms and their Impact *Alexander Kamenskii*	29
3	Administrative Reforms in the Russian Empire: Western Models and Russian Implementation *Andrei Medushevskii*	36
Part III	Peter and Britain	51
4	Changing Perspectives: British Views of Russia from the Grand Embassy to the Peace of Nystad *Janet Hartley*	53
5	Diligent and Faithful Servant: Peter the Great's Apprentices in England *Joan Lane*	71
6	Peter the Great: the Scottish Dimension *Dmitrii Fedosov*	89

Part IV Maritime History — 103

7 British Merchants and Russian Men-of-War: the Rise of the Russian Baltic Fleet — 105
   Richard Warner

8 State, Navy and the Origin of the Petrine Forest Cadastral Survey — 118
   Aleksei Karimov

9 Peter the Great and English Maritime Technology — 130
   W.F. Ryan

Part V Diplomatic and Military History — 159

10 Peter the Great and the Conquest of Azov: 1695–96 — 161
    Graeme Herd

11 Peter the Great and the Baltic — 177
    David Kirby

12 Why St Petersburg? — 189
    Robert E. Jones

13 Seven Years with Peter the Great: the Dutchman Jacob de Bie's Observations — 206
    Thomas Eekman

Part VI The Court and the Arts — 225

14 Catherine I, her Court and Courtiers — 227
    John Alexander

15 Images of Greatness: Portraits of Peter I — 250
    Lindsey Hughes

Index — 271

Plates

1   The actress Letitia Cross as St Catherine. Engraved by John Smith after Kneller (1699?)
2   Peter I by Sir Godfrey Kneller (1698)
3   Engraving of Peter I by John Smith after Kneller (1698)
4   'Peter I in Deptford, 1698' by Daniel Maclise (1857)
5   Topographic drawing of Nizhegorodskii uezd (ca. 1733)
6   Map of pine forests for navy, Nizhegorodskii uezd (ca. 1736)
7   Forest defence line (founded 1706) from Smolensk to Chernigov (early eighteenth century)
8   Forests of Novopavlovskii plantation (1700)
9   Canals and waterways of European Russia
10   Portrait of Catherine I by A.F. Zubov (1726)
11   Print marking the coronation of Catherine as consort by I.F. Zubov
12   Coronation portrait of Peter I. Anon. (1682)
13   Peter I by Jan Kupetsky (1711)
14   Peter I crowned by Victory at Poltava by J.G. Dannhauer (1710s)
15   Round portrait of Peter, attributed to Ivan Nikitin (1720s)
16   Peter on his deathbed, attributed to Ivan Nikitin (1725)

With thanks to the British Museum (Plate 1); Her Majesty's Collection, Kensington Palace (2); L. Hughes (3, 10–11); Royal Holloway (4); Russian Academy of Sciences (5–8); R.E. Jones (9); SSEES Library (12, 13); Russian Museum, St Petersburg (14–16).

Tables

5.1	Russian apprentices to Surrey masters, 1716–18	77
9.1	Part of the bill which the English merchant, Henry Stiles, presented to Peter on his return to Moscow	145
12.1	Number of Ships Using the Port of St Petersburg–Kronstadt, 1718–97	197

Abbreviations

BL	British Library, London
BL, Add. MS	British Library, London, Additional Manuscript
d.	*delo* (file)
doc.	document
f.	*fond* (collection)
fol.	folio
GH	Guildhall
HMC	Historical Manuscripts Commission
ill.	illustrations
l.	*list* (folio)
ll.	*listy* (folios)
MIRF	*Materialy dlia istorii russkago flota* (Material on the history of the Russian fleet)
ob.	verso
op.	*opis'* (section)
r.	recto
RGADA	*Russkii Gosudarstvennyi Arkhiv Drevnikh Aktov* (Russian State Archive of Ancient Documents)
RGIA	*Russkii Gosudarstvennyi Istoricheskii Arkhiv* (Russian State Historical Archive)
RGVIA	*Russkii Gosudarstvennyi Voenno-Istoricheskii Arkhiv* (Russian State Military Historical Archive)
PiB	*Pis'ma i bumagi imperatora Petra Velikogo* (Letters and papers of the emperor Peter the Great)
PRO, CO	Public Record Office, London, Colonial Office
PRO, SP	Public Record Office, London, State Papers
PSZ	*Polnoe sobranie zakonov rossiiskoi imperii* (Complete collection of laws of the Russian empire)

Note on Transliteration and Proper Names

Russian spellings have been transcribed using a modified Library of Congress system. Feminine proper names with alternative endings in -'ia or -iia are generally rendered with -ia, hence Maria, Natalia, Evdokia. Names of monarchs and certain other famous individuals are given in their English equivalent, e.g. Peter (Petr), Catherine (Ekaterina), Sophia (Sof'ia or Sofiia), Alexander (Aleksandr), Alexis (Aleksei). In transcribed citations and titles, however, the originals are rendered in full. The forms 'tsar', 'tsarevna', etc. are preferred, unless in original quotations (Tzar, Czar, etc).

Contributors

JOHN ALEXANDER
Professor of History and Russian and East European Studies, University of Kansas. His publications include *Bubonic Plague in Early Modern Europe: Public Health and Urban Disaster* (Baltimore, MD, 1980) and *Catherine the Great: Life and Legend* (New York: Oxford, 1989). His current research focuses upon the empresses of Russia in the eighteenth century and the emergence of the imperial Russian court as a European-type institution.

ANTHONY CROSS
Professor of Slavonic Studies, University of Cambridge. He is Fellow of the British Academy, Fellow of the Russian Academy of the Humanities and editor of the Newsletter of the Study Group on Eighteenth-Century Russia. Among his principal publications are *By the Banks of the Thames: Russians in Eighteenth-Century Britain* (Newtonville, MA, 1980; Russian translation 1996), *The Russian Theme in English Literature from the Sixteenth Century to 1980* (Oxford, 1985), *Anglo-Russica: Aspects of Anglo-Russian Relations in the Eighteenth and Early Nineteenth Centuries* (Oxford, 1993) and *By the Banks of the Neva: Chapters from the Lives and Careers of the British in Eighteenth-Century Russia* (Cambridge, 1996; awarded the 1997 Alec Nove Prize and the 1998 Antsiferov Prize).

THOMAS EEKMAN
Emeritus Professor, Slavic Languages Department, University of California, Los Angeles (UCLA). He was born in the Netherlands and received his PhD from the University of Amsterdam. He taught there from 1947–66 and then at UCLA until his retirement in 1990. He has published seven books and edited six and written about one hundred scholarly papers.

DIMITRII FEDOSOV
Fellow of the Institute of General History, Moscow. He has a special interest in Russo-Scottish relations, including the history of

the Russian fleet. As well as writing on Scots and their descendants in Russia, he has also organised Highland games and other Scottish cultural events in Moscow.

JANET HARTLEY

Senior Lecturer in International History, London School of Economics and Political Science. Her main publications are *Guide to Documents and Manuscripts in the United Kingdom relating to Russian and the Soviet Union* (London, 1987), *Alexander I* (London, 1994; republished in Russian in 1998) and *A Social History of the Russian Empire 1650–1825* (London, 1999). She is one of the editors of *Britain and Russia in the Age of Peter the Great. Historical Documents*, which was published to coincide with the conference at which the papers in this volume where presented.

GRAEME HERD

Lecturer in the Department of Politics and International Relations, University of Aberdeen. Before 1997 he was Lecturer at Staffordshire University and Projects Officer at the Department of War Studies, King's College London. His PhD was completed at Aberdeen University ('General Patrick Gordon of Auchleuchries, 1635–99: a Scot in Russian Service'). He publishes on post-Soviet security politics, as well as military and diplomatic history of the second half of the seventeenth century. He is particularly interested in the contribution of Scottish mercenaries to Russian political development and modernisation.

LINDSEY HUGHES (ed.)

Professor of Russian History, School of Slavonic and East European Studies, University College London. Her publications include *Russia and the West: Prince Vasily Vasilievich Golitsyn (1643–1714)* (Gulf Breeze, FL, 1984), *Sophia Regent of Russia 1657–1704* (New Haven, CT, 1990) and *Russia in the Age of Peter the Great* (New Haven, CT, 1998). She is convenor of the Study Group on Eighteenth-Century Russia and was the academic organiser of the conference from which this volume is drawn. She is currently writing a short biography of Peter I and planning a longer project on Russian cultural landmarks.

ROBERT E. JONES
Professor of History, University of Massachusetts. He is the author of *The Emancipation of the Russian Nobility* (Princeton, NJ, 1982) and *Provincial Development in Russia: Catherine II and Jakob Sievers* (New Brunswick, NJ, 1984), as well as numerous articles and shorter pieces on the history of eighteenth-century Russia.

ALEXANDER KAMENSKII
Professor of Early Russian History, Russian State University for the Humanities, Moscow. His recent publications include *The Russian Empire in the Eighteenth Century: Searching for a Place in the World* (London, 1997) and books and articles (in Russian) on Catherine II, including *'Under Catherine's Cloak': Russia in the Second Half of the Eighteenth century* (St Petersburg, 1992). He is convenor of the international project on the publication of the papers of Catherine II.

ALEKSEI KARIMOV
Fellow of the Institute of History of Natural Sciences and Technology, Moscow. He received his PhD from the Institute in 1994 ('The History of Exploration and Exploitation of Land Resources in Moscow Province'). He is a member of the Russian Geographical Society and Fellow of the Russian Foundation of Human Sciences. In January and February 1997 he was a British Academy visiting fellow in the UK. He is the author of several articles and is currently working on a comparative study of Russian and English cadastral systems.

DAVID KIRBY
Professor of Modern History, School of Slavonic and East European Studies, University College London. He has specialised in the history of Northern Europe for many years and is the author of *Northern Europe in the Early Modern Period: the Baltic World 1492–1772* (London, 1990) and *The Baltic World 1772–1993: Europe's Northern Periphery in an Age of Change* (London, 1995) He is currently working on a history of the Baltic and North Seas.

JOAN LANE

Senior Teaching Fellow in History, University of Warwick where she has taught since 1979. She has a PhD from the University of Birmingham ('Apprenticeship in Warwickshire, 1700–1834'). She was elected Fellow of the Society of Antiquaries in 1987 and has been General Editor of the Dugdale Society since 1990. Recent publications include *Apprenticeship in England, 1600–1914* (London, 1996), *John Hall and his Patients: The Medical Practice of Shakespeare's Son-in-Law* (London, 1996), *The Making of the English Patient* (London, 1998) and *A Social History of Medicine in England* (London, 1999).

ANDREI MEDUSHEVSKII

Senior Fellow, Institute of Russian History of the Russian Academy of Sciences, Moscow. He also teaches political and constitutional law at the Moscow Higher School of Economics. His interests include the theory and history of state and law, Russian constitutionalism and modern political processes in international perspective. Recent publications (in Russian) include *Administrative Reform in Eighteenth–Nineteenth-Century Russia in Comparative Perspective* (Moscow, 1990) and *The Formation of Absolutism in Russia* (Moscow, 1994).

W.F. RYAN

Academic Librarian, Warburg Institute (part of the School of Advanced Study), University of London. He was previously Lecturer in Russian Language and Literature at the School of Slavonic and East European Studies and before that Assistant Curator at the Museum of the History of Science, Oxford. He is the series editor of the Hakluyt Society and two monograph series at the Warburg Institute, has written extensively on science, technology and magic in medieval and early modern Russia. He is one the editors of *Britain and Russia in the Age of Peter the Great: Historical Documents*. His most recent work is *The Bathhouse at Midnight: An Historical Survey of Magic and Divination in Russia* (London and Philadelphia, 1999).

RICHARD WARNER
Professor of History, Mary Washington College in Fredericksburg, Virginia. He specialises in Russian and maritime subjects and is co-editor of *Boon Island, Including Contemporary Accounts of the Wreck of the Nottingham Galley* (Hanover, NH, 1996). He has published articles in *The New England Quarterly*, *Research in Maritime History*, *Mariner's Mirror* and *Jahrbücher für Geschichte Osteuropas*. He is currently completing a text book on Peter the Great and the modernisation of Russia and a biography entitled *Captain John Deane: Mercenary, Diplomat and Spy*.

Foreword

In 1998 the National Maritime Museum's major international conference, *Peter the Great and the West: New Perspectives*, proved to be one of the highlights of the Museum's year. The conference, held in association with the School of Slavonic and East European Studies, was scheduled to coincide with an exhibition in the Museum's Queen's House that marked the tercentenary of Peter I's expedition to the West. It therefore seemed all the more appropriate to hold such a conference at Greenwich. The Queen's House would have been *in situ* when Peter visited Greenwich Park in 1698. The Museum's 1998 exhibition – which focused on Tsar Peter's stay in Deptford and his visits to the royal dockyards and the Royal Observatory to find out more about ship-building and navigation – added a further dimension to the conference.

Not that the conference was in need of any supplementary interest. The papers covered a range of subjects and addressed both particular aspects of Peter's Grand Embassy and broader questions of modernisation and westernisation associated with Peter's reforms. Speakers included eminent scholars from the Russian Federation and the United States of America as well as the United Kingdom. The programme was carefully balanced to prompt fresh debate.

This volume brings the findings of this successful conference to a wider audience and reflects the productiveness of modern scholarship in Petrine studies. The Museum and the School of Slavonic and East European Studies are grateful to staff in the Museum's Centre for Maritime Research who organised the conference and worked so hard on the day to make it a success.

National Maritime Museum   Richard Ormond
Greenwich   Director
June 1999

Introduction

On 31 December 1996 *The Times* published an editorial article entitled 'The Giant Still Awakening: 400 years ago' to mark the anniversary of Peter the Great's arrival in England in January 1698. The item is significant for a number of reasons, not least of all because the newspaper regarded Peter's visit as an historical landmark of sufficient importance for comment in its editorial column on New Year's Eve. The article drew appropriate parallels between Peter and his modern-day post-Soviet successors, mentioning their common search for Western 'know-how' and their similar experience of the perils and pitfalls of alien influences. The error over the date – which located Peter's arrival in England not only in the wrong year, but even in the wrong century – would not particularly surprise Russian specialists in the United Kingdom, who are more or less resigned to seeing factual inaccuracies about their subject in the media. Among the howlers which appeared in the British press in the anniversary year of 1998 were a reference to 'the nightshirt in which Peter I was murdered' (said to be on show in an exhibition on Russian imperial palaces in the USA; quoted in *The Times*, 20 April 1998, p. 11) and a query in a travel feature as to the 'whereabouts of the axe he [Peter] used to chop off the heads of Ivan the Terrible's followers' (*Daily Telegraph*, Travel Section, 22 August 1998, p. 4). A broadsheet review of my book *Russia in the Age of Peter the Great* (1998), itself a tercentenary offering, was illustrated with a detail from Daniel Maclise's 1857 painting 'Peter I in Deptford, 1698', but unfortunately the editor had mistakenly selected a section of the painting depicting King William III, whose delicate, velvet-clad figure Maclise had purposely contrasted with that of the brawny Tsar-Carpenter, posing with sleeves rolled up ready to do some vigorous sawing.

In general, though, 1998 was a good year for Petrine studies in the UK. A programme of events and publications under the heading 'New Waves', co-ordinated by the city of St Petersburg and the Foreign and Commonwealth Office, endeavoured both to publicise the Petrine tercentenary and to take stock of its wider implications for British–Russian relations today. The year's publications included *Britain and Russia in the Age of Peter the Great: Historical Documents* (School of Slavonic and East European Studies 1998), which originated in a joint British–Soviet archives project and appeared under the editorship of a team which included several of the contributors to the present volume. In November a statue of Peter was unveiled in the grounds of the Russian ambassador's residence in Kensington. Among the highlights of the cultural and academic programme were the National Maritime Museum's exhibition 'Peter the Great in England', held in the Queen's House at Greenwich, to which several papers in this present volume make reference (notably to the prize exhibit, Sir Godfrey Kneller's full-length portrait of Peter, painted in 1698), and the conference at which this collection of papers were delivered. The conference was held in the Maritime Museum's main building from 9 to 11 July 1998.

It was fitting that these two linked Petrine events should have been held at Greenwich, just a mile or so from the site of Sayes Court, the diarist John Evelyn's residence by the Thames at Deptford, where Peter lived for part of his three-month stay in England in order to be close to his shipbuilding work in the adjoining Royal Dockyard, which W.F. Ryan discusses in this volume (Chapter 9). The house survived the notorious acts of vandalism inflicted upon it by the tsar and his companions (the original itemised bill for damages was displayed in the 1998 exhibition), but was demolished in the nineteenth century. Now only a fragment of the garden remains, a few yards away from the evocative Czar Street. Peter visited several other sites in Greenwich area, including the Royal Observatory (where he is said to have caused yet more damage, this time to valuable instruments) and Wren's magnificent new buildings for the Royal Naval Hospital, which Peter so admired that he advised King William to transfer the patients elsewhere and to move in himself. Most of all, Peter loved the river Thames, for ships and sailing were his passion. He hired British naval personnel and took back to Russia many tangible mementoes of British seafaring expertise – ship models, globes, mathematical and navigational instruments, clocks, books and the yacht *Royal Transport* – not to mention a wealth of personal experiences and observations, which he applied to building up his own infant navy. The navy was further augmented in 1712–16 by the purchase of British warships (see Richard Warner's paper; Chapter 7). Perhaps the most enduring legacy of Peter's British experience was in education. Every Russian sailor for more than forty years learned about navigation at the Moscow School of Mathematics and Navigation and its successor, the St Petersburg Naval Academy. The latter was founded by Henry Farquharson, a graduate of Aberdeen University, and his young assistants Stephen Gwynn and Richard Grice, former pupils of Christ's Hospital. Farqhuarson was just one of many Scots in Peter's Russia. Dmitrii Fedosov's paper (Chapter 6) reminds us how much men like the soldier Patrick Gordon and the versatile James Bruce (Iakov Brius) influenced Peter, even though Peter himself never visited Scotland. The saltire-like cross of Peter's own Order of St Andrew – blue on a white background – flew over the ships of the new navy, some of the names of which – Arundel, Richmond, Britannia, London – speak eloquently of British influence.

Britain, of course, was just one of many countries to which Peter turned for expertise and it was appropriate that the 1998 conference should have been an international gathering, attracting delegates from Canada, Denmark, Finland, Germany, Ireland, the Netherlands, Norway, Russia and USA, as well as from many parts of Britain. One of the most enduring of Russian historical images is that of Peter opening a 'window' on the outside world to end centuries of semi-isolation, a window which never quite closed under his imperial successors, slammed shut during the Stalin era, was tentatively unlatched during détente and glasnost in the 1970s and 1980s and was forced wide open again by the collapse of the USSR in 1991. Peter often wielded the cudgel when it came to dealing with his own subjects: he was convinced that he would never achieve anything without harnessing all Russians to the service of the state. However, one of his more attractive qualities was his curiosity about the world and his positive welcoming of foreigners and their influences into Russia, as well as his insistence that selected Russians study abroad ('I am a student and I seek teachers' was inscribed on the seal he carried during the Grand Embassy). In that respect, the 1990s could be said to have marked the dawn of a new Petrine era in Russia. By 1998 the presence of Russian delegates at the Greenwich conference, both invited guests and independent travellers, was no longer an object for particular comment or surprise as it might have been during the Soviet era.

But the process of imitation and assimilation of things foreign remains a sensitive issue. Peter infuriated national sensibilities by discarding native traditions in favour of Western customs, particularly in such visible areas as fashions and hairstyles, but his borrowings from the West took place at a time when the Russian Empire was expanding and its status as a world power was growing, as several papers in this collection demonstrate. Success on the world stage allowed Peter to ignore his critics at home; making Russia great seemed (or was made to seem) more important than keeping it Russian. The economic and political crisis which blew up in Russia in the autumn of 1998 (and which continues at the time of writing, exacerbated by uncertainties over the health of President Yeltsin), not to mention the international repercussions of the events in Kosovo in 1999, underline the complexity and fragility of Russia's relations with the West in the wake of the humiliating territorial loss and military decline experienced in the 1990s.

Foreign visitors to Russia today, like those in Peter's time, find themselves in a country undergoing rapid and bewildering change, a country which bears many of the outward attributes of modern life, but inwardly seems to run according to its own rules. They may well encounter the modern-day equivalents of some of the things which frustrated the envoy Jacob de Bie – as analysed in Thomas Eekman's paper (Chapter 13) – such as sudden changes in taxation requirements and customs dues, fluctuations in the pecking order at court and tampering with the mail. Foreigners could feel like outsiders, with only a tenuous foothold in Russian life, or like virtual captives ('His Majesty cannot stand it when foreigners in his country, blessed by God and by their own diligence, think of returning to their homeland,' wrote de Bie; see p. 220 below). Russians abroad could arouse suspicions, too, like those of the Birmingham metal workers, who feared Russian apprentices would return to 'his Czarist Majesty's dominions to instruct others to the prejudice of the artificers of Birmingham' (see p. 76 below).

The reason why Peter was so loathe to release useful foreigners from his service was, of course, his relentless quest for modernisation – technological, institutional and cultural – a theme which crops up in virtually every paper in this volume, many of which also discuss the associated dilemmas of the modernising process, from the general (see Alexander Kamenskii's examination in Chapter 2 of the problem of reforms which were 'western in form but not in content') to the specific (for example, the language difficulties experienced by the young Russians sent as apprentices to England, as set out by Joan Lane in Chapter 5). Comparative perspectives are useful here. As Andrei Medushevskii demonstrates (Chapter 3), modernisation as experienced in Peter's reign was not a peculiarly Russian phenomenon. Rational solutions to backwardness were adopted by rulers of traditional societies in Japan, Egypt, Turkey, Iran and elsewhere. In all cases, the transformation was accomplished through administrative reform from above and relied on the creation of new bureaucracies and civil servants. Aleksei Karimov's study of forest surveys (Chapter 8) provides a striking illustration of the way in which employing traditional approaches to achieve modern results (in this case, the development of the Russian navy) perpetuated the twin pillars of autocracy and serfdom. The needs of the state overrode any individual claims to personal property rights. Rule from above implied that the crown, in order to fund its costly programmes for the 'common good', had first claim to all resources, be it church bells (requisitioned after the Russian defeat at Narva in 1700) or trees on nobles' land. Peter could also get native manpower cheaply or for free – in the words of Lord John Carteret (quoted by Janet Hartley in Chapter 4) 'the Czar can sail half as cheap again as any other nation, for he gives his men much less pay' – while at the same time profiting from the relative freedom of action enjoyed by foreigners, as when the mayor of Bristol and the member of Parliament Abraham Elton reassured him that they could supply the Russians with new or refitted vessels, 'even in violation of the British Admiralty ... [and] without danger of sanction from acts of parliament' (see Richard Warner's paper; Chapter 7).

Several contributions in this volume deal with the issue of Russia's orientation between east and west in Peter's reign. With the benefit of hindsight, Peter's destiny seemed inexorably linked with St Petersburg and the Baltic (to the extent that the memorably bad NBC mini-series filmed in the 1980s had Peter proclaiming long before the outbreak of the Northern War: 'I shall found a city and call its name St Petersburg'). There were, however, 'alternative scenarios'. Peter first came to Western attention when he captured Azov in 1696, as Graeme Herd narrates (Chapter 10), and it was this victory which provided the impetus for his Grand Embassy to seek aid against the Turks, as well as for the further expansion of the navy and the 'reinvention' of the Russian imperial image. In England in 1698 it was naturally assumed that Peter's navy would be for use against the Tartars and Turks, an assumption which was strengthened by Peter's projects for developing Azov, then nearby Taganrog, for both military and commercial purposes in the early years of the Northern War. Even when he began to concentrate on St Petersburg, as Robert E. Jones shows (Chapter 12), the development of Azov/Taganrog provided a model. Chapter 12 also opens our eyes to some crucial facts: St Petersburg's great advantage in Peter's eyes was its accessibility by water from the Russian heartland, so that in effect it became the sea port of the Volga via the Vyshnii Volochok canal system. But the new capital also posed an irresistible challenge above and beyond practical considerations. Founding a new capital was in itself a calculated 'act of greatness', by which Peter echoed the achievement of the great Constantine and Alexander. By the time all this was happening, as Janet Hartley argues (Chapter 4), it was clear that Russia was no longer concerned primarily with Turkey (hence safely occupied in the east) but on its way to becoming 'the most dangerous enemy our country can have' (Sir John Norris). By the end of Peter's reign, however, the British had come to regard the reorientation as 'containable', to the extent that in the 1740s to 1750s, as Anthony Cross illustrates in Chapter 1, positive (and thoroughly westernised) images of Peter as Northern Hero and Enlightened Monarch prevailed in the British media. In Russia the east to west reorientation was illustrated – as I explain in my own paper (Chapter 15) – by the replacement of the Byzanto-Muscovite image of the holy Orthodox tsar (which at the hands of late seventeenth-century Western artists had often become further orientalised and 'Turkey-like'), by conventional Western iconography based on military attributes (as in Kneller's study of Peter, the contribution of which to British Petrine imagery Anthony Cross describes in Chapter 1) and by Roman imperial symbols.

In the flesh, stripped of conventional 'civilising' attributes, Peter – unpredictable and given to outbursts of clowning and vanddalism – remained perplexing and alarming to Western eyes, adding fuel to the stereotypical perception of Russians as distinctly 'other', as 'barbarians'. As David Kirby points out in Chapter 11, Peter's overriding aim, in his Baltic politics as elsewhere, was to be respected by his fellow monarchs; yet, his 'naughty habits' again and again undermined this aspiration. These habits were observed by Jacob de Bie, whose 'dry and formal' missives by and large confirm the testimony of better-known foreign writers such as Just Juel, Friedrich Christian Weber and Friedrich von Bergholz. Recurring themes include Peter's dislike of formal apartments (which he would often reject in favour of simpler accommodation, thereby offending his hosts) and his heavy drinking. Juel's observations on this latter topic appear in John Alexander's Chapter 14, while Anthony Cross recalls in Chapter 1 some of the taverns which Peter frequented in England. De Bie laconically observed that the 'situation of this court is different from other courts' (see p. 208 below). Despite the fact that Peter had many occasions to witness the practices of other courts, as John Alexander points out, and borrowed the names of his new court officials in barely Russified form (*ober-gofmeister*, *kamer-iunkery*, *freiliny* and so on), Western-style conventions were adopted more or less consistently only for the household of his wife Catherine (a woman of obscure lowly origins), while Peter maintained a sort of anti-court (the best known manifestation of which was the 'All-Drunken Assembly') and deliberately neglected protocol. No wonder foreign envoys felt insecure.

*****

The contents of this volume reflect to a great degree the structure of the conference in which the papers were originally given, although a few changes have been made. The original programme contained five panels and two illustrated lectures. The panels each consisted of two or three half-hour papers under the following titles: Peter and Britain, Maritime History, Diplomatic History, Court and Government, and Military History. The lectures were an introductory one by Anthony Cross and my own concluding talk on portraits. One of the papers, Robert Frost's 'Peter the Great: Military Reform and the Great Northern War', was not offered for inclusion, as it will form part of a book. The presentations of Alexander Kamenskii and Andrei Medushevskii were originally assigned to the session on Court and Government, but in view of the broader issues which they addressed, here they have been reallocated to an introductory section entitled 'The Reforms in Context' (Chapters 2 and 3 respectively). My own paper and John Alexander's, both of which feature personalities and culture, have been joined together to conclude the volume (Chapters 14 and 15). In both cases, it has been possible to include only a fraction of the substantial visual material which accompanied the presentations. The papers presented here vary in length, style and tone and in the density of the annotation provided, some reflecting the immediacy of the spoken word, others adopting a more formal discourse. No attempt has been made to impose uniformity in these respects, but as editor I have tried to introduce consistency into the presentation of proper names and the transliteration or translation of Russian terms; details of this are set out in a note on p. ix. The four Russian speakers all gave their papers and responded to questions in English. Edited versions of their own English texts, as opposed to translations from the Russian, are printed here. In all this I am greatly indebted to the invaluable assistance of Martin Mellor, who acted as copy editor for this volume. As is always the case with collective volumes like this one, the animated discussions which followed the presentations and continued over dinner and in the bar remain only in the memories and notebooks of the participants. It is hoped that the papers presented here will provide readers who were unable to attend the conference with food for thought. The issues over which they range reaffirm – to paraphrase one of the contributors – that in Russia the past, even centuries away, is never dead. The rights and wrongs, successes and failures of the reign of Peter the Great and the lessons which it may or may not teach will no doubt continue to arouse heated debate well into the twenty-first century.

School of Slavonic and
East European Studies
University College London
August 1999

Lindsey Hughes

Part I
Opening Address

1 The Old Man from Cambridge, Mrs Cross, and Other Anglo-Petrine Matters of Due Weight and Substance

Anthony Cross

I am honoured to have been asked to give the opening lecture at this prestigious conference dedicated to Peter the Great, but at the same time I am deeply conscious of the onerous nature of the task confronting me. Given that the delights of a reception and an exhibition await you, I have to sugar the pill of the immediate hour in accord with the traditional eighteenth-century prescription of the *utile* and *dulce*, but with as much emphasis on entertainment as decorum allows. It is nevertheless appropriate that in this commemorative year of 1998 my talk should celebrate Peter's descent on England, and I shall wander down ways and, more often, byways, both familiar and untrodden, which are connected both with that visit and its aftermath. The emphasis throughout will be on the anecdotal and, even more, on the picturesque in both senses of the word, for these reflect the essence of Peter's visit in the popular imagination.

I must also say at the outset that I am inordinately proud of the title of my lecture. Having finally produced it in time for the printing of the programme almost a year ago, I was long paralysed by the prospect of giving what it promises, that is to say, 'due weight and substance'. It does, however, evoke the sort of chapter heading that Daniel Defoe, appropriately enough, and novelists who followed him, such as Fielding and Smollett, frequently provided in their long novels of adventures, peregrinations, and mix of high and low life scenes. Peter was in every respect a fitting hero for such a novel, playing with particular gusto episodes set in taverns, in bedrooms and on board ship. It is nevertheless fully in that spirit of irony which Lermontov liked to attribute to the English while refusing an understanding of it to the Russians that I refer you in particular to Fielding's novel *The Life of Jonathan Wild the Great* and its first chapter entitled 'Showing the wholesome uses drawn from recording the achievements of those wonderful productions of nature called GREAT MEN'. Fielding's specific target was here, as it was in some many of his earlier works, Sir Robert Walpole, but whenever the cap fits, let it be worn, and it is salutary, certainly in the eighteenth-century context, to hear what Fielding has to say. The whole chapter deserves quotation, but I will confine myself to the following paragraph:

> But before we enter on this great work, we must endeavour to remove some errors of opinion which mankind have, by the disingenuity of writers, contracted: for these, from their fear of contradicting the obsolete and absurd doctrines of a set of simple fellows called, in derision, sages or philosophers, have endeavoured as much as possible to confound the ideas of greatness and goodness, whereas no two such things can possibly be more distinct from each other: for greatness consists in bringing all manner of mischief on mankind, and goodness in removing it from them. It seems very unlikely that the same person should possess them both; and yet nothing is more usual with writers, who find many instances of greatness in their favourite hero, than to make him a compliment of goodness into the bargain, and this without considering that by such means they destroy the great perfection called uniformity of character. In the histories of Alexander and Caesar, we are frequently, and indeed impertinently, reminded of their benevolence and generosity and kindness. When the former had with fire and sword overrun a vast empire, had destroyed the lives of an immense number of innocent

wretches, had scattered ruin and desolation like a whirlwind, we are told, as an example of clemency, that he did not cut the throat of an old woman and ravish her daughters, but was content only with undoing them.[1]

I shall stop the quotation there, not that what Fielding goes on to say about Caesar – and Peter was compared to both Caesar and Alexander in eighteenth-century hagiographies – is not appropriate, but that the instance of sexual gratification provides a more than convenient transition to the Mrs Cross of my title. If that were not of itself suitable justification, then I might also refer you to Chapter 10 of Fielding's novel, entitled 'A discovery of some matters concerning the chaste Laetitia which must wonderfully surprise, and perhaps affect, our reader.' It is the reputation of Letitia Cross and the honour of the family name that I must now most earnestly defend.

It was recently remarked by two American scholars that the liaison between Peter and Letitia is virtually unknown to historians of the English stage,[2] although it is notoriously familiar to Russian and Western historians of matters Petrine, but, I should stress, purely Petrocentrically, that is, in general ignorance of the true nature and talents of Letitia. Letitia was about twenty years old, possibly less (her date of birth is disputed), when Peter first set eyes on her. She had been in the theatre from an early age and if noted for her singing above her acting, had nevertheless already played significant parts in comedies and tragedies during the two seasons preceding Peter's arrival. These included the role of Miss Hoyden, described in the cast list as 'a Great Fortune, Daughter to Sir Tunbelly Clumsey, a Country Gentleman', in the première of John Vanbrugh's *The Relapse; or Virtue in Danger* in November 1696. This play was performed again at Drury Lane on 5 January 1698, only days before Peter's arrival, and Letitia may well have played the role on that occasion; however, no cast list survives. It has been suggested that 'Hoydenish roles seem to have been her speciality, and Vanbrugh may have tailored her role in *The Relapse* to her special talents.'[3] This play and Vanbrugh's next comedy, *The Provok'd Wife* (1697), were the subject of particular attack by the non-juring divine Jeremy Collier (1650–1726) in his *A Short View of the Immorality and Profaneness of the English Stage*, published within a week or so of Peter's departure from England. The controversy had begun earlier during Peter's stay and it is a nice irony that in Narcissus Luttrell's chronicle of daily events mentions of the tsar's visits to theatres and masquerades should alternate with references to King William's support for a bill 'against prophaneness, swearing, drunkenness, and whoring'.[4] In his *Short View* Collier protested against attacks and criticism of the clergy, asserting their high status in various parts of the world, including Muscovy, where 'the Bishops have an Honourable Station; and the Present Czar is descended from the Patriarchal Line.'[5] Vanbrugh made an immediate reply in his *Short Vindication of the Relapse and the Provok'd Wife, from Immorality and Profaneness* stating, *inter alia*, that an English gentleman who had allegedly written a speech in *The Relapse* to which Collier had taken exception, had 'gone away with the czar who made him Poet-Laureate of Muscovy'.[6] The late M.P. Alekseev, who drew attention to this intriguing reference,[7] was inclined to look for a real Englishman who was in the ranks of the many recruited by Peter; I, for my part, interpret it as Vanbrugh's *jeu d'esprit*, hitting back at Collier with an example of the new enlightened Russia and not unmindful of 'Hoyden' Letitia's recent involvement with the tsar. Coincidentally, at just this same period Letitia's elopement to the Continent was also in part 'blamed' on Collier: 'O Collier! Collier! Thou's frighted away Miss Cross. / She, to return our Foreigners Complaisance, / A Cupid's Call, has made a Trip to France.'[8]

It was during the 1697–98 season that Letitia was consistently billed as 'Mrs Cross', while previously she had occasionally been so dubbed, alongside 'Miss'. This was an indication not of married status, but of her acceptance as a mature actress. She was in fact to marry in 1706 a Martin Weier, who promptly left for Marlborough's army in Flanders and was killed, but she kept the name of Mrs Cross throughout her long career (she died in 1737, but acted until 1732).[9] During Peter's time in London, Letitia played Eromena in *The Fatal Discovery; or, Love in Ruines* (author unknown), Salome in John Crowne's *Caligula* and spoke the prologue in Charles Gildon's *Phaeton; or the Fatal Divorce*, but Peter is not known to have seen any of these. He was present at performances of Thomas Betterton's opera *The Prophetesse; or, the*

History of Dioclesian and Nathaniel Lee's *The Rival Queens; or, the Death of Alexander the Great* and attended another opera, the identity of which has not been established, and was at two musical evenings in York Buildings on the Strand, where possibly Letitia sang.[10] Thus it is difficult to say where precisely the tsar and she met, although it is insinuated by Bogoslovskii that it was at the time of Peter's visit to see *The Prophetesse* on 15 January and that the entry in the *Journal* (*Iurnal*) for the following day: 'byli doma i veselisis' dovol'no' ('we remained at home and had a whale of a time') involved the company and more of Letitia.[11]

As far as contemporary sources go, there is no reference to any liaison between tsar and actress and, like so many of the anecdotes connected with Peter, it suddenly appeared in print long after the alleged events. John Mottley in his very successful compilation *The History of the Life of Peter I, Emperor of Russia* (3 vols, 1739), borrows most of his information about Peter's time in London from John Perry's highly influential *The State of Russia under the Present Czar* (1716); however, whereas Perry had contented himself with asserting that Peter 'was prevail'd upon to go once or twice to the Play, but that was what he did not like', Mottley, writing just two years after the death of the actress, went on to add: 'yet it was whispered about, that one of the actresses, Miss Cross, had found the way to please him, and had been once admitted into his Company.'[12] This was elaborated into a whole little drama three years later, in Eléazar de Mauvillon's *Histoire de Pierre I, surnommé le Grand*, when 'Quelques présens assez considérables achevérent de vaincre les scrupules de la belle Actrice, si l'on peut appeller scrupules les premières facons que font les Femmes de cette profession, pour garder quelque espèce de bienséance.'[13] It is this mercenary element that is developed in what was also the most scabrous variant of the alleged Peter–Letitia liaison, which appeared in a collection of anecdotes compiled by Peter's famed instrument-maker and mechanic Andrei Nartov, who had himself been in England in 1719. Nartov's collection, allegedly finished in 1727, was much added to at a later date and frequently culled its so-called 'authentic' materials from printed sources (including Mauvillon); it was printed for the first time in its entirety only in 1891. The relevant anecdote reads as follows:

Tsar Peter Alekseevich, being as a young man in London in 1698, became acquainted through Menshikov, who was inseparable from him during his travels and drowned in luxury and sensuality, with an actress, named Cross, whom sometimes during his stay in England he took for amorous dalliance [*dlia liubovnoi zabavy*], but he never let his heart be enchained by any woman, so as not to slow down the advances which the monarch expected from the initiatives he had taken for the benefit of his country. His love was not a tender and powerful passion but a mere response to nature. But when at the time of his departure he sent her via Menshikov five hundred guineas, then Cross, dissatisfied with this gift, complained about the Russian tsar's meanness and asked him to tell his master. Menshikov did as she asked and reported to his majesty, who said in reply: 'You, Menshikov, think that I'm as big a spendthrift as you. For five hundred guineas old men serve me with zeal and intelligence, but this woman served me badly with her fore-parts [*khudo sluzhila svoim perëdom*].' To which Menshikov replied: 'Let the payment fit the job.'[14]

This of course tells us far more about Peter (and Menshikov as pimp) than it does about Letitia who, even if she had offered her body, as most commentators sadly seem to agree, would not possibly have rejected a sum of 500 guineas. In her later career, when she was generally acknowledged to be 'one of the best Comedians upon the English stage', she was only earning £100 a year.[15] Far more probable is that Peter would never have offered anywhere near that amount, if he offered anything at all, although the anecdote catches well his generally cynical attitude to women. It would seem that despite Perry's – and Bogoslovskii's – assertions to the contrary, Peter was much taken with the theatre, which he and most of the members of the Grand Embassy had witnessed for the first time in their lives just weeks before in Amsterdam. It was a place of wonder and of temptation where, since the Restoration, actresses performed women's roles for the first time in plays which became increasingly free in their language and in the themes they treated and where, as Macaulay puts it, 'nothing charmed the depraved audience so much as to hear lines grossly indecent repeated by a beautiful girl, who was supposed to have not yet lost her innocence.'[16] Be that as it may, I can only offer you, ladies and gentlemen, innocence without the obscene verses in this engraving, probably dating from 1799, of Letitia Cross as St Catherine from the original painting by Sir Godfrey Kneller (see Plate 1). An English rose broken on the wheel of a Russian tyrant's lust – need one say more.

It is Kneller who provides me with my next bridge, for of course it is Kneller's portrait of Peter that has made the artist known in a Russian context and that gave both Russia and the West its most influential representation of the young tsar. It is the portrait that adorns the programme of our conference and, brought from its home in Kensington Palace, the portrait that awaits you at the end of one of the exhibition rooms (see Plate 2). Horace Walpole in one of his many acidic moments said of Kneller that 'where he offered one picture to fame, he sacrificed twenty to lucre.'[17] Whether his portrait of the fair Letitia was for lucre, possibly from an admirer, cannot be established; certainly Peter would never have paid, given his already quoted assessment of the lady's charms and performance. Kneller's portrait of Peter, however, was certainly an offering to fame. It was hailed as an excellent likeness, so much so that the Dutch traveller and artist Cornelius de Bruyn, who had seen the original painting in Kneller's studio in London, was able instantly to recognise the tsar in the flesh in Muscovy in 1702.[18] In one of the newsletters of the day it was written that it was 'drawn to the life at full length in a Roman habit, a Marshall's Staff in his hands and the Regalias lying by him and shipps storming a fort on the Sea Side'.[19] This seems an anticipation of Peter's dress in Falconet's Bronze Horseman rather than an accurate description of the shining black armour and luxurious cloak fully after the fashion of the Baroque martial portrait that Kneller and his predecessor Sir Peter Lely had executed over preceding decades.[20] The naval scene in the background is said to be the work of the outstanding Dutch marinist Willem Van der Velde, but it was also frequent practice for Kneller, having drawn the face, to leave the rest of a painting to be completed by his studio. I might say, however, that what you read in a portrait, and Peter's in particular, seems much conditioned by conflicting influences. J. Douglas Stewart, the leading British expert on Kneller, finds 'the swagger and springiness of a Russian dancer; and in the face there is exposed the ruthlessness and intelligence of this semi-barbaric giant,' while Ian Grey, the author of a biography of Peter, written in 1960, sees, rather more plausibly, I feel, 'a lively, open and handsome face with strong features and large dark intelligent eyes. There is something almost chivalrous and benevolent in this picture of the young tsar, caught in a moment of calm.'[21] At least they agree on the intelligence, and you will soon have the opportunity to make your own interpretation.

That Peter began to sit for Kneller in London at the end of January 1698 is well attested.[22] However, over more than a century Russian art historians have so successfully encouraged the notion that Kneller first painted the tsar in Utrecht in September 1697 that even Western scholars have begun to believe it. This is not the occasion to refute it – my attempt to do that will be published later this year – and I only draw your attention to it as an example of how the myths surrounding Peter continue to grow.[23] There is, however, an anecdote, originating in the late eighteenth century, which gives a version of how Kneller came to paint Peter that is even more distorted than the story about Peter and Letitia and has never hitherto been recounted, as far as I am aware, in English. Peter Krekshin, who had served under Peter and preserved to the end of his life a completely uncritical and idolatrous attitude towards the tsar, recounts in a work published in 1794 how Queen Anne of England, years of course before her accession, asked Peter to sit for his portrait. She then:

> sent to Italy for the famous painter Gotfried Kneller and the engraver the famous Smith. When the said masters arrived she invited the tsar to dinner in her house. She asked the tsar to sit in a chair facing her and thus Petr Alekseevich sat facing the wall and in the corner of the room by the window there were hanging tapestries, behind which the painting master Gotfried Kneller secretly stood.

It had been agreed that a cup of wine would be brought to the queen when Kneller had finished; but the work continued long after dinner had drawn to an end, so further sweetmeats and fruit were brought and the queen decided to regale Peter with an account of early English history. Finally the wine was brought and the queen ordered Kneller to show the painting to the tsar, who was not pleased (or, as the Russian text has it, 'Nepriiatno bylo tsariu Petru Alekseevichu videt' personu Svoiu, no otobrat' uzhe bylo ne vozmozhno'). Whereupon the queen commanded the engraver Smith to make 'several thousand' engravings on parchment and on ordinary paper and present them to ministers and Parliament and foreign ambassadors and to distribute the remainder free to whomever wanted them.[24]

It was indeed through the engravings made from Kneller's portrait that its fame spread. The most celebrated of them all was by John Smith, Kneller's favourite engraver whom, in a splendid conceit, Kneller painted in 1696, holding his own engraving of the artist's self-portrait.[25] It was Smith's engraving (see Plate 3) which became the model for numerous other engravers, who introduced their own fanciful variations on the tsar's features, clothing and pose. The Russian art critic V.V. Stasov believed that Kneller's portrayal of Peter's face was already 'too idealised', but 'idealization and cosmetic improvement [*prikhorashivan'e*] were even more noticeable' in the work of all who copied him, engravers and painters alike.[26] Smith's engraving was half-length and it is revealing that no engraving of Kneller's full-length portrait has ever been executed. Hot on the heels of Smith's engraving came the exotic and effeminate variant produced by William Faithorne in 1698 and, two years or so later, the anonymous version, captioned 'Peter Alexeewitz the Great Czar of Muscovy who sat down before Nerva in the year 1700 with an Army of 100 000 Men', so rare that only one copy is known to exist, almost inevitably in the St Petersburg Public Library.[27] Some years later, however, the Smith engraving was used in a completely unexpected and novel way.

Luttrell mentions that on Sunday 27 February 'the czar and his priests were at Lambeth house to see the archbishop ordain a minister of the church of England.'[28] The minister in question was Christopher Clarke, born in Norwich in 1671 or 1672, and therefore the virtual coeval of Peter, and a graduate of Christ's College, Cambridge, where he was to be remembered as an important benefactor, providing the money for 'casing with freestone the front of the College from the great gate southwards'.[29] That work was completed in 1740, the year in which the noted mezzotint engraver

John Faber, Jr produced an engraving of Clarke from an original painting (present whereabouts unknown) by J. van Diest. Clarke was then Archdeacon of Norwich and living at Marlingford Hall, where he died two years later, in 1742. The long inscription beneath the engraving details his various offices and includes as a particular distinction the fact that he was 'Ordained Priest, in Lambeth Chappell 27th February 1697 [*sic*] by the Rt. Rev. John, Lord Bishop of Norwich (in the presence of that Renown'd Emperor, Peter the First, Czar of Muscovy, Present also His Grace the Most Rev. Thomas Lord Archbishop of Canterbury, & the Rt. Rev. Gilbert, Lord Bishop of Sarum &c).' What is more, the three-quarter-length portrait shows Clarke in wig, gown and bands standing by a table with his right hand on the Bible, while he points with his left at a wall niche in which there is a bust of Peter. No such bust, however, ever existed and it is obvious that the artist created it from the engraving by John Smith, under whom he may indeed at one time have worked.[30]

I now intend to offer you two further British representations of Peter which, like the one in Clarke's portrait, do not figure in the more conventional iconography of the Russian tsar. Both are uniquely available in a Russian publication in which their significance was not recognised and the captions accompanying them were uninformative, when not erroneous. My slides (shown during the conference lecture) are made from that publication and their value for your edification and entertainment more than outweighs, I believe, their poor quality. Both relate to the period of the Great Embassy, although both are productions of later years.

The first, however, relates to the famous first encounter between Peter and William III, which took place not in England but in Utrecht on 1 September 1697. The official meeting was between the ambassadors of the Great Embassy and the British king with his plenipotentiaries at the negotiations for the Peace of Ryswick, but there followed a secret meeting between William and Peter, which took place in a small gallery at the inn, in the presence of very few attendants who included Franz Lefort, the 'first ambassador' of the Great Embassy, and the Burgomaster of Amsterdam, Nicolas Witsen, acting as interpreter. The Russian standpoint, from the time of that meeting up, indeed, to the present day, is that nothing is reliably known of what was said. There was no official communiqué – after all, the meeting was secret – and the versions of the texts that surfaced subsequently have been rejected as fabrications, not least, I suspect, because Peter is reported to have said so many nice things about William. Within weeks there was a French version of the speech published in London – by the very printer, it should be noted, who was responsible for publishing the English version of Peter and Ivan's 1689 edict, offering refuge to French Huguenots after the revocation of the Edict of Nantes. Luttrell gave what he called 'an abstract' in his diary, and in the following decades various other French and English variants appeared. The controversy was revived when Professor George Barany wrote a little book entitled *The Anglo-Russian Entente Cordiale of 1697–98: Peter I and William III at Utrecht* (New York, 1986), to which he was inspired by the discovery of a contemporary English manuscript version of the speech among the Sutherland Papers in the National Library of Scotland. Although no Dutch version of the speech has ever been discovered – Peter would have given his speech most probably in Dutch (if not in Russian) – circumstantial evidence seems to support the reliability of the French and English versions of 1697. What has been hitherto completely overlooked is that in 1982 in the book by the late Academician Alekseev, to which I have already alluded in connection with the Letitia Cross, there appeared a photograph of a *printed* English version of the speech (virtually the same text as the one in the Sutherland Papers) but captioned as follows: 'Hand-coloured engraving, London, 1698, British Museum, London.' However, my inspection with a magnifying glass of the engraving revealed that it was in fact published by Jacob Robinson, a printer known to be active between 1737 and post-1758, and it was dedicated by him to Arthur Onslow, the Speaker of the House of Commons, a position he occupied between 1728 and 1761. The date of the publication seems to be 1757 (possibly 1753), but why it appeared precisely when it did cannot be established. For our purposes the engraving has its added interest in the representation of the two monarchs and we see them in a setting almost resembling a theatre and with Peter in declamatory pose. To the various mysteries surrounding the publication may be added a further one concerning the location of any copy, for all my enquiries at the British Museum and British Library have brought no results: there is no entry in any catalogue.

Things do, however, re-surface, as my second example from the same source demonstrates.

Peter's ability – before, during and after the Great Embassy – to do justice to the occasional glass of wine, grog, beer or anything that came within reach is not to be disputed and he is known to have graced more than one English hostelry with his presence. A plaque is to be placed, with the encouragement of the Russian Embassy, on the wall of the inn in Godalming, Surrey, where Peter and his companions caroused on their way to Portsmouth, and the same would be done for taverns in Deptford and elsewhere, if they were still standing or traceable. However, during Peter's lifetime at least one tavern took his name and the acquiring of the pub sign was one of the more successful incidents in the visit to England in the first years of the nineteenth century of Lev Savel'evich Vaksel' (or Waxel). Mentioned by Bogoslovskii in his great work on Peter as 'a certain Vaksel' [*nekii Vaksel'*], probably a collector of curios', he was in fact a nephew of Admiral Mordvinov, an archaeologist, antiquarian, draftsman, a member of the Scottish Society of Antiquaries and a Corresponding Member of the Russian Academy of Sciences. The story – as given in John Barrow's anecdote-ful *Memoir of the Life of Peter the Great* (1832) and reproduced by Bogoslovskii – goes as follows:

> Having finished their day's work, they [Peter and his companions] used to resort to a public-house in Great Tower Street, close to Tower Hill, to smoke their pipes and drink beer and brandy. The landlord had the Tzar of Muscovy's head painted and put up for his sign, which continued till the year 1808 [in fact 1804], when a person of the name of Waxel took a fancy to the old sign, and offered the then occupier of the house to paint him a new one for it. A copy was accordingly made from the original, which maintains its station to the present day, as the sign of the 'Tzar of Muscovy', looking like a true Tartar.[31]

Ian Grey, a biographer of Peter whom I have already mentioned, failed in his attempt to locate the inn in Deptford,[32] not that Great Tower Street is there, but it was Alekseev who looked for the sign, which was discovered in the Public Library in St Petersburg, where it had been deposited in 1858.[33] It is in need of restoration and the panel is split; it has never been exhibited. My slides are from the only known published photographs, revealing the slightly differing images of Peter on the front and reverse sides and indeed showing him, if not 'looking like a true Tartar', then certainly neither as Kneller chose to see him. In fact, he looks a bit like a Lord Mayor of London but with the rounded face reminiscent of the Caravaque portrait of 1723. The sign, I would suggest, dates from the second half of the eighteenth century; it was in 1751 that the *Universal Magazine* published an engraving by Anthony Walker, made via P. Soubeyran's engraving (1743) from Caravaque's original painting, and this may have provided the model.[34] Finally, the sign presents a problem I would be delighted to solve: after the publican's name, Edward Wilde, appears the place (?) Hasted. Where is Hasted?

My pursuit of British artists who undertook to produce portraits of Peter now takes me into the nineteenth century and to an encounter with a noted British painter, whose authorship of vast canvases on Petrine themes in a St Petersburg museum was only relatively recently re-established by Elizaveta Renne, Keeper of English Paintings in the Hermitage.[35] Sir Robert Ker Porter is the painter in question, whose long love affair with Russia, beginning with a first visit in 1805 and ending with his sudden death on a visit in 1842, included a very real romance with a Russian princess, Maria Shcherbatova, whom he married in 1812. It is solely his first visit, however, which is described in his *Travelling Sketches in Russia and Sweden*, published in 1809. He had been commissioned by Alexander I to paint a series of paintings, dominated by a portrait of the great Peter, to adorn the Council Chamber of the Admiralty, which was in the course of reconstruction under Zakharov. Porter writes:

> A large full length portrait of the immortal Peter is to be placed at the upper end of this state apartment, under a rich canopy of crimson velvet and gold, draperied in regal style,

and surmounted with every insignia of the imperial dignity. I am now painting on this picture. It is ten feet by seven and a half. I represent my illustrious subject surrounded by naval and military trophies. He rests his right hand upon an anchor, also holding in the same charts of the Caspian and Black Seas; ... At his feet lie the colours of his great northern rival, whose fortune he made stoop on the dreadful day of Pultowa; and over his head waves the imperial flag of his marine. The back ground is a view of Cronstadt, with fleets of men of war and merchant ships, to shew the progress of arms and commerce under his cherishing auspices.[36]

In his desire for authenticity Ker Porter roamed St Petersburg, looking at prints and paintings, visiting the Kunstkamera to see clothes and objects associated with Peter, measuring his height (6' 7") from a nail driven into a door jamb and studying carefully the wax figure of Peter, although he got a bit confused about the authorship of the head: 'The face was modelled from his own, by a lady, during his life; and from it Monsieur Falconet drew some of the sublimest features of his statue. I acknowledge myself to be not less obliged to the fair artist.'[37] How closely he followed Anne-Marie Collot's version of Peter's face we unfortunately cannot say, for the present whereabouts of the painting is unknown – how do you lose a 10' × 7½' canvas? It was last described hanging in its appointed place in the Admiralty in 1819; for some reason, it seems not to have been with its accompanying two paintings, when they were finally transferred, a century later, in 1921, to the Central Naval Museum in St Petersburg. The latter two paintings do survive and they give us other Porter representations of Peter.

Ker Porter went on to describe the two other paintings which he was contemplating: 'of eight feet by seven: one, the Emperor saving the lives of a boat's crew who were perishing in the Lake Ladoga: the other, his Imperial Majesty's naval victory over Admiral Ehrenshield [Ehrenskjöld]'; and there were to be more, as yet undecided but reflecting 'the most eminent acts of his all-glorious life'.[38] In the event, although he does not mention it, Ker Porter substituted Peter at 'The Taking of Azov' for the Ladoga episode, but he duly completed a scene from the battle of Hangö of 1714, showing the captured and wounded Swedish admiral Ehrenskjöld in centre stage, looking up at Peter as if at God and about to offer him his sword. The Peter in this painting was possibly modelled on Karl Moor's famous portrait of 1716, but it is difficult to say on which portrait Peter at the taking of Azov in 1696 could be plausibly based. The former painting has most recently been on display in the exhibition 'Unforgettable Russia: Russians and Russia through the Eyes of the British, 17th–19th Centuries' at the Tretiakov Gallery in Moscow and is reproduced in the catalogue.[39]

By a curious coincidence, another Scottish artist, William Allan, also arrived in St Petersburg in 1805. He soon travelled south, where he was to paint over the next few years picturesque scenes, such as 'Bashkirs Conducting Prisoners to Siberia' and 'Frontier Guards', both of which, incidentally, were on display in the Moscow exhibition I have just mentioned and also, even more recently, in the Hermitage. In 1844, Allan, by then a baronet and a Royal Academician, returned again to Russia, where, at the invitation of Nicholas I, he began a large painting called 'Peter the Great Teaching His Subjects the Art of Shipbuilding'. He took it back with him to London, where he completed it and it was exhibited at the Academy in 1845, before being dispatched to St Petersburg to be hung in the Winter Palace. Sadly, it seems never to have got there; the Hermitage's curator reported in January 1846 that he had only seen the painting in its unfinished state two years previously. Its fate, like that of Ker Porter's portrait of Peter, is thus unknown. Perhaps the loss was not too great; a reviewer in *The Athenaeum* had described the painting as 'characterless, feeble, and unworthy of a place of distinction'.[40]

Finally, we turn our attention to a canvas which, unlike those by Ker Porter and Allan, awaits you in the exhibition. It has not travelled far, only across London, from Royal Holloway College, where it is part of the collection formed by Thomas Holloway and was purchased by him in 1883.[41] It is of course Daniel Maclise's 'Peter I in Deptford, 1698' (see Plate 4), exhibited in 1857 at the Royal Academy, at the schools of which he had won the gold medal for historical composition back in 1829 and of which he had become an Academician in 1840. The Irishman Maclise was nothing if not a man of epic vision, churning out innumerable paintings on historical subjects, reflecting great moments in British history and enjoying enormous popularity with patriotic Victorian England.

Peter, the worker-tsar, learning all the tricks of shipbuilding from English masters, was a self-recommending subject. It is amusing to reflect that it was precisely the subject Horace Walpole suggested to Sir Joshua Reynolds, when the artist was commissioned by Catherine the Great to paint an historical painting on a subject of his own choosing.[42] Reynolds went for 'The Infant Hercules'; given the empress's negative reaction to the delivered painting, he would have done well to have followed Walpole's advice. Be that as it may, we know nothing of the reasons why Maclise selected Peter at precisely this period of his career and the so-called *Memoir*, published in 1871, the year after the artist's death, lists the painting and nothing more.[43] Maclise did supply the painting, which was originally untitled, with a long description which revealed his reliance on Bishop Burnet's characterisation of the tsar as well as other well-known sources. Unlike Ker Porter, Maclise did not have to search far for the appropriate Petrine face; he simply adopted Kneller's, and why not. As for the rest of Peter, he has been given the arms and legs of a shot-putter and he affords a formidable contrast to the thin, pallid, ill-looking, almost effeminate William. The rest of the scene is a stage set in the best or worst traditions of academic historical painting, which were equally obvious in the canvases of Ker Porter, painted half a century earlier. We have a gallery of Russian types, including dwarves, three adoring young ladies, one of whom is allegedly the fair Letitia, the notorious monkey, which is supposed to have jumped at King William on his first visit to Norfolk Street, and a whole array of tools, many of them so modern in appearance that they could be bought today at your local DIY shop. The painting was widely mentioned in reviews in the London papers. There was strong criticism of the painting's static character, the over-crowding and exaggeration, the constant full-glare and lack of subtlety; there was praise, however, for the draughtsmanship and for separate parts in an imperfect whole. One particularly swingeing review ended with the verdict that:

Colour is also everywhere crude and unqualified by general tone. Indeed a footlight effect seems to glare upon the whole; and this, together with the general *mise en scène*, the attitudinising, and the painted faces, would lead us for a moment to fancy we were assisting at a representation of 'L'Etoile du Nord', and that this incident was included.[44]

This quotation and the mention of Letitia suggest that we should finish our Petrine ramble by returning to the theatre, but enter this time by the front door as spectators rather than as stage-door johnnies. By a happy coincidence it is exactly 100 years since the last play written by a British playwright on the theme of Peter ran for a total of thirty-eight performances at the Lyceum Theatre in London. To complement our examination of British pictorial 'representations' of the tsar we can survey briefly his dramatic 'embodiments'.

Peter as a character in a play staged in a British theatre made his debut back in 1748. In that year a so-called 'new historical drama', entitled *The Northern Heroes; or, the Bloody Contest between Charles the Twelfth, King of Sweden, and Peter the Great, Czar of Muscovy*, played at a booth at Bartholomew Fair. Peter makes his delayed entrance at the beginning of Act II, when, as the stage direction informs us, he is appropriately surrounded by 'a model of a Ship, a Globe, and mathematical instruments'. The time is Poltava and Peter is obliged to 'forsake the peaceful Arts, / And lovely Science change for hostile Arms', while he deals with 'this hair-brain'd King, this wild, romantic Hero', who is otherwise known as Charles XII, the Lion of the North.[45] For all its insubstantiality, the play captures well the image of Peter that dominated the British consciousness in the 1740s and 1750s, a period when the idea of Britain and Russia as 'faithful allies' gained ground and a spate of laudatory biographies appeared, beginning with Mottley's already mentioned best-seller in 1739 and ending with W.H. Dilworth's revealingly entitled *The Father of His Country; or, the History of the Life and Glorious Exploits of Peter the Great, Czar of Muscovy*, twice issued in 1758 and 1760. The Peter of *The Northern Heroes* is not quite the God of War of Kneller's portrait and is certainly not Maclise's artisan tsar which chimed in so well with the Victorian cult of 'the working man'; he is rather the ideal Monarch of the Enlightenment: wise, considerate, educated, devoted to his country and its people, peace-loving but prompt to just defence; he was as unlike, indeed, to the real Peter in most respects as was the Peter in further dramatic roles in the eighteenth century. In Joseph Cradock's 'historical tragedy', *The Czar* of 1776, Peter is a flawed colossus, a man with, as Cradock puts it, 'some imperfections'. In some respects he is the tsar familiar to us, extolled by British poets such as Aaron Hill and James Thomson, who commands 'from chaos light and order rise', but he is also, as befits a tragic hero, beset by 'Passions [which] by turns, like storms o'erwhelmed his mind'.[46] An altogether different Peter appears in John O'Keeffe's comic opera of 1790, *The Czar Peter*, which is the first play to reflect the tsar's visit to England and work in the Deptford yards. He is a curious amalgam of buffoon, self-satisfied prig, who makes pronouncements such as 'by your false pursuit of London pleasures, you've gather'd weeds in a flower garden – most contemptible, the degenerate noble who plumes himself upon the illustrious actions of his ancestors', and, of course, lovesick swain, who serenades his beloved with lyrics such as:

> Should wordly cares oppressing
> Encircle us with woes;
> Wilt thou, my earthly blessing!
> Then soothe me to repose.[47]

Let us swiftly bypass several early and mid-nineteenth-century dramas, comedies and, in one case, a full-blown opera, to return to 1898 and the five-act tragedy, entitled *Peter the Great* and written by Laurence Sydney Brodribb Irving. Irving had spent three years in St Petersburg and was something of a Russian scholar, much taken with Dostoevskii and Gor'kii, whom he translated, and, in the view of his biographer, irredeemably affected by Russian 'gloom'.[48] He was also the son of Sir Henry Irving, who headed the star-studded cast, 'fum[ing] and bluster[ing] in the character with an amazing expenditure of energy', as one unkind reviewer suggested; he was supported by Ethel Barrymore as Euphrosine, the Tsarevich Alexis's mistress, and by Ellen Terry as Catherine I, a somewhat minor role for such an actress but, as one critic reflected, her 'first appearance in male attire [was] not easily forgotten'.[49]

Irving's treatment of his subject was as liberal in its treatment of historical fact and chronology as almost every other British or foreign drama or piece of fiction (and, of course, there were lots of novels about Peter which I simply cannot mention). Thus, the seven years before the battle of the Pruth in 1711 and the trial and death of the tsarevich in 1718 are conveniently lost to provide a dramatic opening to the play. Rumours of Peter's capitulation to the Turks led his opponents to acclaim Alexis as tsar. Peter returns and the confrontation between father and son, which is the core of the drama, begins. As *The Times* put it, 'for the purposes of the play we are asked to regard Peter as at heart a kind and indulgent father, who is nevertheless strong enough or misguided enough to subordinate his paternal affections to the interests of the State.'[50]

British opinion of the historical Peter had by the end of the nineteenth century nose-dived since the heady days of the eighteenth and early nineteenth centuries and in the aftermath of the Crimean War and the widespread effects of the apocryphal but highly damning 'Testament of Peter the Great'. Most of the reviewers of the tragedy had harsh words to say about the tsar and the following bears quotation for its condemnation and for the identity of the author. Castigating Peter for 'his personal stinginess [which] was almost as remarkable as his personal poltroonery', it continues:

> it is impossible to make an authentic hero out of him. It was of course a sufficiently extraordinary accident that a seventeenth-century Russian, with the vitality of a man of genius, and a gigantic childishness that saw civilisation as an imaginative boy sees a box of toys, should have been born as free from medieval scruples and superstitions as a nineteenth-century American millionaire; and there is no denying that the childishness offered a rare opportunity to literary and courtly idolisers after his death.[51]

These are the words of George Bernard Shaw, drama critic of *The Saturday Review*, who didn't see the play performed but read the text and was positive about the dramatist's 'frank, contemporary, vernacular English' and the 'essentially modern and realistic' characterisation. The play, however, was never published and thus, in the absence of even a manuscript text, cannot be revived. For another reviewer that would have been just as well, for he believed that:

> it would have been strange indeed had it been reserved to a young dramatist to discover an effective subject in the life of Peter the Great, since so prominent a feature of history must already have presented itself to many minds, only to be discarded. So far, we believe, it has never been successfully treated on the stage without the aid of music ...[52]

Thus the curtain comes down on Peter, who has not been the subject of either painting or play in Britain in the twentieth century (and I exclude with every good reason the NBC television spectacular). Peter has become very much the object of attention from historians and he has lost much of his appeal to the popular imagination. The year 1998 has, of course, done something to restore him to public view; however, if newspaper comment so far is taken as representative it has not done much.[53]

I realise that you have been waiting patiently for the 'old man from Cambridge' to make his promised appearance. The moment has come, although I regret that his is only a bit part and his entrance only in the last act; at least, though, it rates him a first mention in a Petrine context. As you may remember, Peter, according to Nartov, was supposed to have said that in contrast to Letitia, 'for five hundred guineas old men serve me with zeal and intelligence.' Unfortunately, it is impossible to say whether the old man from Cambridge was in their number. It is just that in a long list of items of expenditure for which the merchant Henry Stiles, who was much in attendance on Peter during his stay in London, received later reimbursement. There was, alongside such things as £4 10s for two magnets, £50 for a gold watch, £5 for wigs and £5 12s for twelve pairs of stockings, the entry 'given to the old man who came from Cambridge [*stariku dano chto prishel iz Kambrich*] £2 10s'.[54] No identification of this worthy is, however, possible. Three hundred years on, I'm afraid that you have had to make do with me, an old Cambridge don, who has come to Greenwich today to pay his tribute to the great Peter.

NOTES

1 Henry Fielding, *The Life of Jonathan Wild the Great*, New York, 1962, pp. 22–3.
2 Judith Milhous and Robert D. Hume, 'Theatrical Politics at Drury Lane: New Light on Letitia Cross, Jane Rogers, and Anne Oldfield', *Bulletin of Research in the Humanities*, 85, 1982, p. 412.
3 *Dictionary of Actors, Actresses, Musicians, Dancers, Managers & Other Stage Personnel in London 1660–1800*, 4, Carbondale, IL, 1975, p. 63.
4 Narcissus Luttrell, *A Brief Historical Relation of State Affairs from September 1678 to April 1714*, 4, Oxford, 1857, p. 349.
5 Jeremy Collier, *A Short View of the Immorality, and Profaneness of the English Stage, Together with the Sense of Antiquity upon this Argument*, London, 1698, pp. 133–4.
6 *The Complete Works of Sir John Vanbrugh*, 1, London, 1927, p. 200.
7 M.P. Alekseev, *Russko-angliiskie literaturnye sviazi (XVIII vek – pervaia polovina XIX veka)*, *Literaturnoe nasledstvo*, 91, Moscow, 1982, p. 70.
8 From the Epilogue to *Love and a Bottle*, quoted in *Dictionary of Actors*, p. 63.
9 Milhous and Hume, pp. 424–5.
10 William Van Lennep, ed., *The London Stage*, Part 1 (1660–1700), Carbondale, IL, 1965, pp. 490–4.
11 M.M. Bogoslovskii, *Petr I*, 5 vols, Leningrad, 1941, II, p. 302.
12 John Perry, *The State of Russia under the Present Czar*, London, 1716, p. 166; John Mottley, *History of the Life of Peter I, Emperor of Russia*, 2 vols, Dublin, 1740, I, p. 99.
13 Eleazar de Mauvillon, *Histoire de Pierre le Grand, surnommé le Grand, empereur de toutes les Russies*, Amsterdam and Leipzig, 1742, p. 67. Mauvillon says that he began to translate Mottley, but realised that there were many other sources to tap; however, he declines to name them. See Voltaire's version in his 'Anecdotes sur le czar Pierre le grand' (1748): 'il alla à la comédie anglaise, où il n'entendait rien; mais il y trouva une actrice, nommée Mlle Groft. Dont il eut les faveurs, et dont il ne fit pas la fortune' (*Oeuvres complètes de Voltaire*, 23, Paris, 1879, p. 284).

14 L.N. Maikov, ed., *Rasskazy Nartova o Petre Velikom*, St Petersburg, 1891, p. 9.
15 Milhous and Hume, pp. 420, 426.
16 Lord Macaulay, *The History of England from the Accession of James the Second*, 1, London, 1913, p. 392.
17 Horace Walpole, *Anecdotes of Painting*, quoted in J. Douglas Stewart, *Sir Godfrey Kneller*, London, 1971, p. 6.
18 Cornelius de Bruyn, *Travels in to Muscovy, Persia, and Part of the East-Indies*, 2 vols, London, 1737, I, pp. 21–2.
19 Quoted from a newsletter of 17 February 1698 in Lady Newton, ed., *Lyme Letters 1660–1760*, London, 1925, p. 209.
20 It was, however, fashionable at the time to portray sitters in silken 'Civil Vests' or 'Togas', which Stewart says were then regarded as 'antique': J. Douglas Stewart, *Sir Godfrey Kneller and the English Baroque Portrait*, Oxford, 1983, p. 47.
21 *Ibid.*; Ian Grey, *Peter the Great, Emperor of All Russia*, London, 1960, p. 116.
22 See the dispatches of the Austrian and Brandenburg Residents: Bogoslovskii, *Petr I*, II, p. 310; British Library, Ad. Ms. 30 000B, f.16.
23 See my 'Did Peter Sit for Kneller at Utrecht in 1697?', *Study Group on Eighteenth-Century Russia Newsletter*, no. 26, 1998, pp. 32–42.
24 [P.N. Krekshin], *Kratkoe opisanie slavnykh i dostopamiatnykh del Imperatora Petra Velikogo, ego znamenitykh pobed i puteshestvii v raznye Evropeiskie Gosudarstva ...*, 3rd edn, Moscow, 1794, pp. 49–53. This anecdote is reproduced in full by D.A. Rovinskii, *Podrobnyi slovar' russkikh gravirovannykh portretov*, 2 vols, St Petersburg, 1889, II, cols 1301–2, and in part by Bogoslovskii, II, 583. For an interesting interpretation of this anecdote in a different context, see M.B. Pliukhanova, 'Istoriia iunosti Petra I u P.N. Krekshina', *Uchenye zapiski Tartuskogo universiteta*, no. 513, 1981, pp. 27–8.
25 *Dictionary of National Biography*, 18, London, 1889, p. 112.
26 V.V. Stasov, *Gallereia Petra Velikogo v Imperatorskoi Publichnoi biblioteke*, St Petersburg, 1903, p. vii.
27 *Ibid.*, pp. 11–12; *Anglo-Russian Relations in the Eighteenth Century*, exhibition devised and catalogue compiled by Anthony Cross, Norwich, 1977, p. 6.
28 Luttrell, 4, p. 351.
29 John Peile, *Biographical Register of Christ's College 1505–1905*, 2, Cambridge, 1913, p. 106.
30 *DNB,* 18, pp. 112–13. (Faber, incidentally, engraved in the 1730s Kneller's portraits of members of the Kit-Cat Club.)

31 [John Barrow], *A Memoir of the Life of Peter the Great*, London, 1832, p. 83. Cf. Bogoslovskii, *Petr I*, II, p. 317, where the inn is called 'Czars of Moscow Tavern'!
32 Grey, *Peter the Great*, pp. 117, 457, note 5.
33 Stasov, *Gallereia Petra Velikogo*, p. xi. (Vaksel' apparently presented the sign to the Academy of Sciences on his return from England.)
34 *Universal Magazine of Knowledge and Pleasure*, 9, 1751, facing p. 7. The sign also reproduces the caption 'Czar of Muscovy'. Cf. Rovinskii, II, col. 1352.
35 E.P. Renne, 'Robert Ker Porter v Rossii', *Trudy Gos. Ermitazha*, 25, Leningrad, 1985, pp. 105–9.
36 Robert Ker Porter, *Travelling Sketches in Russia and Sweden during the Years 1805, 1806, 1807, 1808*, 2, London, 1809, pp. 8–9.
37 *Ibid.*, p. 10. Cf. pp. 15, 38–38–9.
38 *Ibid.*, p. 9.
39 *Nezabyvaemaia Rossiia: russkie i Rossiia glazami britantsev XVII–XIX vek*, Moscow, 1997, p. 157. Small black and white photographs of both paintings are in Renne, p. 107.
40 *The Athenaeum*, 1845, p. 466, quoted by Elizaveta Renne, 'British Artists in Russia in the First Half of the Nineteenth Century', in Brian Allen and Larissa Dukelskaya, eds, *British Art Treasures from Russian Imperial Collections in the Hermitage*, New Haven, CT and London, 1996, p. 110.
41 I am most grateful to Dr Mary Cowling, Curator of the Holloway Collection, for the information she generously supplied about the painting.
42 Cf. a letter by Hannah More of 10 May 1786 to one of her sisters: *Horace Walpole's Correspondence*, ed. W.S. Lewis, 31, New Haven, CT, 1961, p. 243.
43 W. Justin O'Driscoll, *A Memoir of Daniel Maclise, R.A.*, London, 1871, p. 121; Algernon Graves, *The Royal Academy of Arts: A Complete Dictionary of Contributors and Their Work from its Foundation in 1769 to 1904*, 5, London, 1906, pp. 156–7.
44 Quoted in Jeannie Chapel, *Victorian Taste: The Complete Catalogue of Paintings at the Royal Holloway College*, London, 1982, p. 110.
45 *The Northern Heroes*, London, 1748, p. 16.
46 Joseph Cradock, *Literary and Miscellaneous Memoirs*, 1, London, 1828, p. xlii.
47 *The Dramatic Works of John O'Keeffe, Esq.*, 3, London, 1798, pp. 205, 165.
48 Austin Brereton, *'H.B.' and Laurence Irving*, London, 1922, pp. 174, 177.

49 *The Times*, 3 January 1898, p. 10; *The Era*, 8 January 1898, p. 15.
50 *The Times, op. cit.*
51 *The Saturday Review*, 8 January 1898, pp. 42-3.
52 *The Times, op. cit.*
53 See, for instance, *The Independent*, 28 March 1998; *The Sunday Times*, 12 April 1998.
54 'Zapis' Oruzheinoi palaty o vydache deneg angliiskomu kuptsu A. Steilsu v vozmeshchenie raskhodov ... 17 ianvaria 1700', RGADA, f. 196, Sobraniia Mazurina, op. 3, delo 195, f.1.

Part II
The Reforms in Context

2 The Petrine Reforms and their Impact

Alexander Kamenskii

The impact, the results and the consequences of the Petrine reforms is one of the most controversial problems of Russian history. From 1725, when Peter the Great passed away, to the present day it has been widely discussed by writers of various kinds: historians, politicians, thinkers, authors of historical fiction and so on. On the one hand, this illustrates the vitality of Peter I as a topic in Russian history and thought. On the other, it once again illustrates that the past, even centuries away, is never dead in Russia and that people feel that to a great extent it determines the present and the future. This means that interest in the Petrine reforms is not just academic but also, perhaps chiefly, of a political nature. Marc Raeff was absolutely right to say that 'the historiography of Peter the Great provides an almost perfect mirror for the Russian intelligentsia's views on the past and future of Russia, their relationship to the West, and the nature of social and political problems confronting their country'.[1] But, politics aside, it is quite evident that the Petrine reforms are a complex phenomenon which cannot be treated in straight-forward terms of good or evil. The same should be said about their impact. It was felt in almost all areas of Russian life and, while some of the results of the reforms seemed very good in the 1720s or 1730s, they turned to be not so good afterwards, and vice versa. More than that, some of the consequences at first were not visible at all and showed themselves only much later. This paper aims to sum up the most important results of the Petrine reforms, to indicate which of them had a long-term significance for Russian history and to demonstrate their contradictory nature.

The first point to be identified is that the reforms allowed Russia to overcome the systemic crisis that occurred in the second half of the seventeenth century.[2] Russia no longer lived under the threat of losing its independence or part of its territory. On the contrary, it became one the world's leading powers and with a modern army and access to the Baltic could claim a corresponding place in the world economy. So from this point of view the reforms appeared to be a kind of a medicine which cured the Russian state of a serious illness. But as often happens, the recovery was not complete and the medicine started to have negative side effects.

The second most vivid result of the reforms was the westernisation and modernisation of the most important political institutions, of the system of government and of the life of society in general. The changes were most striking in the cultural sphere and in everyday life. It was not only that a large and the most active part of Russian society changed into European dress, started to live in houses built in European style, ate European dishes and adopted European types of social and private activities, as well as information and leisure; it was also and, most importantly, that all these material changes to the way of life in turn affected the way of thinking and system of values. Russian society became more dynamic and more receptive to anything new. Assimilation of European cultural values – as well as closer acquaintance with those of them which included elements of civil society – found expression in the fact that some Russians now felt themselves to be not the object but the subject of history. All of the above certainly took place very slowly and gradually while, for a long period of time, elements of the new culture were mixed up with traditional perceptions, sometimes producing fantastic combinations. This was the result of very rapid changes and was linked with a radical rejection of Russian cultural traditions, which in its turn could not but have a negative effect on Russian culture and national consciousness.

As far as government is concerned, the rational principles of its organisation were in a large part merely copied from European models, while the newest ideas of European thinkers were used for its construction. Modernisation left its mark on the names of the offices, posts within them, their hierarchy, the system of control over them, the introduction of permanent salaries and so on. It should be emphasised that these manifestations of modernisation had a strong impact on social consciousness since at least until the reforms of Alexander II in the middle of the nineteenth century there was almost no spheres of social activity outside state service.

Another manifestation of modernisation showed itself in the economy. In the course of the Petrine reforms Russia managed to do away with its technological backwardness. But the judicial and social basis of the new industry with its usage of servile labour and lack of conditions for the appearance of a free labour market meant that the reform did not favour future industrial development. On the contrary, the small elements of a free market economy which could be found in seventeenth-century Russia were destroyed in the course of tax and regional reforms.

The fourth vital manifestation of modernisation concerns the social structure. The destruction of some marginal social groups and the promulgation of some new laws provided at least a theoretical possibility for the formation of European-type estates. But it was here where the contradictory character of the reforms showed itself more than anywhere else, revealing that in fact they were western in form but not in content. In some respects, the social structure of Russian society became similar to that of most European countries but in others the reformer made the future estates even less free than before. The idea of a well-ordered police state as well as the idea of doing one's duty in life-long service to the state for the 'common good' meant the introduction of strict control over all spheres of private life, while the new fiscal system tightly bound everyone either to a definite place of residence, or to a profession or to a social group. To a great extent this seems to be the result of the fact that the formation of a new social structure was not the aim of the reform but its by-product, and the state was not inclined to give the estates the rights without which they could not in fact become real estates. This was even more true in view of the fact that a full-scale legal status within an estate implied a certain degree of self organisation which in its turn meant a certain degree of independence from the state. The conflict between the state and the estates later became an important element in Russian political history. And this conflict was manifested most obviously in the relations between the state and the nobility. It was the nobility who had the most favourable conditions for evolving into a real estate. At the same time, however, the nobility became more dependent on the state than before. Also, simultaneously, the realm of new ideas, secular education and opportunities to learn more about the life of noblemen abroad made a Russian nobleman reflect more thoroughly on his own way of life, his corporate rights and needs. From Peter the Great's time the process of transformation of the Russian nobility into a real estate was in fact a process of consolidation, of gaining rights and privileges and of emancipation. In the course of time the nobility became a mighty political force as every step of its emancipation made it politically stronger. There would have been nothing disastrous in this process if it were not for the fact that the corporate rights of the Russian nobility were tightly bound to those of the peasants.

The strengthening of serfdom appeared to be one of the most glaring contradictions of the results of the Petrine reforms. But Peter still considered peasants to be his subjects, part of the state mechanism with tax paying functions without which it would have been impossible to have a regular army and by whose service to their landlords the service of the army officers and officials was maintained. Noblemen becoming independent meant that the peasants ceased to be the subjects of the state but turned into the landlords' property. In other words, the state was losing control over the larger part of its population. As the nobleman gained more and more rights, so the peasant lost his. One of the most striking peculiarities in the history of the Russian nobility was that their rights to own serfs became part of their rights as an estate. But the process of the formation of the Russian nobility into a real estate, especially its corporate consciousness, was deformed by serfdom because being a member of the nobility meant not only having a high social status, as in other European countries, but also the right to own serfs. It is also quite obvious that the peculiarities of the Russian nobility's corporate consciousness could not but affect national consciousness in general. Also, serfdom made the formation of a middle class very difficult as industry depended on servile labour; therefore the entrepreneurs dreamed of raising their social status by entering the nobility. That is why they did not oppose the nobility but sought a compromise with it. A general conclusion to be drawn is that with serfdom there was no way for synchronous development of an estate order, which in fact gave rise to what is called 'the golden age of the Russian nobility'. As far as the peasantry was concerned, serfdom affected its psychology on a great scale, as well as making it socially passive.

The Petrine reforms also had a very contradictory influence on the Russian economy. On the one hand, there appeared many new works and branches of industry. On the other, industry based on servile labour was doomed to be always short of workers and to develop very slowly. There was certainly no way for a free market to form, and there were also no opportunities for foreign investment. The structure of industry was aimed mostly at satisfying the needs of the state but not the basic needs of the people. That is why it comes as no surprise that before long Russian industry was again lagging behind.

It was due to the Petrine reforms that secular culture appeared in Russia. Without it Russia would not have become a member of the European cultural community and made its contribution to world civilisation. In fact, the new culture was adopted by only a small minority of the population which was split into two unequal parts. This cultural split turned out to be another tragedy of Russian history as the gap between those who adopted the new culture and those who did not became wider and wider with time.

The rapid changes which occurred under Peter made members of the educated elite reflect upon what was going on. It is no accident that at this time Russian memoirs and Russian historical scholarship first appeared. An educated man gradually became frustrated by the discrepancy between the European cultural values on which his education was based and the national cultural tradition. Another discrepancy, he started to realise, was between the imperial ideology and the reality of cultural dependence on the West. All this turns out to be the background for a new national consciousness which was taking shape up to the beginning of the nineteenth century, with bifurcation as one of its most characteristic traits. I am of the opinion that it is here where the origin of the Russian intelligentsia, with its sense of guilt towards the common people, lies.

Another aspect of the consequences of reform concerns the state itself. Owing to the reforms there was no longer any threat of the country disintegrating. Russia became an Empire with a strong centre, a complex but uniform bureaucratic machine, fiscal system, police, army and navy. The regional reform carried out when the Empire was still in the process of formation consolidated a strictly centralised system of governance with political decisions taken only in the centre. This reform contributed a great deal to making Russia 'united and indivisable', to making it a unitary state with a very durable power system. This state now declared itself to be the supreme good and inevitably gave birth to fear and distrust that people felt towards it.

Making Russia an Empire, a kind of a superpower, determined its foreign policies for a long time to come. It is quite natural that Russians were proud of their country. However, in order to maintain this status a strong and large army and navy were needed, which was extremely difficult with an economy based on serf labour, vast unused territories, lands with an unfavourable climate and a low density of population. That meant that maintaining superpower status was possible only at the expense of the people's living standards.

One more important thing should be mentioned. It was due to the Petrine reforms that the transformation of the concept of the tsar and his power occurred. Peter himself did his best to show his subjects that he too was a servant of the state, working hard for the 'common good'. He set the example of an ideal monarch and as a result there appeared a set of criteria by which people now could evaluate any new tsar. Since then society considered that it had the right to demand that the tsar behave himself in a way it thought appropriate. That meant, although it seems paradoxical, the appearance of certain limits on autocracy and also was one of the causes of the so-called palace revolutions of the eighteenth century.

It is quite obvious that the impact of the Petrine reforms was manifested not only in what is mentioned above but also that they had a crucial impact on almost all areas of life and on Russian history in general. Its main contradiction seems to be the preservation of serfdom, which influenced culture, the economy and the social order and formed the basis of a new systemic crisis. In other words, in fighting one crisis the reforms gave way to another.

NOTES

1 M. Raeff, 'Suggestions for Additional Reading' in Raeff (ed.), *Peter the Great Changes Russia*, 2nd edn, Lexington, MA, 1972, p. 195.
2 See A. Kamenskii, 'The Systemic Crisis in Seventeenth-Century Russia and the Petrine Reforms', in A. Cross (ed.), *Russia in the Reign of Peter the Great: Old and New Perspectives*, Proceedings of an International Workshop, held at the Villa Feltrinelli, Gargnano, Italy, 17–20 September 1997, Cambridge, 1998, pp. 1–11.

3 Administrative Reforms in the Russian Empire: Western Models and Russian Implementation

Andrei Medushevskii

TRADITIONAL SOCIETY AND MODERNISATION

Traditional society in the Russian Empire, as opposed to West European models, was characterised by three common features:

- Landed property in principle was concentrated in the hands of the state and was distributed and redistributed by the state bureaucracy in order to realise its military and civil purposes.
- The main social groups were formed by the state or with the intermediate participation of the state according to the whole logic of the 'service state'. That implies the close interdependence of all social groups with each other, on the one hand, and with the state administration on the other. In this system, the *raison d'être* of each social group was determined by its service functions within the framework of the whole system of financial, military and civil government, at the centre and in the provinces. The system of Russian service land tenure is at the very core of this administrative organisation of the state, which was traditionally interpreted by West European analysts, from Montesquieu to Wittfogel, as 'Oriental Despotism'. In spite of such

moral criticism of the system, I would like to stress here that the service state in the Russian Empire lasted a long time and was obviously effective for a traditional society of this kind. The originality of this form of organisation consists in the system's permanent potential for maintaining its stability and reproducing itself under different conditions. This system makes it possible to create and promote an effective military and administrative system on the basis of natural economy and to mobilise economic resources and troops in crisis situations by a command service system from top to bottom without spending a lot of time and money (the military service estate system in Russia).

- The third main feature of the Russian empire is the concept of unlimited monarchical power, embodied in the Orthodox Christian idea of the incorporation of the church hierarchy into the administrative system of the imperial government. In this concept all forms of independent social control over the monarch were eliminated, in theory and in practice.

The main consequences of these principal features of the social and political organisation of the Russian Empire were reflected in the great autonomy of the administrative superstructure and bureaucracy, which became the main instrument in the process of modernisation.

THE RUSSIAN MODEL OF WESTERNISATION AND MODERNISATION: ADMINISTRATIVE REFORMS AS THE INSTRUMENT OF MODERNISATION

The development of economic relations, geographical discoveries, the spread of new means of communication and technical knowledge in modern times unified the world into a single system, each element of which was only a fragment or a part of the whole system. In such a situation, any loss of tempo by a state and any retardation in its development posed a threat to the sovereignty of that state, to its very independence. In such a situation of international competition, the patterns of military, economic and administrative organisation of the most developed states became the models for traditional or underdeveloped states.

This process of reorganisation of society according to new principles and ways of life is known as modernisation. Since in the modern era the most attractive patterns came from Western Europe, this process can also be described as westernisation or, in Max Weber's words, rationalisation. Today we can also use the term globalisation. All the main features of the process of modernisation – the reorganisation of traditional social structures and institutions, the implementation of new European patterns of culture and technology, and the secularisation of life – were represented in the Russian Empire and the other great empires of Eastern Europe and Asia. In these traditional empires, which lacked developed elements of European civil societies, they had to concentrate first of all on administrative reforms from above and on the creation of a new bureaucracy and civil servants, which were simultaneously both the product of modernisation and its main instrument. From this point of view, the whole historical period of the last two centuries of the Russian Empire's existence was a period of bureaucratic modernisation, of reforms and counter-reforms, which can be interpreted as an original strategy for the self-regulation of traditional systems in new world conditions and as the mode of adaptation of the ruling classes to the modernisation process.

From this comparative perspective we can better understand, on the one hand, the similarity of the reform process in Russia and other empires during the eighteenth and nineteenth centuries. On the other hand, this comparative approach gives us the opportunity to consider the fundamental difference between the Russian and other national strategies of modernisation. This difference resulted first of all in the fates of different states in the twentieth century, when Soviet Russia after the civil war became a world superpower and totalitarian state, while other empires disintegrated or, like Turkey in the wake of Kemal Atatürk's revolution, became underdeveloped, Western-oriented states with unstable democratic processes.

In this long-term perspective we can construct two models of modernisation: the revolutionary model and the evolutionary model. For a better understanding of the genesis of these different models, we can analyse the actual mechanism of reforms in Russia and other empires and the specific implementation of Western patterns in different cases.

THE CHARACTERISTIC FEATURES OF REFORMS IN THE RUSSIAN EMPIRE

The most important feature of the reforms in Russia in the eighteenth century was the process of consolidation of property and the creation on this basis of a new ruling class, a process which reached its highest point in the era of Peter the Great. The real social significance of this evolution consisted in the equalisation of the legal status of the conditional service type of land tenure (*pomest'e*) and the permanent hereditary type of land tenure (*votchina*). This process started earlier and developed gradually in the seventeenth century, but judicial legitimation of the equal status of these two main types of landed property became a fact only in the first quarter of the eighteenth century. The unification of property relations on the land and the parallel formation of serfdom formed the social basis for the separation of the ruling class from the rest of the population and stimulated the consolidation of the homogeneous service elite of the state with its stereotyped patterns of culture and the equal participation of its different groups in administration and decision-making processes. In place of the archaic pyramid of different estates under the tsar's court, a ruling class of a principally new type emerged. The most active role in the creation of this new class was played by the state, which strove to maximise its control over the ruling elite and use it as an effective instrument of administration.

A clear demonstration of this tendency in the social politics of Russian absolutism was Peter the Great's idea of limiting the hereditary rights of the landowners by the introduction of the Law of Single Inheritance into Russia (1714) in order to prevent the economic degradation of the ruling class as a result of the endless division of land tenures with each new generation of landowners and at the same time with the aim of providing sufficient staff for the military and civil service.

The main result of this policy was the reorganisation of the ruling class according to new rational principles, as embodied in the well-known legal act the Table of Ranks (1722). Its main principles are as follows:

- The ruling class received a unified structure.
- New principles of social mobility were established (the principles of hereditary priority or *mestnichestvo* were replaced by those of administrative competence and efficiency).
- The Table strengthened the dependence of the ruling class on state power (because career and civil service based on the regular payment of salaries abolished the legal possibility of using other traditional sources of enrichment).
- It accelerated the rationalisation of the ruling class and its internal organisation, which were determined now, on the one hand, by civil rank (and not by its earlier estate position) and, on the other hand, by its functional effectiveness (membership of the military, civil or court branches of administration).

All these features of the new social order were focused in the bureaucratisation of the state apparatus and in the concentration of power in the hands of the ruling elite (the *generalitet*, which consisted of the top four ranks in the Table) and the monarch.

Modern studies written by Russian and foreign historians (including the author[1]) has shown the possibility of placing the Table of Ranks in the broader context of the administrative history of European absolutist states, such as Prussia, Sweden and Denmark, where strict analogies from this time can be found. Important documentation was also provided by the Russian embassies in Great Britain, France and Austria. At the same time archival research into the sources of the Russian Table of Ranks has revealed some documents of Turkish origin (in Russian translation) on military administration, which were probably taken into account in the process of elaborating the Table (for example, lists of military and naval officers and officials with some information about the range of their responsibilities).

Great interest was shown in French and English models of government, in the mechanism of relations between different branches of power – Monarch, Parliament and King's Council – and in the structure of the ruling class in England. We have at our disposal a very detailed description of the political structure of English government, which was written by a close adviser especially for Peter the Great, in order to provide comparative information for the composition of the Table of Ranks. The author of the document was Andrei Artamonovich Matveev (the son of the guardian of the tsar's mother, Natalia Kirillovna Naryshkina, killed during the *strel'tsy* revolt of 1682). One of the most educated men of his time, Matveev was Russian ambassador in Holland, France and England (1707–08) and later became president of the College of Justice. A collection of Matveev's reports was in use and was kept in Peter the Great's Kabinet, his personal chancellery and the supreme political archive of the Empire. I discuss this collection of documents in detail in my book *The Foundation of the Russian Absolutism* and here I want only to cite some important facts.

- Matveev comments on the English Statute of Queen Anne (1707) and underlines the separation of powers of the Monarch and Parliament, explains the position of King's Councils, prerogatives, and the special rights and privileges of the highest officials of the State.
- Another object of investigation for Matveev was the question of mutual relationship or correlation between noble origin and high rank or the political role of the leading officials of the Kingdom. What the Russian diplomat found astonishing was the democratic nature of the social behaviour of the English aristocracy and its openness to the incorporation of gifted representatives from the lower classes and other social groups. In connection with this general idea, he mentioned the possibility of the Admiral-General bestowing noble titles and ranks on the heroes of sea battles. The democratic character of the behaviour of the English aristocracy in Parliament, King's Councils and generally in private and social life contrasted with the patterns of social and political behaviour which predominated in Russia in all spheres of life.

In the broad context of the administrative rationalisation process, the Russian Table of Ranks can be interpreted not as something peculiar and specific to Russia, but as the most impressive realisation of a general modern trend towards more rational government and the formation of a new ruling class and bureaucracy, first of all in countries where the absolutist state became the instrument for the modernisation of traditional patriarchal or feudal structures and landed aristocracies. (That was the case with the old boyar aristocracy, which was absorbed by the new noble ruling elite in Petrine times.)

The modernisation of the state apparatus was realised in the rational principles of its construction, in the creation of a new network of institutions (Senate and colleges instead of the traditional administration by *prikazy*) and the development of planning and efficiency controls. In comparison with the *prikaz*-type administration of old Muscovy, the qualitatively new features of the Petrine administration are the unification, centralisation and functional specialisation of the state apparatus and also its militarisation, which was typical for all absolutist regimes of the period. The most typical traits of the rationalised organisation of power were represented in a unified system of legal norms, different regulations (*reglamenty*), instructions and rules for the functioning of colleges and other institutions; a new formalised hierarchy of levels of administration, institutions and bureaucracy; and new norms for controlling the status and material level of different categories of officialdom and their social mobility. This created the basis for the formation of a genuine corporate ethos in the bureaucracy as a special social stratum and led to a steady increase in its quality from Peter's time onwards. Reorganisation of the state apparatus therefore reflects the deeper changes in the social basis of the absolutist regime and unstable mutual relations between different social structures: the new ruling elite, the bureaucracy in formation and the new regular army.

Another key feature of Peter the Great's administrative modernisation and westernisation is the genesis of the phenomenon of Russian constitutionalism in the past and present. A central concept of Peter's administrative reforms was the ideal of the 'Regular State', which implies a systematic, symmetrical state organisation, functioning in agreement with what are considered correct legal procedures on the basis of established and, in principle, unchangeable laws (not the traditional customs or precedents which prevailed in the previous administrative system). This approach brings us to the vital question of whether the major administrative reforms and political modernisation were a bridge to the creation of a modern Russian constitutional system.

Modern Russia saw a great number of constitutional attempts which failed, but their real impact on the creation of the liberal tradition and political culture in general has not been properly analysed. In my new book on the Russian constitutionalism[2] I trace its origins and critically analyse its nature, main trends and political structure. I examine the process of transition from pre-revolutionary autocratic rule to constitutional monarchy and a democratic social order and, following that, the rebirth of an authoritarian regime. Modern attempts in this direction also can be characterised as an organic part of this original and genuine political tradition, the most important feature of which is the permanent struggle between the idea of representative government and bureaucratic power.

It is remarkable that the English political experience was known and exploited by all those aristocratic opponents who aimed to limit monarchical power in Russia just at the time of the foundation of absolutism and especially after the death of Peter the Great. English models of constitutional monarchy in process of formation was one of the main subjects of discussion in all political projects in Russia in the eighteenth and nineteenth centuries.

The need to introduce some kind of constitutionalism was felt by the Russian ruling elite soon after Peter the Great's death and found its first expression in 1730 in the so-called Conditions (*Konditsii*), addressed to Empress Anna by the Russian aristocratic elite (members of the Supreme Privy Council, the so-called *Verkhovniki*). Other projects from the era of Enlightened Despotism (the second half of the eighteenth century) also aimed at further enlarging the powers and legislative functions of the Senate and other ruling organs. Considerable interest has been shown in comparative analysis of the different forms of Russian legal ideology (in different political projects):

- the oligarchical constitutionalism of the most influential court parties of eighteenth-century Russia with their prototypes from England, Sweden and Poland;
- the concept of a true or legal monarchy with the existence of fundamental laws, which Montesquieu considered to be most important for Enlightened Absolutism (it was realised first of all by Catherine the Great in her Instruction to the Legislative Commission (1766) and later in the policy of official constitutionalism at the beginning of the nineteenth century);
- the modernising bureaucratic absolutism of the nineteenth and early twentieth centuries with its policy of semi-constitutional reforms from above (the projects of M.M. Speranskii and later N.A. Valuev and S.Iu. Witte; the Manifesto of 17 October 1905 drafted by Nicholas II).

Another part of the Russian constitutional tradition, as represented by the constitutional projects of the leading figures of the Decembrist movement, deeply influenced Russian political thought before the reforms of the 1860s. In many respects this path was revolutionary. It envisaged the abandonment of the old patriarchal system through the abolition of serfdom and the monarchical regime and the introduction of a European model of government and judicial system (in republican or constitutional monarchical form). In my book I outline the main features of Russian bureaucratic constitutionalism after the liberal reforms of the 1860s. Throughout this period the driving force of Russian constitutionalism was the enlightened bureaucracy, which tried in fact to preserve the monarchical government through this reformist path. It was a form of bureaucratic constitutionalism from above. Educated liberal society and its most important thinkers (B.N. Chicherin, K.D. Kavelin, A.D. Gradovskii and S.A. Muromtsev) contended that only a strong centralised state could simultaneously keep order and promulgate sweeping civil reforms, for when nations lacking democratic experience embark on extensive reforms, the absence of a powerful state apparatus may lead to uncontrolled revolutionary ferment. The 1905 revolution brought to light the urgent need for political and constitutional modernisation in Russia (the projects of P.B. Struve, S.A. Muromtsev and F.F. Kokoshkin). But the autocratic regime showed itself incapable of promoting those political measures through which it might modernise itself and Russian society as a whole.

From this viewpoint we can sketch the true meaning of the term 'constitution' as it appears in juridical literature and political projects in the period after the French revolution. Between the end of the eighteenth and the beginning of the nineteenth century the constitutional question aroused great controversy inside the Russian government. In eighteenth-century Russia the meaning of the word constitution was different from the one that the reformist movement would give it in the nineteenth century. The term meant, in fact, political system, implying the strengthening of the autocratic regime. In the early twentieth century, Russia was ruled by an institutional system commonly defined as constitutional monarchy. This term, however, encompasses a variety of forms and expressions. Along with some generally shared characteristics, the type of regime shows features that vary from country to country.

Within this general framework I outline the constitutional systems of three countries (England, France and Germany) that exerted the deepest influence on European institutional arrangements and Russian legal consciousness. From this point of view, I demonstrate the crisis of the absolutist framework as a constitutional model and the path towards the new principles of a modern liberal state. According to that position I distinguish the typological variety, developmental alternatives and different forms of legitimisation of such a regime and explore the evolution of this phenomenon from the French to the Russian revolution, through to the political transformations of more recent times in the Soviet Union and modern Russia. My comments and criticisms are based therefore on a study of the major imperial and constitutional systems of modern times from both a theoretical and political-science point of view.

The reforms of Peter the Great seen from this perspective created a new model of transition from traditional to modern society. That model contained all the essential traits of all previous global reforms in world history (from Ancient Egypt and the reforms of Constantine the Great in Byzantium to Akbar in the Great Mogul empire). Examples of these traits are changes in religion, transfer of the capital city, geopolitical changes such as the struggle for communications by sea and changes in the administrative apparatus. The principal novelty of Peter's reforms consists in their orientation towards the world geopolitical system and changes in it. From this viewpoint. we can identify the principal new traits in reforms of this type. Among them we would emphasise the planned character of reform (because the purposes and instruments of reform are determined in advance); the conscious general orientation towards a process of modernisation; and the adoption of the best European patterns and forms of socio-economic and military organisation as the model (and source of inspiration).

The very abrupt character of Peter the Great's reforms applied the new features to a model of socio-political transformation, which in its turn became the stereotype or principal reform model for Russia and some West European countries in the era of Enlightened Absolutism (the administrative reforms of Frederick the Great in Prussia, Joseph II in Austria, Catherine the Great in Russia, and Struense's attempts at reform in Denmark). But Peter's model of modernisation was most influential in the Orient, where it was described by many proponents of modernisation. Tanzimat in the Ottoman Empire, the Meiji revolution in Japan and the Hundred Days of Reforms in China were typical examples of the same strategy. However, I have in mind primarily the importance of the Russian model for the Ottoman Empire in Tulip Time and later in Selim III's reign (1789–1807). Peter's model of reform also influenced Ottoman Egypt, where at the beginning of the nineteenth century the governor Mehmet Ali declared himself a follower of Peter the Great and consciously imitated all the principle reforms of the Russian tsar. We can also find traces of influence of this modernisation model in the Tanzimat period. Examples of such influence are a policy of secularisation and persecution of the religious conservative opposition in both countries; the destruction of traditional Jannissary troops by a westernised 'New Model' Army in Mehmed II's reign (1451–81) and the similar elimination of patrimonial *strel'tsy* guards by Peter; and elaboration of the Table of Ranks in the Ottoman Empire at the beginning of the Tanzimat era. However, the revolutionary character of Peter the Great's reforms is matched most closely by the revolutionary character of the reforms of Kemal Atatürk. In both cases we see a radical systematic transformation of traditional society according to broad programmes of nation building and the use of appropriate Western models in order to provide conditions for the modernisation, rationalisation and secularisation of society by using the same instruments: the army, bureaucracy and new educational technologies. After the Second World War examples of such reforms can be found in Gamal Abdel Nasser's Egypt and in the monarchical regimes of Haile Selassie in Ethiopia and Mohammed Pahlavi in Iran. In spite of the great differences in the historical context and political situations in these underdeveloped countries and the actual consequences of reforms, we can see a number of common trends:

- the driving force behind the reforms: modernisation and westernisation of traditionalist societies in order to support and guarantee national survival;
- the forms and methods of their implementation: everywhere this process corresponded with the strengthening of state power, in the absence of a middle class as the leading force of reforms;
- ideology: nationalism and patriotism instead of religion;
- complete reorganisation of ways of thinking and behaviour: the opening of the world and the struggle for seas, the creation of a new capital as an anticlerical and symbolic act, reforms of the way of life such as introduction of a new calendar, alphabet, dress, etc.

Last, but not least, we must note the personal role of the great reformers and charismatic leaders of their nations, of men such as Peter the Great or Kemal Atatürk, who were able to oppose national and religious prejudices and adopt modernisation as their personal destiny.

STAGES OF MODERNISATION

The development of the modernisation process in the Russian Empire has gone through five main stages, in common with other countries of Eastern Europe. I have discussed this problem in three special monographs on the Russian socio-political process in comparative perspective: *The History of Russian Sociology* (Moscow, 1993); *The Foundation of the Russian Absolutism* (Moscow, 1994) and *Democracy and Authoritarianism: Russian Constitutionalism in Comparative Perspective* (Moscow, 1998).[3] Here I want only to emphasise the possibility and fruitfulness of this comparative approach for reconstructing the five common stages in the modernisation process of great empires.

- The radical modernisation of traditional society beginning with Peter the Great's Grand Embassy to the West in 1697–98. The experience of Peter the Great's reforms was very instructive for Ottoman society and immediately after his military triumph the idea of reforms became very popular. (The Turkish Embassy to the West.)
- The second stage of administrative reforms came into existence under the influence of the European Enlightenment and can be interpreted as an attempt to realise the idea of Enlightened Absolutism, on the basis of fundamental laws. In Prussia, Austria, Russia and the Ottoman Empire this idealistic principle could not be codified in laws nor realised by Friedrich the Great, Joseph II, Catherine the Great or Selim III.
- The third stage was the era of liberal reforms of the nineteenth century, with the main purpose of creating civil society and the state of law from above. In all empires the main social strata interested in this process were the enlightened bureaucracy and intellectuals. They stressed the need to transform the patriarchal monarchy into a constitutional monarchy. From this perspective, the abolition of serfdom and the creation of new liberal legal institutions in Russia may be compared with the ideas of liberal bureaucrats in Germany, the Meiji reformers in Japan and Tanzimat reformers in the Ottoman empire.
- The fourth main stage (the end of the nineteenth and beginning of the twentieth centuries) can be called the constitutionalist period. It was a period of the spread of liberal constitutionalism as the ideology of German and Russian liberals, and Young Turks, elaboration of constitutional projects and a time when the

last monarchical constitutions were drafted and promulgated (in the Ottoman empire in 1876 and in Russia in 1905).
- The fifth stage is the phase of the decline and fall of the Russian, German, Austrian and Ottoman Empires after the First World War and national revolutions (1917 in Russia, 1918 in Germany and 1922 in Turkey).

COMPARISON OF MODELS

However, in spite of this parallelism in the process of using Western models, there were great differences between national conditions and between the strategies of the implementation of Western forms. The core of the differences lies in the approach of reformers to their traditional heritage. In the Russian case, the traditional system of the service state and the corresponding system of administration and ruling class were abruptly broken by Peter the Great and his successors. The new westernised nobility, established by absolutism, lost its previous social function as the military service estate and became a leisure class, separated from the mass of the population and national cultural traditions. The abolition of serfdom in 1861 completed the process of the disintegration of the traditional service state and created the elements of a civil society in the German sense of the term (*bürgerliche Gesellschaft* and *Rechtsstaat*). At the same time, however, this reconstruction destabilised the economic and administrative positions of the ruling class and failed to provide stable vertical channels of communication between traditional structures of agrarian society and the elite. In contrast, the reformers of the more developed German Empire and more traditionalist Ottoman Empire used a properly evolutionary or moderate strategy of social transformation (known as re-traditionalisation) in order to achieve a more adequate implementation of Western models. In reality, to quote the well-known expression, it was the effective realisation of the 'advantages of backwardness'.

NOTES

1 See A.N. Medushevskii, *Administrativnye reformy v Rossii XVIII–XIX vv. v sravnitelno-istoricheskoi perspektive: nauchno-analiticheskii obzor*, Moscow, 1990; *Istoriia russkoi sotsiologii*, Moscow, 1993; *Reformy Petra I i sudby Rossii: nauchno-analiticheskii obzor*, Moscow, 1994; *Utverzhdenie absoliutizma v Rossii: sravnitel'noe istoricheskoe issledovanie*, Moscow, 1994.
2 *Demokratiia i avtoritarizm: rossiiskii konstitutsionalizm v sravnitel'noi perspektive*, Moscow, 1998.
3 See notes 1 and 2 above. None of these works is currently available in English translation.

Part III
Peter and Britain

4 Changing Perspectives: British Views of Russia from the Grand Embassy to the Peace of Nystad

Janet Hartley

When Peter I visited England in 1698 he was regarded with curiosity but not with fear. Russia was perceived as being of only peripheral importance in Europe and of no threat to England. The tsar's victory at Azov in 1696 was noted but this was not seen to be a matter of great concern, although it was remarked that 'It is an extraordinary thing for a Monarch like him to travel hundreds of leagues from his dominions when he has on his hands a great war against the Turks and the Tartars'.[1] It was assumed that Russia's interests lay almost entirely in the East (the congratulatory poem celebrating Peter's arrival in England refers to Russia's 'Glist'ning Sabre on proud *Asia* Gleams ... Its Conquering Steel shall to the *East* give Law'),[2] or at the most were confined to those countries which bordered her. Peter's own views about the current European situation, and the possible implications for Poland, were noted by Matthew Prior, Secretary to the embassy in Paris, but without further comment, as a matter of record rather than of serious concern:

> His [Peter's] own inclinations oblige him to carry on a war with the Turk, and for that purpose to get a fleet ready for the Black Sea. He is absolutely against the French, and that

aversion may contribute a good deal towards settling the crown of Poland upon the Elector of Saxony.[3]

Indeed, John Ellis, Under-Secretary of State in The Hague, wrote sarcastically to William Trumbell, Secretary of State, that Peter would be far better occupied elsewhere:

> Towards the end of the week wee are to expect ye Empr & his Rabble here ... It were to be wishd the Czar loving ye Sea as he does, might discover ye North passage (if there be any such) into Persia, which would be a real advantage that would justify his ramble.[4]

It seems to have been assumed by diplomats at the time that Peter had come to the West to study, as in the words of Wolfgang von Schmettau in The Hague, 'countries more civilised than his own, and especially nations who have developed a Navy, which is his master passion'.[5] But Russia was not seen as a serious naval competitor: the English government did not regard it as dangerous that the king should give Peter the warship the *Royal Transport*, at the time one of the fastest ships which had been built in Britain. Nor was it considered harmful to allow Peter to take English shipbuilders into his service. It was generally assumed that a Russian fleet would be used in the south against the Tartars. Bishop Burnet commented that Peter 'designed a great Fleet at *Azoph*, and with it to attack the *Turkish* Empire'.[6]

Where Russia was seen as important in 1698 was as a potential market for British exports and, in particular, to open up the lucrative market in tobacco to British merchants at the expense of the Dutch who dominated the trade. In return for the gift of the *Royal Transport* and £4000 (and bills of exchange for a further £8000) Peter had permitted Lord Carmarthen and a group of city merchants to import into Russia 3000 hogsheads (one and a half million pounds) of tobacco in the first year, 5000 in the second and 6000 hogsheads thereafter, at a duty of four and a half kopecks per pound. That the tobacco enterprise failed, and the *Royal Transport* was wrecked off the Swedish coast in 1715, does not detract from the fact that this was seen as the main opportunity arising from Peter's visit.[7]

By the early 1720s, Russia's international status had been transformed. The victory over the Swedes at Poltava in 1709, the development of a Russian fleet in the Baltic, the quartering of Russian troops in Mecklenburg in 1716–17 and the territorial acquisitions made by Russia at the Treaty of Nystad in 1721 all meant that British ministers now regarded Russia as a country of considerable military and naval strength which could pose a genuine threat to the European order in general, and British interests in particular. I shall examine the three main areas of concern to the British government:

- first, the potential Russian naval threat to Britain;
- second, the consequences for British trade of the rise of Russia; and
- third, the impact of Russia's new-found strength on the balance of power in Europe.

*****

British interests were most clearly affected by Russia's newly established naval strength, and particularly by her naval presence in the Baltic and territorial acquisitions on the Baltic coastline. By 1719, the British government was sufficiently concerned about the Russian naval threat to attempt to bring home British seamen and craftsmen employed in naval construction in Russia. As James Jefferyes, the British Minister in Russia, warned in the spring of 1719:

> whether it will be for the Interest of great Britain to be a spectator of so growing power as this [Russia], especially at sea, and brought about by her own subjects, I humbly submit to yr Lps [Lordships] consideration ... it is high time that they be called out of the service ... the Czar hath lately said in full Company that his Fleet and that of Great Britain are the two best in the world; if then at present he looks upon his Fleet to be preferable to that of Holland or France may it not be supposed that in some years time he will look upon it to be

equal, if not preferable to ours likewise ... the ships that are built here are as good as any in Europe ...[8]

There were also accusations that British seamen were being seized and forcibly conscripted into the Russian navy.[9]

British ministers were conscious that Russia had several advantages vis-à-vis Britain as a serious naval power. Jefferyes commented in 1719 that:

> no sooner is one ship launched but another is sett on the stocks; all the necessary requisites are the product of his own country; the timber is brought from Casan, but at so cheap a rate, that I have been told he can fitt out a Man of War (reckoning the other requisites proportionally) at 2 thirds less charges than one of the same biggness will cost in great Brittain ...[10]

Lord John Carteret, British minister in Stockholm, wrote in the same year:

> Now 'tis notorious that the Czar can sail half as cheap again as any other nation, for he gives his men much less pay. Provisions are exceeding cheap in his country and he likewise has all the materials of shipping at home for nothing, and the building of his shipping in a manner costs him nothing, the common labourer having no wages, only victuals.[11]

In addition, it proved difficult for the British to man the Baltic fleet. Charles, Viscount Townshend, Secretary of the Northern Department, wrote to William Finch, British envoy in Stockholm, in April 1721 that 'Our seamen have taken such an aversion to the Baltick service' that men had to be press-ganged 'which has given no small offence to our Merchants and occasioned new Clamours'.[12] It had also proved impossible in practice to force British craftsmen to leave Russian service, where they received better pay and conditions than they would at home.

The British maintained a naval presence in the Baltic during the Great Northern War. Initially this took the form of armed convoys to protect British merchants from Swedish privateers, but in the later stages of the war the naval presence was supposed to curb the ambitions of Russia. In 1719 (and for several years thereafter) Sir John Norris was dispatched with a British fleet to the Baltic to intimidate the Russians and oblige them to come to terms with Sweden. The British government was aware of the potential naval threat of Russia in this area which made it imperative that Russian pretensions should be checked before it was too late. Norris himself was both confident but respectful of the Czar's power, writing in July 1719:

> my utmost endeavours shall not be wanting to the total destruction of the Russian naval force, and hope, when it is to be attempted, it may be concerted with a reasonable probability of success, because I think the Czar by his situation, numerous army, and disposition towards the water, to be the most dangerous enemy our country can have.[13]

Norris, however, was unable to subdue the Russians (as he appealed in 1720 '...for God sake lett sumthing be formed to end with this Russian bare for, unless a man be maid with such a hide this climate is insufferable ...').[14] Indeed, the skilful way in which the Russians used their galley fleet in the shallow waters and narrow passages in the Baltic archipelago meant that Norris was unable to engage the Russian fleet at all and exposed the limitations of British fleet as a punitive force. The failure of Norris meant that Peter, far from being tamed, was emboldened as a result of the British expedition. Charles Whitworth, minister in Prussia but previously British envoy in Russia, who had been confident of British success at the beginning of May 1721 ('Sir John Norris's arrival in the Baltick, has certainly blasted all his [Peter's] Designs') wrote to Norris less than three weeks later that 'when you first came into the Baltique, the Czar was as quiet as a Lamb, and all his great threats and Projects were lay'd aside' but that now 'He is grown again as bold as a Lion ...'[15]

Despite this setback, there was still a certain complacency in government circles about Britain's ability to maintain her naval supremacy. Whitworth, who had the direct experience of having lived in Russia and who was strident in his warnings about the increase of Russian power, nevertheless commented in 1721 that 'and for his main Fleet and Forces, they must pass the Sound before they can be formidable or troublesome to Us ...'[16] A constant theme of British ministers in the early 1720s was that other countries had more to fear from Russia as a naval power than had Britain, and that it was the duty of British ministers abroad to convince their hosts that this was the case so that they would join an anti-Russian coalition with Britain or, at least, not be drawn into an alliance with Russia. James, Earl Stanhope, Secretary of the Northern Department, wrote in 1719 to Alexander Hume-Campbell, Lord Polwarth, British envoy in Denmark, that 'I am sure it [the growing power of Russia] concerns Denmark, if they understood their own interest, even more than it does us ... The Czar has already double the force by sea that Denmark can aver ...'[17] In similar vein, Townshend wrote to James Dayrolle, British minister at The Hague, in 1721:

> by not only opening their [the Dutch] Ports to him, but also equipping as it were a whole Fleet for his [Peter's] service; which may very soon prove of the utmost ill consequence not to our Navigation alone, but to that of the Dutch and others in these parts ... for as to us Wee have no need to fear these Muscovites so much, being always in a condition to make them repent their undertaking anything against his Majesty or his subjects.[18]

*****

Russian possession of the Baltic littoral had a potential affect on British trade. Whitworth frequently warned that Russia's ascendancy would be 'intirely destructive to the English Trade in the North'.[19] In early 1721 Whitworth gave Townshend a comprehensive description of the possible impact on British trade of Peter's success at Nystad:

This Peace will leave the Czar Master of allmost all the Naval Stores in the Baltick. The most & best Tarr, & fyr-planck are drawn from Wybourg and Keksholm; Hemp & Flax from Revel; and the finest Masts with vast quantities of hemp, oak-planck & pipe-staves down the Dvina from Riga: As there will be but one market for these Commodities, the trade will be precarious, & prices & terms at least imposed upon our Merchants at pleasure: The Moscovites by their near Situation to Germany, will be tempted in time, to fetch most of their course Cloaths from Saxony, Silesia, & those parts, in return for Russia Leather, Wax, & Ashes, which must lessen the Consumption of our northern Cloaths, & Kersies there: But the worst Consequence of all is, that when the Czar finds himself well settled in Livonia by the Peace, Your Lordp may depend upon it, He will soon begin to send the Product of all his Dominions, to forreign Markets, in his own Vessels; Not only for the gain of the Trade, but to breed up his Sea-Men by those voyages: And as his Navigation increases, Ours in the Baltick must diminish ...[20]

In the 1720s the Dutch still had more ships passing through the Sound than the British[21] and Whitworth himself acknowledged that the Dutch were therefore more vulnerable than themselves ('the Dutch will loose the most by it, for they were the greatest Carriers to those Parts ...').[22] But the Great Northern War, and poor British-Russian relations in the years following it, affected British imports from Russia which had shown a particular decline in the years 1719–23.[23] During the Northern War British merchants had suffered mainly at the hands of Sweden not Russia: Sweden had declared a monopoly on tar in 1703 which affected British imports; British merchant ships were subject to confiscation by the Swedish navy; Swedish privateers were also highly effective. These activities, the Russia Company reported in 1717, led to 'their very great Loss & discouragement of Trade'.[24] The problems had, however, been exacerbated by Peter's instruction in 1713 that British merchants must in future use the ports of St Petersburg and Riga, now in Russian hands, rather than Archangel, which not only made British merchants vulnerable to the activities of the Swedish navy and privateers but also, as the Russia Company reported in 1724, meant that 'the chief Navigation to and from Russia now passes thro' the Sound, to the great increase of the Dutys and port Charges there'.[25]

The British ambassadors in Sweden were instructed to raise the issue of British grievances and the British navy reluctantly provided convoys for British merchant ships in the Baltic. (Merchants complained that the navy used its poorest and least seaworthy ships for these duties.) These actions had little practical affect. In fact the British government had a long history of ignoring or being unsympathetic to the claims of the Russia Company. Indeed, during Peter's visit in 1698 the Company was infuriated that the tobacco contract had been made not with themselves but with a group of new city merchants led by Carmarthen. The British government was concerned, however, by one important aspect of the Baltic trade: the import of naval supplies from the Baltic area. These included masts (the best masts came through the port of Riga), tar and hemp (needed for rope). Britain's lack of self-sufficiency in naval stores made her particularly vulnerable to shifts in power in the Baltic area. In 1721 the House of Commons expressed the fears of the consequences of the peace of Nystad: 'Nor are we yet satisfied, that the peace by us mediated, and concluded in the *North*, hath not made the provision of naval stores for our fleet, more precarious than formerly, though on that single article, the safety of the kingdom may possibly depend.'[26]

The government's concern for naval supplies meant that it was prepared to sacrifice the interests of the Russia Company to ensure reliable and cheap imports of vital goods. In 1724, the Russia Company appealed to the Lords Commissioners for Trade and Plantations for a monopoly to import hemp from Russia to Britain. The Company claimed that their trade was being undermined by 'cheap Freights in the Netherlandish Ships' with the result that the Company could lose a 'great part of their Trade to Muscovy, and more than Fifty Sail of Brittish Ships will be laid by as useless, and the Navigation of this Kingdome diminished and discouraged'.[27] But the Lords distrusted the idea of creating a monopoly in the hands of the Russia Company and found that such a suggestion would 'not be for the Benefit either of Trade or Navigation to restrain the importation of Hemp of the Growth of Russia in the manner desir'd by the Muscovia Company'. In particular, the Lords believed that it would be cheaper to import hemp via Holland than directly from Russia. They also feared that a monopoly could make the navy vulnerable as 'The Czar is already grown so powerful in the Baltick that such an Alteration would make your Majesty's Subjects too much dependent upon him for their Supplies in Naval Stores.'[28]

The concern about overdependence on Russia also led the government to consider ways of stimulating the production of naval supplies in the colonies during the Great Northern War. After 1722, timber and hemp were imported duty-free from North American colonies but this never became a substitute for supplies from the Baltic, not simply because of quality but also because freight and labour costs were so much cheaper in Russia. In 1727 Britain imported 2842 masts from Russia and the Baltic region and only 219 from the American colonies.[29]

Nevertheless, even those ministers like Whitworth who gave dire warnings about the threat to British trade believed that, in the end, Britain and Russia were natural trading partners and needed each other. Whitworth's conclusions in early 1721 were that Britain could best preserve her interests by coalition with other countries to get as favourable a peace as possible; but by October 1721, having digested the peace of Nystad (10 September), he was more confident that:

> The Czar tho' he may & probably will affect our trade by new Designs and Regulations, can not be dangerous to the safety of Great Britain ... As for the Czar himself, all which in my Opinion England has to wish, is only a common intercourse of Civility and Trade: All further engagements are unnecessary, and may be dangerous ...[30]

*****

In 1698 Russia had clearly been regarded as a peripheral power; by the early 1720s British ministers debated the extent to which Russia now had the potential, and the desire, to disturb the whole European order. Both during and after the Great Northern War, Britain attempted to restrain Russian ambitions through the formation of coalitions against her, which is itself indicative of a new respect for Russian power. Foreign ministers, as it has been seen, were urged to stress the potential naval danger of Russia. Ministers also warned of the military threat which Russia now posed to central Europe. Townshend informed James Scott, British minister in Poland, in March 1721 that he had warned the Austrian court of 'the dangers & disadvantages that may arise from letting the Muscovites grow so great and formidable as they do both by Sea & Land'.[31] Whitworth warned the Prussians in April of that year that Peter 'would perpetually hang over Prussia, like a Storm ready to break, & thereby oblige them, almost blindly, to follow the Dictates of his Will'.[32]

There is no doubt that Britain did view Russia by the early 1720s as a power of European significance and a potential disturber of the European peace. George Tilson commented in 1722 that 'I see we shall find ye Czar growing upon us every way ... all Europe might soon tremble before him.'[33] There was certainly an awareness that Peter could, at the very least, cause trouble. Baron Johann Casper von Bothmar, Hanoverian minister of George I, commented in December that 'It appears to me that the empire will always have enough to do as the Czar, to all appearance, intends to keep us occupied.'[34] In particular, Peter was now able to *meddle* in European affairs, which was troublesome but not necessarily dangerous. Whitworth expressed this clearly: 'He [Peter] will only plague you now with intreagues and jealousies, which will cost him little or nothing';[35] 'All our attentions on this side of the world are turn'd on the Czar and his motions which are very extraordinary, but I believe rather desined to amuse than to begin new broyls.'[36] The tsar's capacity to cause consternation was demonstrated by the almost hysterical reaction amongst European powers to a threatened, what one historian has called, 'insignificant naval expedition', in 1723, which in the end came to nothing except that 'the Czar has made a Flurry with a Fleet in the Baltic, and put all his neighbours in alarm.'[37]

British perceptions of their own spheres of influence, and the Russian challenge to them, also changed. In 1698 it seemed of little interest that Peter had beaten the Turks at Azov; by the end of the Great Northern War British interests in the Middle East were seen to be directly affected by Russian advance. John Carteret, 1st Earl

Granville, instructed Abraham Stanyan, the British minister in Constantinople, in 1723 that he should stress the

> inconveniences and dangers, which will attend the Porte, if the Czar should succeed in his designs ... find some means, if possible, to encourage the just apprehensions, which the trading Turks are under, of the entire loss of their Trade ... Russia would be so able to under sell Turkey, that the Trade of the Turkish Empire would be soon swallow'd up, and the Czar in process of time be able to set up again the Grecian Empire at Constantinople itself.[38]

English trade was the crucial concern here as the instruction continues 'The King is particularly concerned for the Trade of His Subjects.' On the other hand, this was also seen as an area where Peter could be usefully distracted from European affairs and where his troops could be diminished by warfare and plague (James Scott commented to Townshend in late 1722 that the Persian campaign had led to many losses 'par les maladies et par la Desertion').[39] Tilson expressed the view to Whitworth in 1722 that he hoped the Persian conflict would 'embroil him, and quell that boiling temper, wch will otherwise diffuse itself on all his neighbours',[40] and in the following year John Campbell, Lord Glenorchy, British envoy to Denmark, hoped that 'the Czar may have work enough next summer on that side and not have time to disturb us here'.[41]

The most direct way in which Peter could directly affect British national interests was through his support of the Jacobite cause. Yet in practice Peter only toyed with the Jacobites, and their high hopes of him were dashed.[42] Although the British government were concerned and kept informed of Russian plans, it was not a central issue in their diplomacy with Russia. Even the ever-vigilant Whitworth dismissed this as a serious threat, writing in 1721 that 'The notion of his [Peter] fitting out ships in forreign Ports to favour the Pretender and joyn with Spain in any such design, is so great a Chimera, that it does not deserve a serious Refutation.'[43] Eight months later he commented, rather less emphatically, that:

tho' there is reason to believe, that He [Peter] was early apprised of the Jacobites designs in England: And without doubt encouraged them by great Promises, in hopes of disturbing yr. Affairs at Home: But He is too poor to supply them with Money; And I am persuaded knows his own Situation too well, to think really of assisting them any other way.[44]

Finally, despite Peter's victory over the Swedes, the Russian threat was seen to be containable. There was a belief that coalitions could be formed against Peter, once other countries were made aware by British foreign ministers that their best interests lay with Britain. As Tilson wrote in May 1721, a concert of powers 'would put a stop to his [Peter's] ambitious views, and make him think twice before he would disoblige such powerfull Allys'.[45] Furthermore the Russian threat was perceived as limited. As Stanhope expressed in early 1721:

And as to the Czar, we are not much in pain how he takes our Reasonings with respect to his Interests ... And when that [the War] is over, it may be in the Choice of the Czar whether he will be well or ill with us, without much concern on our part, he knows very well the Benefits of our Friendship, but if he chuses rather to have us still his Enemys, a Squadron of 12. or 15. Men of War ... will soon let him see what a stop we can put to all his great projects of Grandeur both in Strength and Commerce by Sea.[46]

Even Whitworth became more reconciled to Russia's newfound strength and came to believe that only particularly unfavourable European circumstances would allow Peter to be a serious threat to Britain, writing in 1722 that:

The Czar may be a Bug-Bear to his Neighbours; But neither his Power, nor Designs can immediately affect Great Brittain, nor indeed be of any great Importance to us, but in Case of a general War, and by the Diversion he might then make in the Empire; But I hope the Prudence of his Majesty's Councils, will be able to remove so disagreable an Incident, at least for some years; and in that time Providence may change the State of Affairs to our Advantage ...[47]

Or, as he put it a few days later, in a letter to Tilson: 'I agree with you that the Northern Serpent will be always hissing, and as certainly sting, when it finds occasion: But that does not seem to be so near, except the King of Polands death should cause new Troubles.'[48]

Indeed, it was felt that Russia had benefited from the weakness of others. Whitworth commented that had Sweden been in a position to fight after the death of Charles XII: 'nor would his [Peter's] force be found so terrible as is generally imagined if it was once brought to a real tryal ... his success has been more owing to the weakness of his enemies and their rash measures than to his own strength or conduct.'[49]

*****

British policy towards Russia changed according to domestic circumstances. When Admiral Norris was instructed to destroy the Russian fleet in 1719, all ministers accepted the feasibility of such an active policy. But shortly afterwards, in 1720, the British government was shaken by the South Sea Bubble crisis. This not only undermined the government's confidence but meant that it was less easy to fund expensive and risky expeditions. Townshend stated that it was difficult to put together a squadron considering 'the decay of our publick Credit'.[50]

Furthermore, there was a significant change in personnel in government in the early 1720s which led to a more conciliatory attitude towards Russia. Firstly, Stanhope died in February 1721 and was replaced as Secretary of the Northern Department by Townshend (James Craggs, Secretary of the Southern Department, died a few days later and was replaced by John Carteret). Stanhope had been frank, writing to Norris, 'you should have used your utmost endeavours to do all the mischief you possibly can to the Muscovite fleet, than which a greater service cannot be done to your country.'[51] Townshend had shared the optimism of Norris's expedition but was more inclined to come to terms with the Russians than his predecessor had been and believed that good relations could be established between the two nations, commenting in February 1721 that: 'As soon as the Peace shall be made between Sweden and His Czarish Majesty, there will not remain any difficulty on our part why we should not be well with Muscovy; it is the Interest of both Nations to entertain a mutual good Intelligence ...'[52]

The deaths of Stanhope and Craggs coincided with the rise to power of Robert Walpole, who was appointed as Chancellor of the Exchequer and First Lord of the Treasury in April 1721, and who dominated the administration from 1722. He believed in maintaining neutrality in the Baltic and in not wasting unnecessary expenses on adventurous foreign policy, writing in 1723 that: 'My politics are in a narrow compass, to keep free from all engagements as long as we possibly can. If we keep perfectly well with France and the Czar I am under no alarm of foreign disturbance, which alone can confound us here.'[53]

In 1724 Walpole replaced the Secretary of the Southern Department, Carteret, who had been the minister in Stockholm during the Nystad negotiations, and who had wanted to send a fleet against Russia when Peter carried out his naval exercise in 1723, with Thomas Pelham-Holles, Duke of Newcastle, who was content to follow Walpole's lead.[54]

Finally, Peter remained an enigma to the British; as George Tilson wrote to Whitworth in March 1722, 'I long to hear something certain of ye Czar's designs: he throws out so many contrary hints, as if he design'd to amuse ye world ...'[55] The threat of Russia was often equated with the threat posed by her unpredictable ruler. In turn, fears of Russia were always tempered by the possibility of the tsar's death. Peter's uncertain health gave some cause for optimism. As Polwarth wrote to Tilson in early 1720: 'By a letter I have from Dantzick of the 14th the Czar had relapsed and was very ill of a cholick. If he should drop off it will make matters very easy.'[56]

And ministers assumed that Russia would be weakened by his death. Townshend reported to William Finch in early 1725 that the 'News we have had here of the late great Event in Muscovy by the Czar's death, will undoubtedly have a considerable effect on most countrys in Europe ...'[57] In this, in the short term at least, they were correct. As Vice-Admiral Sir Charles Wager wrote in 1726: 'the Muscovites do not seem to be such a terrible people as they were when the Czar was living ... I have no notion of their galleys being any use ...'[58]

It was ironic that by this date the economic links between Britain and Russia were so strong that there were fears that if Russia became too weak this could have harmful economic consequences. These fears were expressed in March 1730 in the *British Journal*:

> [W]as the City of Petersburgh swallowed up in the sea, as is not unlikely to be its fate in a few years; and were the Ports of Riga, Narva, Revel and Wyburgh, lost to the Muscovites and become Swedish again as they were before, yet we should never want for hemp, Pot ashes, Russia leather, and other valuable Importations from thence, as we had them before, when those towns were in the hands of the Swedes. But the inland trade of Muscovy for the consumption of British Manufactures, that will never be restored, unless the Empire of Russia rouses itself from under the lethargic slumber, which it is now fallen into; their furred Gowns and long Petticoats will return upon them; and all the sordid affectation of a singularity from all the world, which made them so truly contemptible before, will do the like again and where shall our trade be carryed on?[59]

NOTES

1 *HMC Report on the Manuscripts of the Marquess of Downshire*, I, London, 1924, p. 746: Wolfgang von Schmettau to Sir William Trumbell, 4/14 June 1697.
2 Quoted in Leo Lowenson, 'People Peter the Great met in England: Moses Stringer, Chymist and Physician', *The Slavonic and East European Review*, 37, no. 89, 1959, p. 459.
3 *HMC Calendar of the Manuscripts of the Marquis of Bath*, III, London, 1908, p. 161: Matthew Prior to the Marquis of Winchester, The Hague, 19 September 1687.
4 London, British Library, Additional Manuscript (hereafter BL, Add. MS) 28 900, f. 11: John Ellis to Trumbell, The Hague, 3 September 1697.

5 *Manuscripts of the Marquess of Downshire*, I, p. 746: Schmettau to Trumbell, 4/14 June 1697.
6 *Bishop Burnet's History of His Own Time*, II, London, 1734, p. 221.
7 For a more detailed analysis of the relevance of Peter's visit for the tobacco monopoly see W.F. Ryan, 'Peter the Great's English Yacht: Admiral Lord Carmarthen and the Russian Tobacco Monopoly', *Mariner's Mirror*, 69, 1, 1983, pp. 65–87.
8 London, Public Record Office, State Papers (hereafter PRO, SP) 91/9, f. 134v, f. 196v: James Jefferyes to James, Earl Stanhope, St Petersburg, 3 April 1719 OS; the same to the same, 15 May 1719 OS.
9 PRO, SP 91/9, f. 229: Jefferyes to James Craggs, Reval, 6 August 1719 OS.
10 PRO, SP 91/9, f. 217: Jefferyes to Craggs, Reval, 16 July 1719.
11 *HMC Report on the Manuscripts of Lord Polwarth*, II, London, 1916, p. 331: Lord John Carteret to Alexander Hume Campbell, Lord Polwarth, Stockholm, 29 September 1719.
12 PRO, SP 104/155, pp. 246–7, Foreign Entry Books: Sweden 1714–1724: Charles, Viscount Townshend to William Finch, London, 7 April 1721.
13 Quoted in David Denis Aldridge, 'Sir John Norris and the British Naval Expeditions in the Baltic Sea 1715–1727', PhD thesis, University of London, 1972, p. 250.
14 *Polwarth Papers*, II, p. 559: Sir John Norris to Polwarth, Gothland, 26 May 1720.
15 BL, Add. MS 37385, f. 113: Charles Whitworth to George Tilson, 6/17 May 1721; f. 255, Whitworth to Norris, Berlin, 31 May / 11 June 1721.
16 BL, Add. MS 37386, f. 185: Whitworth to Townshend, the Hague, 3/14 October 1721.
17 *Polwarth Papers*, II, p. 276: James, Earl Stanhope to Polwarth, Hanover, 16 August 1719.
18 PRO, SP 104/84, f. 19v–20: Foreign Entry Books: Holland, Secretary's Letters, Townshend to James Dayrolle, London, 8 August 1721.
19 BL, Add. MS 37384, f. 302: Whitworth to Norris, Berlin, 15/26 April 1721.
20 BL, Add. MS 37384, ff. 348v–349: Whitworth to Townshend, Berlin, 22 April / 3 May 1721.
21 Jacob M. Price, 'The Map of Commerce, 1683–1721', in *New Cambridge Modern History*, VI, Cambridge, 1970, p. 871.
22 BL, Add. MS 37388, f. 270: Whitworth to Tilson, Berlin, 7/18 April 1722.

23 G.A. Nekrasov, *Russko-shvedskie otnosheniia i politika velikikh derzhav v 1721–1726 gg*, Moscow, 1964, p. 60.
24 London, Guildhall Library (hereafter Guildhall), MS 11 741, IV, p. 477: Russia Company Court Minute Books, 1708–19, 30 December 1717.
25 Guildhall, MS 11 741, V, p. 167: Russia Company: Court Minute Books, 1817–35, 2 February 1724.
26 *A Collection of the Parliamentary Debates in England*, VIII (1721–22), London, 1741,pp. 207–8.
27 Guildhall, MS 11 741, V, p. 127: 4 February 1723; also at PRO, Colonial Office (hereafter CO) 388/24, f. 76: Correspondence 1722–24.
28 PRO, CO 389/28, pp. 145–6: Lords' Commissioners Papers, 1721–31, 20 March 1724.
29 Douglas K. Reading, *The Anglo-Russian Commercial Treaty of 1734*, New Haven, London, 1938, pp. 28–30.
30 BL, Add. MS 37 386, ff. 185, 186v: Whitworth to Townshend, The Hague, 3/14 October 1721.
31 PRO, SP 104/123, Foreign Entry Books: Poland/Russia, 1712–21, Townshend to James Scott, London, 10 March 1721.
32 BL, Add. MS 37 384, f. 180: Whitworth to Townshend, Berlin, 1/12 April 1721.
33 BL, Add. MS 37 388, f. 315: Tilson to Whitworth, London, 17 April 1722.
34 *Polwarth Papers*, III, p. 74: Baron J.C. von Bothmar to Polwarth, Copenhagen, 25 November / 6 December 1721.
35 BL, Add. MS 37 387, f. 67: Whitworth to Tilson, Berlin, 2/13 December 1721.
36 *Polwarth papers*, III, p. 115: Whitworth to Polwarth, Berlin, 7/18 April 1722.
37 Quoted in Grzegorz Krol, 'The Northern Threat: Anglo-Russian Diplomatic Relations 1716–1727', PhD thesis, University of London, 1992, p. 217.
38 BL, Add. MS 22 518, ff. 109–10: Carteret Papers, John Carteret to Abraham Stanyan, 5 January 1723. See also A.C. Wood, 'The English Embassy at Constantinople, 1660–1762', *English Historical Review*, 40, 1925, p. 551.
39 PRO, CO 389/46, Petitions 1720–24: Scott to Townshend, Berlin, 21 November 1722.
40 BL, Add. MS 37 389, f. 8: Tilson to Whitworth, London, 4 May 1722.
41 *Polwarth Papers*, III, p. 311: John Campbell, Lord Glenorchy, to Polwarth, 12/23 October 1723.

42 See Maurice Bruce, 'Jacobite Relations with Peter the Great', *Slavonic and East European Review*, 14, 1936, pp. 343-62, especially pp. 348-51; also Król, p. 202: 'Jacobite hopes for Russian support were based on the somewhat illusory conviction that Peter the Great was warmly inclined towards them.'
43 BL, Add. MS 37386, f. 185: Whitworth to Townshend, The Hague, 3/14 October 1721.
44 BL, Add. MS 37389, f. 95: Whitworth to Tilson, The Hague, 8/19 June 1722.
45 BL, Add. MS 37385, f. 67: Tilson to Whitworth, London, 2 May 1721.
46 BL, Add. MS 37383, ff. 109-109v: Stanhope to Whitworth, London, 27 January 1721.
47 BL, Add. MS 37388, ff. 134-34v: Whitworth to Scott, Berlin, 6/17 March 1722.
48 BL, Add. MS 37388, f. 180: Whitworth to Tilson, Berlin, 17/28 March 1722.
49 *Polwarth Papers*, III, London, 1931, p. 54: Whitworth to Polwarth, Berlin, 5/16 March 1721.
50 PRO, SP 104/155, p. 246: Townshend to Finch, London, 7 April 1721.
51 Quoted in J.F. Chance, 'The Northern Pacification of 1719-20', *English Historical Review*, 22, 1907, p. 714.
52 BL, Add. MS 37383, f. 201: Townshend to Whitworth, London, 14 February 1721.
53 Quoted in Basil Williams, *Carteret & Newcastle. A Contrast in Contemporaries*, Cambridge, 1943, p. 54.
54 In the word of Plumb, a biographer of Walpole, 'The Czar let Carteret down' in 1723 by pulling back from open conflict and so making his position untenable. J.H. Plumb, *Sir Robert Walpole. The Making of a Statesman*, II, London, 1960, p. 58.
55 BL, Add. MS 37388, f. 141v: Tilson to Whitworth, London, 9 March 1721/22.
56 *Polwarth Papers*, II, p. 469: Polwarth to Tilson, Copenhagen, 16/27 February 1720.
57 PRO, SP 104/125, Foreign Entry Books: Russia 1722-26, Townshend to Finch, London, 23 February 1725.
58 Quoted in Aldridge, *Sir John Norris*, p. 330.
59 Quoted in Jeremy Black, 'Russia and the British Press 1720-1740', *British Journal for Eighteenth-Century Studies*, 5, 1, 1982, p. 90.

5 Diligent and Faithful Servant: Peter the Great's Apprentices in England

Joan Lane

In the year of the Grand Embassy, Peter I could not have been aware what a controversial topic apprenticeship would shortly become in England and could certainly never have thought that his later activities in sending Russian youths there for training might actually contribute to the whole debate. Apprenticeship had existed in England since the eleventh century, a simple arrangement for training in occupational skills in which a child lived *en famille* in the master's household for a fixed period of years (the term), was taught the master's craft, became a qualified journeyman and was admitted into the craft guild. The young man was then able to practise an occupation for life in his own right, eventually hoping to become a master. It was in fact breaking the law to trade as a carpenter, gunsmith, apothecary or any other skilled occupation without having served an apprenticeship. The whole system protected masters by controlling the intake of recruits, by fixing prices and thus limiting competition and also, it was claimed, ensured that customers had the quality of their goods or services controlled, with minimal risk of unskilled workmanship. The majority of all apprentices at all times were male for, although girls could be indentured, they were invariably bound to the poorest, least acceptable occupations and sweated trades. It was never possible for them to be apprenticed in the highly-skilled, profitable male occupations.[1]

Apprenticeship came to England with the Normans and altered little until after the mid seventeenth century, when family fortunes, changed by the civil war, considerably increased the numbers of young boys becoming apprentices. Those who had prospered could place their sons in more superior occupations than would have been possible before 1660, while families who had suffered in the war might find that they were obliged for the first time to apprentice their sons to trades. An expanding English economy based on consumerism, although really a mark of the eighteenth century, can be clearly seen in the closing years of the seventeenth century and there were, thus, more openings for apprentices as masters expanded their businesses, especially after the 1688 Revolution brought the promise of peace to the country.

By the time of Peter's Grand Embassy, English apprenticeship had developed all the features it was to retain for over a century, until its controlling Statute of Artificers[2] was repealed in 1814; on his visit Peter would have observed apprentices and masters actively engaged in a huge variety of trades in both London and the provinces. There were three categories of apprentices in the eighteenth century, of whom the most numerous were the pauper children, bound by their parish officials, the Overseers of the Poor, as an economy for the ratepayers and an effective form of social control as the population swelled. Pauper apprentices might be orphans, illegitimate or simply from a family overburdened with children for whom the parish was legally responsible. Thus it was far cheaper to place a pauper with a distant master, saving the cost of maintenance for many years and eventually giving the child a legal right of support in the parish where the master lived. The middle category of apprentices, a small minority, were the children bound by a charity into a good trade, usually literate, invariably orphans whose own fathers had had a respectable occupation. The most prosperous apprentices in England, amongst whom were the Russian youths, were those placed by their own parents or guardians in large numbers to a wide variety of livelihoods.

The most difficult aspect of apprenticeship to assess after some two centuries is how particular occupations were viewed by eighteenth-century society and therefore considered as more or less desirable careers for boys and girls. Certain occupations changed little in public esteem, some always well regarded for their valuable end-product (silversmithing, cabinet making), others deplored as poorly paid and with no career prospects (brick making, chimney sweeping). Some trades were particularly susceptible to changes in fashion, briefly valued but then declining when tastes altered (button making, wig making). However, one feature common to all occupations that can serve as a yard-stick was the apprenticeship premium, a lump sum paid to the master when the indenture or agreement was signed. The premium was always a reliable indication of an occupation's prosperity and social standing, as well as the apprentice's future earnings and prospects as a journeyman. Premiums were not generally paid until the later seventeenth century and Daniel Defoe noted that they originated in the gift a prospective apprentice might take to the new master's wife to ensure that she would take motherly care of him.[3] Slowly the gift changed into cash and informal scales of payments can soon be discerned, with high premiums to some occupations and very low sums to others. Defoe was extremely critical of large premiums for making apprentices unmanageable and unwilling to undertake menial tasks, and he contrasted the biggest sum (£200) paid in the 1660s and 1670s to Levant merchants in London which had risen to £1000 by 1720.[4]

There were, however, always larger premiums in certain circumstances, most commonly in the professions (surgeon, apothecary, attorney) and in the higher crafts and occupations (stuccoist, cabinet maker, bookseller) and clearly related to the apprentices' future earnings and status. Apprentices to famous men also paid more than the average master would demand, so that William Cheselden, the London lithotomist, took between £150 and £350 with his apprentices in the years 1712-30[5] and Arthur Devis, the artist, required 150 guineas with a boy.[6] Such apprentices often later joined their master in business or even married into his family, thus gaining a prosperous, secure future.[7] Other men who commanded a big premium were those in whose occupations there was high profit but also considerable risk, such as merchants and manufacturers. Since premiums reflected the economic condition of their area, apprentices in London, county towns, fashionable spas and cathedral cities always paid more to their masters than those in small towns and villages.

A minority of apprentices, however, were more difficult to place and for these larger sums would also be paid as an incentive to the masters, so that, for example, disabled children clearly needed special arrangements, including a bigger premium. Children from overseas, although English, came in this category, indentured far from home, sometimes orphaned, usually with no family support during their term. Peter the Great's apprentices were clearly also in this group, with the additional and substantial problems of language and cultural barriers between master and apprentice. The premium covered the costs of keeping the apprentice during the term, his clothes, board and lodging, and also paid the master for instruction, as well as recompensing him for the work the apprentice might spoil or the customers he might offend through his lack of experience. No wages were paid and the master would have benefited from the apprentice's labour only in the last year or two of the term. The value of apprenticeship must have been apparent to Queen Anne's government because they decided to tax premiums in 1709 and the Stamp Act[8] produced an income of £3792 10s. in its first year. The tax was paid on the premiums of all non-pauper apprenticeships. There was a sliding scale of 6d. in the pound for premiums up to £50 and of 1s. in the pound for larger sums. It was so successful a source of revenue that the Act was not repealed until 1804. The tax came into force on 1 May 1709. Tax was collected and recorded on a county basis and the great apprenticeship registers, each of over five hundred pages, are now in the Public Record Office; thirteen volumes cover the years 1710-60 and there are a further nineteen for the rest of the century.[9] In addition to tax details, they record the apprentice's name, home, parentage, premium and term, as well as the master's place and occupation. The original duplicate indentures were retained by the two parties to the agreement, the master and the apprentice's parent or guardian. A written document was essential for an apprenticeship to be legal; an oral agreement was not adequate or binding. The indenture set out the precise obligations and duties for both master and apprentice (Appendix 5.1). In exchange for the premium, the master was to teach the apprentice the art and skill of his trade 'as best he can' and to provide the apprentice with sufficient meat, drink, clothes, lodging, washing and necessaries during the term.

The demands on the apprentice, however, covered both the requirements of the trade and limits on his personal behaviour. The prosperous apprentice was to keep his master's secrets, obey his lawful commands, not harm his master nor see him harmed, not waste nor lend his master's goods and neither buy nor sell without permission. The apprentice's few leisure hours were also controlled by the indenture: he was not to enter a tavern or playhouse, nor to gamble. He was not to be absent from the master's house day or night and he could neither 'commit fornication' nor marry. An apprentice's finances would not normally have allowed him to indulge in any of these activities, since he had no wages. However, the handful of apprentice diaries that have survived for the early eighteenth century show how dissatisfied many were with their circumstances and how they broke various clauses in their indentures. The trade companies were aware of how troublesome apprentices might be and the London Company of Carpenters issued advice to apprentices reminding them:

> You shall do diligent and faithful Service to your Master for the Time of your Apprenticeship, and deal truly in what you shall be trusted. You shall often read over the Covenants of your Indenture, and see and endeavour yourself to perform the same to the utmost of your Power ... You shall be of fair, gentle and lowly Speech and Behaviour to all Men.[10]

An indication of how well-established the indentures were may be judged from the fact that law stationers sold printed apprenticeship forms from the mid seventeenth century, with a space left blank for the premium to be inserted as they were signed.

*****

Although I had worked on the apprenticeships of over 40 000 Warwickshire children and their masters in the eighteenth century, I felt only amazement to find in the London register for 1718 the entry on 22 July for 'Theodore Klepanicen, a Russian' indentured to Samuel Freeth of Birmingham, an edgetool maker, for five years and with a premium of £70, on which the duty was paid on 24 February 1719.[11] I initially presumed a family link as the reason for his coming to Warwickshire, where there were certainly a few English apprentices from overseas serving their terms. However, in the month before Klepanicen's tax was paid, the ironmongers and smiths of Birmingham petitioned parliament against the 'large and unusual sums' paid by 'Muscovites [who have] lately put apprentices to this place to learn the arts of making our iron manufacture.' The Birmingham metal workers feared the Russians would return to 'his Czarist Majesty's dominions to instruct others to the prejudice of the artificers of Birmingham'[12] and in 1719 the Russian Resident in London, Fedor Veselovskii, reported to Peter that complaints had been made to parliament about 'the Russian apprentices who are studying there ... that the training of them was highly prejudicial to England, because on their return to their homeland they would carry on the trades they had learned here and thereby affect the sale of British manufactured goods.'[13] In fact, only Klepanicen was registered as serving an apprenticeship in Birmingham; however, his huge premium of £70 certainly justified local fears if other youths were also indentured at this rate, although under-registration and tax avoidance has long been suspected. Samuel Freeth's trade was not a populous one in Birmingham and the few other edgetool makers there always took premiums of £5 or £10 and for seven years, making the premium worth less because it covered a longer period. However, unlike the majority of masters, for whatever reason, Freeth bound no other apprentices, although most men took two or more at appropriate intervals during their working lives.

As my research progressed, I moved on to the apprenticeship records of other English counties and was delighted to find fifteen more Russian apprentices in the London area.[14] These, however, were all indentured to the shipbuilding trades grouped in the eastern part of Surrey (see Table 5.1), situated south of the Thames, in Southwark, Rotherhithe, Lambeth and Newington. Five were bound to boat or barge builders and three to anchorsmiths, as well as two each to painters, to joiners and to auger makers. There was also a single youth bound to an upholsterer, not necessarily a maritime occupation.

Table 5.1 Russian apprentices to Surrey masters, 1716–18

Date	Apprentice	Term	Premium	Master	Place	Trade
5 Jan 1716	Andres Rogofschi	5 yrs	£40	Wm Norris	Rotherhithe	anchorsmith
5 Jan 1716	Simon Condratur*	5 yrs	£40	Rd Wright	Rotherhithe	joiner
9 Jan 1716	Nick. Goribsoff*	7 yrs	£40	Jas Methurst	Southwark	anchorsmith
9 Jan 1716	Metrius Navikoff*	7 yrs	£60	Thos Jeffery	Southwark	ship's joiner
9 Jan 1716	Stephen Protapopoff*	7 yrs	£60	Jas Knight	Newington	painter
9 Jan 1716	Gregory Asteramuoff*	7 yrs	£60	Wm Parker	Rotherhithe	painter
17 Feb 1716	Andrew Cuzmin*	5 yrs	£80	Thos Bevois	Rotherhithe	boat builder
13 Feb 1716	Tichon Juraskoff*	5 yrs	£55	Henry L'Mar	Lambeth	boat builder
13 Feb 1716	Ivan Schipiloff	5 yrs	£55	Daniel Woodden	Lambeth	boat builder
17 Aug 1716	John Bassanoff*	7 yrs	£50	George Warren	Redriffe	anchorsmith
24 Feb 1717	Stephen Jurassoff	3 yrs	£50	John Coffen	Lambeth	barge/boat bldr
7 Oct 1717	John Uslumoff*	3 yrs	£120	Wm Hayes	Southwark	upholder
13 July 1717	Ivan Schirisoff	3 yrs 7 mths	£30	Thos Dyson	Lambeth	boat builder
24 Apr 1718	John Dejaff*	5 yrs	£70	Thos Roberts	Redriffe	auger maker
24 Apr 1718	John Ulianoff*	5 yrs	£70	John Ellis	Redriffe	auger maker

* apprentice listed in the Ambassadorial Chancellery list (see Appendix 5.2)

The area in which they lived lay close to Deptford, visited by Peter the Great nearly twenty years earlier. Rotherhithe (also called Redriffe) was a separate village, its wet dock built in the years 1696-1700, with a two-mile 'ribbon of wharves and cottages' reaching almost to the edge of Deptford at the Naval Victualling Yard.[15] When its population was about 6000 in 1725, the incumbent noted the majority of inhabitants were 'ordinary traders, gardeners, or such as depend upon the sea'. Lambeth was the site of the fashionable New Spring Gardens (later Vauxhall) in the seventeenth century, although the northern part of the parish along the riverside was highly industrialised, producing glass, pottery and stoneware. With a population of some 7000 in 1725, the parish also contained St Thomas's Hospital and Lambeth Palace, where Peter had met the Archbishop of Canterbury in 1698. Southwark, known from medieval times for its inns, theatres and prisons, was the largest community to which the Russian apprentices were sent, with a population of some 43 000 in the early eighteenth century divided among its three parishes. The Russian youths can be contrasted with those bound by Southwark's seven parochial apprenticing charities, which could pay premiums of only £3 to £5 to indenture deserving local children to various trades and handicrafts. Newington, situated between Southwark and Lambeth, was a smaller and poorer parish in the early eighteenth century, with 'no families of note' in 1717 when Stephen Protapopoff lived there.[16]

*****

These Russian apprentices came to England in groups in 1716, 1717 and 1718, completing their terms in the period 1720-23. Their ages are not known and it seems very possible that they were older than the average English apprentices, who began the term at fourteen and completed it at the age of twenty-one. They might even not have been novices, but have had instruction in their various crafts in Russia before coming to England. The most striking difference between these Russian apprentices and their English counterparts, however, is the size of the premiums that were paid. In 1747 Campbell published his *London Tradesman* as a guide to parents and youths in choosing a career, its prospects, demands on the child and the cost of the premium. For the maritime trades to which the Russians were bound he noted very modest premiums: from £5 to £10 for an edgetool maker, up to £10 for an anchorsmith, from £5 to £10 for a boat builder and from £5 to £20 for a ship's painter, with only the upholder (upholsterer), catering for a luxury market, able to command from £20 to £50 with an apprentice. For all these trades, the hours of work were from 6 in the morning until 7 or 8 o'clock at night.[17]

At this stage, I did not know of the existence of any other Russians coming to England for technical training, but when the Ambassadorial Chancellery file of 1717 was published in translation, it became clear that Peter the Great had sent as many as forty-two youths to England to learn a variety of skills in the years 1715-17, as well as some to Holland.[18] Although there are often discrepancies between the names phonetically written in the London registers and those recorded in the Chancellery list, many are recognisable, especially as their trades were given in the 1717 file (Appendix 5.2). It is also noticeable that five sets of brothers or relations, named Baranov, Chebotaev, Jurass(k)off, Karashev and Martynov, travelled to England together, although indentured to different occupations. It is significant that Peter wished his apprentices to learn more than maritime skills, for of the forty-two names listed, there were a total of ten indentured to furniture making, locksmithing and the 'decoration of beds and other ornaments', as well as two to the making of mathematical instruments, all important for his westernisation plans.

One of the most difficult aspects of these Russian apprenticeships is to ascertain to what calibre of master the youths were sent. Fortunately, of the three bound to furniture making, Fedor Martynov, noted as Theodore Martinoff in the English records, was indentured on 24 April 1718 to George Nix, a cabinet maker of St Paul's, Covent Garden, with the very substantial premium of £100. This was more than six times the sum (£15) he had received two years earlier when indenturing a joiner's orphan son.[19] However, Nix provides a good example of the London cabinet maker of his day, who had, 'although of low origin', according to a contemporary, 'raised himself to eminence in his profession, and from the honest frankness of his conversation, was admitted to the table of the great, and to the intimacy of Lord Macclesfield.'[20] He gained minor commissions from some grand patrons, including tables and chairs for Earl Fitzwalter at Moulsham Hall, tables for Lord Monson at Burton Hall and a kettle stand for the Earl of Leicester at Holkham Hall. Against such a background the Russian apprentice was trained, unfortunately not still with Nix when the latter carried out his finest commission, making and renovating furniture at Ham House for the 4th Earl of Dysart in the years 1729 to 1734. Nix was paid a total of £430 13s 6d for this work[21] and the splendid set of oak chairs in the Great Hall can still be seen there, clear evidence of his own skills being passed on to the Russian youth. An interesting aspect of this particular apprenticeship is that George Nix's earlier apprentice, Edward Halfhide, would have served most of his term as senior to Theodore Martinoff in the workshop.

Unfortunately, since apprenticeship was essentially a personal one-to-one relationship of master and apprentice, not all such arrangements were successful. Hogarth's popular series of engravings, *Industry and Idleness* (1747), powerfully illustrates how the virtuous apprentice, Frank Goodchild, could prosper, finally marrying his master's daughter and becoming Lord Mayor of London, in contrast to the gallows death of Tom Idle, who gambled and generally enjoyed the capital's low life. An indenture could be legally broken in specific circumstances, as, for example, if the master went bankrupt, absconded or died. If the apprentice ran away, the missing time was added on to the existing term when he was caught and returned to the master. However, apprenticeship failed most often because either master or apprentice repeatedly broke the terms of the indenture and because apprentices complained of physical abuse or other forms of cruelty. Masters were *in loco parentis* in the eyes of the law and were thus allowed to chastise apprentices, except for life and limb. For many men physical punishment was the only way they knew to correct a youth for spoiled work, indolence or disobedience and, especially in the poorer trades, there were many examples of cancelled indentures because of a master's cruelty in all eighteenth-century English county quarter sessions. However, not all apprentices were dutiful and some were clearly unmanageable, repeatedly breaking the conditions of the indenture and, on occasions, physically attacking the master or absconding from his service. Such breakdowns were rarest of all in the high-premium occupations, where apprentices were literate and could communicate with their family, who would protest to a brutal or incompetent master on their behalf.

The Russian apprentices were obviously youths and young men in exceptional circumstances, in an unfamiliar culture, far from home, presumably with a substantial language barrier, and facing many years ahead of them living with unknown masters. Not all the Russians settled happily in their new homes and by November 1720 the Resident in London, Bestuzhev, had to inform Peter the Great that two of them, Klepan[i]tsyn and Rokotov, 'constantly run away from their teachers and sell their clothes off their backs. There is nothing good in them and they do not want to learn and their masters do not want to keep them.' The two runaways were to be sent back to Russia, via Holland, and a survey was to be made of the other apprentices' progress. If satisfactory and out of their time, they were to be returned by sea to Archangel in the spring of 1721. There clearly was a degree of disquiet about the role of the apprentices in British-Russian relations, for the royal reply in December 1720 emphasised:

> And if you think that they [the apprentices] will be able to finish their studies in England, because, as has been explained above, we intend no hostile action against Englishmen in our realms, then tell them to remain there; but if you think that they will not be allowed to remain there, then in that case, order them to go to Holland and to complete their studies there.

Prince Kurakin replied on 10 January 1721 that:

> The students who are pursuing studies in England will remain the full time to complete them, since they run no danger. But I am also reporting to Your Majesty that six people who have completed their year will be sent home in spring; and that 10 of the students have written to me that they have acquired the skills in their speciality, but have not yet completed the years required by contract, and they demanded permission of me to leave their masters and go to Holland, and to be sent home from Selby [?]. Not only did I refuse them this, but I wrote in

threatening terms that they were on no account to do this because otherwise no nation would ever accept Russians again.[22]

The actual means by which masters were sought and apprentices allocated is unclear, although there were obviously many formal and other links between Britain and Russia by the early eighteenth century, including men who worked in both countries. In the very early years of the century, when non-apprenticed young men came to England to study, Thomas Stiles, whose brother served the tsar for many years, seems to have been involved in such arrangements in London. In 1708 he reported on two young men, in England for seven years, working in ship-building, who were in financial difficulties. A year later there were accounts of 'dissolute and unruly' young 'volunteers' in London, unable to live within their means. The problems encountered in coping with some Russian pupils in London were vigorously stressed by Samuel Holden, a member and later Governor (1729-31) of the Russian Company. In November 1721 he wrote to Peter the Great requesting payment for the tasks he had undertaken in caring for the Russian apprentices in England during a period of six years. He wished to be recompensed for finding masters for those who did not have them, 'the best masters for them in different arts', providing them with 'necessary things', looking after the sick and sending home those who had finished their training. In addition, he had sent away those who 'fell into debt and were put in prison before their time was up'. He noted finally that there were still twenty-five Russians in England, due to finish their studies in the spring of 1722.[23]

How such arrangements could be initiated can be seen in 1706 when a group of thirty young students were sent to England at the suggestion of Charles Whitworth, the English envoy in Russia. They came as the best pupils from the Moscow School of Navigation and Mathematics to further their naval skills by travelling to England for 'advanced practical training', but they were clearly not apprentices and some were aristocrats. They were described as 'lusty young men and few or none under twenty years old'.[24] Among these students was Ivan Bezsonov, a priest's son, who seems to be the same young man who was apprenticed to an anchorsmith, George Warren of Rotherhithe, for seven years in August 1716; this would support the suggestion that Peter's apprentices were far older than the English boys and already had certain basic skills.[25] Another example of extended training was the case of Andrei Tret'iakov, sent to England to learn barge building in 1715. In April 1722, presumably after a term of seven years, Veselovskii, the Russian ambassador, requested that Tret'iakov be accepted 'to improve himself in the knowledge of that Art' at the Royal Foundry at Woolwich, only to be refused because the Master Founder there was too busy instructing English youths and therefore 'Excused from Entertaining him'.[26]

Since full details of every apprenticeship cannot be traced, it is not possible to match up the seventeen recorded premiums with the sums 'transferred to England to pay for tuition and keep' of the forty-two names in the Ambassadorial Chancellery list of 1717 (Appendix 5.2). Apparently the Admiralty paid the (unknown) charges for 1715-17, but for 1717 the total was £2870, for 1718 it was £920 and for 1719 a total of £518 7s 2d.[27] However, the wide range of high premiums that could have been paid makes precise arithmetic impossible. Since most masters in all trades took more than a single apprentice in their careers, bringing in welcome capital and providing junior trainees at the bottom of the workshop hierarchy, it is striking how most known masters with Russian apprentices apparently eschewed doing so. However, William Hayes, an upholsterer in St George's, Southwark, indentured his own son in 1713, as well as John Uslumoff for four years in 1717, while John Ellis, an auger smith at Rotherhithe, had taken an apprentice in 1715 for seven years with only £10, in contrast to the £70 for five years he received in 1718 with John Ulianoff.

Contemporary English opinion does not appear entirely to have welcomed the Russian apprentices and, although it is clear that a larger than average premium would be required to compensate the master for the additional difficulties in teaching and lodging a foreign pupil, it is also likely that the substantial sum recompensed the master for the lack of other apprentices, enabling him to give undivided attention to his one solitary pupil. Masters might also have been ostracised by their fellow craftsmen for unpatriotically training foreign youths in skills that were important to the country's economy and defence and have found difficulty in trading in their community after the Russian apprentices had left. The antagonistic sentiments expressed by the Birmingham metalworkers could well have been felt elsewhere against those who allowed Russians to share English secrets and skills. The forty-two youths apprenticed in 1716-18 were clearly the largest cohort to come to England as students, as against the thirty named in 1706, and it seems reasonable that apprenticeship was undertaken for this later group because of the strict social and economic controls that the masters could exert. As mentioned above, masters were responsible for the apprentices' welfare and the necessities of life and, under the terms of the indentures, the young Russians would not have been allowed to behave wildly or become destitute while being trained. Craft apprentices were, in any case, more manageable than the wealthy young nobles sent abroad to be taught naval and other skills and on whom there were few constraints.

The question remains: what inspired Peter the Great to decide to send youths to England to become apprentices as part of his modernisation schemes?[28] He would personally have viewed apprenticeship as a good method of training and would have seen apprentices working along the Thames on his visit to London two decades earlier. He greatly admired English ships and shipbuilding and must have seen the obvious advantages of having young workmen trained in English skills living permanently in Russia rather than simply importing older foreign craftsmen to work there. Recent research has shown that apprenticeship, at least in Moscow, existed from the late seventeenth century, although it was less developed and more flexibly defined than in England. It is striking, however, that by 1721 Peter instituted craft guilds in Russia and fixed apprentices' terms at seven years, exactly as in the English system.[29]

The problem of knowing what level of communication existed between master and apprentice remains unsolved. It is inconceivable that the English masters had any knowledge of foreign languages, and certainly not Russian, and, although gesturing and observation could be used in demonstrating practical skills, there were definite limitations. It is, of course, feasible that the apprentices gained some knowledge of English before leaving Russia, where there were numbers of skilled Britons serving the tsar. Many of them probably acquired a good knowledge of English during the period of their apprenticeship. It is equally an open question as to whether all the apprentices returned to Russia and how their careers developed if and when they did so. The whole amazing phenomenon of the Russian apprentices in England can best be summed up by the comments of Gilbert Burnet, Bishop of Salisbury, whom Peter was visiting as part of the Grand Embassy in February 1698. Burnet noted that as he had 'good interpreters' he had 'much free discourse with him [Peter] ... he was, indeed, resolved to encourage learning, and to polish his people by sending some of them to travel in other countries, and to draw strangers to come and live among them.'[30]

Appendix 5.1 A typical apprenticeship indenture, 1705

John Beale of Woolscot in the County of Warwick puts himself apprentice to William Edwards surgeon of Kenilworth to learn his art and with him after the manner of an apprentice to serve for four years from this date. During the term the apprentice shall faithfully serve his master, his secrets keep, his lawful commandments gladly obey; the apprentice neither to do damage to his master nor see it done; the apprentice not to waste his master's goods nor lend them unlawfully. The apprentice not to commit fornication nor contract matrimony during the term; the apprentice not to play at cards or dice or any unlawful game that may cause his master loss. The apprentice not to haunt taverns nor ale-houses nor be absent day or night from his master's service but in all things behave as a good and faithful apprentice towards his master.

William Edwards, in consideration of the sum of £53 16s, shall teach the apprentice all the art he uses by the best means he can. William Edwards shall find the apprentice in meat, drink, washing and lodging during the term.

1 May 1705 [signatures of William Edwards, John Beale and two witnesses]

Source: Warwickshire County Record Office, CR 556/364.

Appendix 5.2 Ambassadorial Chancellery list of apprentices sent to England, 1715-17

Name	Occupation	Name in London register
Ivan Alfer'ev	metal working	
Ivan Bakaev	mathematical instruments	
Antip Baranov	house joinery	
Boris Baranov	chairs, tables, dressers	
Ivan Bezsonov	boat building	John Bassanoff
Rodion Chebotaev	boat building	
Vasilei Chebotaev	ship's joiner	
Ivan Deev	gimlet making	John Dejaff
Mattvei Drozzhin	barge building	
Vasilei Iudin	mast making	
Ivan Ivanov	metal working	
Aleksei Karashev	locksmithing	
Mikhaila Karashev	decoration of beds, other ornaments	
Semen Katsiberdeev	mathmatical instruments	
Fedor Klepanitsyn	carpentry equipment	Theodore Klepanicen
Semen Kondrat'ev	joiner	Simon Condratur
Andrei Kozmin	boat building	Andrew Cuzmin
Ivan Kostiantinov	metal working	
Boris Malochkin	saw making	
Ivan Maliutin	mast making	
Matvei Manturov	house joinery	
Aleksandr Martynov	locksmithing	
Fedor Martynov	chairs, tables, dressers	Theodore Martinoff
Dmitrei Novikov	ship's joiner	Metrius Navikoff
Grigorei Opushkin	saw making	
Grigorei Ostroumov	ship's painter	Gregory Asteramuoff
Stepan Protopopov	ship's painter	Stephen Protapopoff
Vasilei Rokotov	carpentry equipment	
Ivan Salmanov	house joinery	
Andrei Sarygin	chairs, tables, dressers	

Osip Selunskoi	locksmithing	
Iakov Shishkovskoi	oar making	
Andrei Skobel'tyn	metal working	
Petr Sokolov	oar making	
Ivan Suvorov	decoration of beds, other ornaments	
Andrei Tret'iakov	barge building	
Tikhon Turasov	barge building	[? Tichon Jurasskoff]
Ivan Ul'ianov	gimlet making	John Ulianoff
Ivan Usliumov	cannon founding	John Uslumoff
Aleksei Usov	house joinery	
Nikita Zherebtsov	anchorsmithing	Nick. Goribsoff
Petr Zhukov	mast making	

Source: S. Dixon *et al.*, (eds), *Britain and Russia in the Age of Peter the Great: Historical Documents*, School of Slavonic and East European Studies Occasional Papers 38, London, 1998, p. 193.

NOTES

1 See O. J. Dunlop and R. V. Denman, *English Apprenticeship and Child Labour*, London, 1912, and Joan Lane, *Apprenticeship in England, 1660-1914*, London, 1996, for accounts of the history of apprenticeship.
2 Act of Parliament, 5, Eliz. I, c. 4.
3 Daniel Defoe, *The Complete English Tradesman*, London, 1738, p. 138.
4 Daniel Defoe, *The Great Law of Subordination Consider'd*, London, 1724, pp. 10-11.
5 P. J. and R.V. Wallis, *Eighteenth-Century Medics*, Newcastle upon Tyne, 1988, p. 112.
6 E. Hughes, *North Country Life in the Eighteenth Century*, London, 1965, pp. 93-5.
7 Dick Whittington symbolised the apprentice from relatively humble beginnings who prospered and married his master's daughter.
8 Act of Parliament, 8, Anne, c. 5.
9 Public Record Office, I.R.1. 41-48 cover the years 1710-25. The returns for Bedfordshire, Surrey, Sussex, Warwickshire and Wiltshire have been published by their respective county record societies.

10 George Unwin, *The Gilds and Companies of London*, London, 1908, p. 240.
11 Public Record Office, I.R.1, 46/74. Russian names were often garbled when transcribed into Latin script (on the basis of sound rather than consistently transcribed from the original Cyrillic spelling). Compare the spellings on p. 77 below with the names in modern transcription in Appendix 2.
12 House of Commons Journals, XIX, 21 January 1718/19, p. 78.
13 Cited in Anthony G. Cross, *'By the Banks of the Thames' : Russians in Eighteenth-Century Britain, 1700-1800*, Newtonville, MA, 1980, p. 155.
14 Hilary Jenkinson, ed., *Surrey Apprenticeships, 1711-31*, Surrey Record Society, X, 1928.
15 Bridget Cherry and Nikolaus Pevsner, *The Buildings of England: London 2 South*, London, 1984, p. 559.
16 W. R. Ward, ed., *Parson and Parish in Eighteenth-Century Surrey: Replies to Bishops' Visitations*, Surrey Record Society, XXXIV, 1994, pp. 53, 39-40, 56-64, 154-5.
17 R. Campbell, *The London Tradesman*, London, 1747, pp. 240, 299, 323, 169.
18 S. Dixon *et al.*, (eds), *Britain and Russia in the Age of Peter the Great: Historical Documents*, School of Slavonic and East European Studies Occasional Papers 38, London, 1998, p. 193.
19 Geoffrey Beard and Christopher Gilbert, (eds), *A Dictionary of English Furniture Makers, 1660-1840*, Furniture History Society, 1986, pp. 648-9.
20 Lord Teignmouth, *Memoirs of the Life ... of Sir William Jones*, London, 1806, I, p. 10.
21 *A Dictionary of English Furniture Makers*, p. 233.
22 *Britain and Russia*, pp. 233-4.
23 *Ibid.*, p. 235.
24 Cited in Cross, *'By the Banks'*, p. 148.
25 *Britain and Russia*, p. 58.
26 *Ibid.*, p. 194.
27 *Ibid.*, p. 193.
28 On education and learning, see L. Hughes, *Russia in the Age of Peter the Great*, London, 1998, pp. 298-331.
29 See J. Hartley, *A Social History of the Russian Empire, 1650-1825*, London, 1998, pp. 162-170.
30 Cited in Paul Dukes, *The Making of Russian Absolutism, 1613-1801*, London, 1990, p. 68.

6 Peter the Great: the Scottish Dimension

Dmitrii Fedosov

> ... Behold the matchless Prince,
> Who left his native throne, where reign'd till then
> A mighty shadow of unreal power ...
> And roaming every land, in every port ...
> Gather'd the seeds of trade, of useful arts,
> Of civil wisdom and of martial skill.
> Charg'd with the stores of Europe home he goes!
>
> James Thomson of Ferniehill on Peter the Great

One of the earliest announcements of international events in Russia's first newspaper, *Vedomosti*, founded by Peter I in December 1702, dealt with the meeting of commissioners for the Anglo-Scottish union and the final decision on the matter was duly reported in the same source in June 1707.[1] Peter's realm, just then bursting onto the European stage, could not fail to notice the exit of one of its long-standing actors, especially since the first permanent Russian minister to Britain, Andrei Artamonovich Matveev, arrived there at the very time of the Union. As a consequence, Russo-Scottish relations were never established on the official level, although they did prosper in many other ways.

Matveev belonged to a family which embodied novel trends in seventeenth-century Muscovy: his father rose from obscurity to become a confidant of Tsar Alexis and head of the foreign policy of the tsardom; his mother sprang from Scottish Hamiltons, some of whom had fought in the Russian army since the days of Ivan the

Terrible, received lands in reward and eventually changed their name to Khomutov.[2] The Matveev palace, graced with paintings, porcelain, mirrors, chiming clocks and even a private theatre, was the wonder of Moscow, while its hostess, Evdokia, quite unlike diffident Russian matrons of the period, often entertained her husband's guests. In this same place Tsar Alexis met a young ward of the Matveevs, Natalia Naryshkina, who became his second wife and gave birth to Tsarevich Peter in 1672. The kinship of the Hamiltons and the Naryshkins was further sealed by the marriage of Evdokia's niece and namesake to an uncle of the tsarina. Thus, newcomers from the West, and Scotland in particular, gained access to the future reformer of Russia almost from his cradle, and their presence at court soon told on him, despite all the grumblings of intolerant boyars and Orthodox clergy.

Despite the lack of direct evidence, N.V. Charykov has shown convincingly that young Peter's first foreign tutor was Colonel Paul Menzies of Pifodels (1637–94), a scion of a substantial clan in Aberdeenshire.[3] As a graduate of the Scots College at Douai and competent in all the major European languages, Menzies acquired considerable learning. His exploits as a soldier and Russian envoy to German and Italian states were equally impressive. A French acquaintance of his, Foy de la Neuville, reported that Menzies remained in charge of Peter's studies (a position which implies exceptional trust) until falling from favour with the new regime in the early 1680s.[4] We do not know what subjects he taught, but stories of his own travels across Europe would have been sufficient to stir the imagination of his pupil. Peter's regard for Menzies is manifest in the latter's promotion to major-general, in Peter's frequent visits to his mansion in Moscow and in one of the grandest funerals given during that reign.

Peter's passion for things military can be traced to his tender years, and it never left him. What started as a game soon asserted itself as stark necessity. Besides, military reform in Russia had already progressed a long way by the time Peter staged his mock battles, and in this respect, more than any other, he upheld the cause of his predecessors who had also relied on Western, not least Scottish, experience. In the half century between the 1650s and Poltava in 1709 no less than fifteen men of Scottish birth or origin held a general's rank in the Muscovite forces, in addition to numerous colonels and lesser officers. Foremost among them was the figure of Patrick Gordon (1635–99), Peter's chief advisor and bosom friend, who on two occasions virtually saved the throne for his sovereign. Gordon's singular achievements are borne out by contemporary sources, including his own detailed and impartial diary.[5]

A firm adherent (like Menzies) of the Stuarts and a Roman Catholic from the north-east of Scotland, Gordon distinguished himself in the Chigirin (1676–78) and Crimean campaigns (1687–89), reaching the dignity of full general and the most high-ranking foreigner in Muscovy. However, his true rise only began in the late 1680s. Commanding one of the best regular units, the Butyrskii regiment, Gordon supplied Peter's 'stableboy' or 'play' troops with his well-trained men and helped to forge them into the tsar's 'Life Guards', a term which first appears in the General's diary. In 1689 Gordon faced a difficult choice between Regent Sophia – whose prime minister, Prince Vasilii Golitsyn, was his patron – and Peter – who challenged Sophia's power from the Trinity–St Sergius monastery. In the event Gordon rallied foreign officers to support Peter; his journal gives a matter-of-fact conclusion: 'Our going to Troitza [Trinity monastery] was the crisis of this business, for all begun to speak openly in the behalfe of the yongest Tzar.'[6] Peter emerged victorious and, not surprisingly, the very first invitation to a feast in Moscow's Foreign Quarter that he accepted came from Patrick Gordon, whom he honoured with a visit on 30 April 1690.[7]

From then on the tsar hardly ever parted with his trusty old general. Gordon supervised all the army manoeuvres and ensured Peter's first significant conquest, the capture of Azov from the Ottoman Empire in 1696. His final triumph was the suppression of the *strel'tsy* mutiny, which posed a formidable menace to his own person and to the Russian government at large, while Peter was touring the West with the Grand Embassy in 1698.[8]

Contrary to his own modest confessions, Gordon's interests and successes were not confined to the military sphere. He produced perhaps the best chronicle of seventeenth-century Russian and East European history, went on diplomatic missions to Britain and secured the foundation of the first Roman Catholic church in Muscovy. For years his political weight prevented Russia from recognising the outcome of the so-called 'Glorious Revolution' in

Britain, and, as *de facto* Stuart ambassador in Moscow, he paved the way for Admiral Thomas Gordon, Sir Henry Stirling and other Jacobites active at Russian court throughout Peter's reign and beyond.[9] His influence on Peter (if not quite his merit) was rivalled only by Franz Lefort who used to serve under his command. Although Gordon did not turn into a full-fledged Russian, his sincere efforts to do his best for his adopted country as well as his attachment to its young ruler are beyond doubt. Peter could not contain his tears at Gordon's deathbed and closed the eyes of the man who had indeed fought a good fight.

It is tempting to imagine Patrick Gordon in charge of Russian troops at Narva in November 1700 against the Swedes, whose tactics he know perfectly well. As it happened, at the outset of the Great Northern War Tsar Peter suffered a shattering reverse, while Colonel James Gordon, having replaced his father at the head of the Butyrskii regiment, was among the prisoners in that battle along with three of his clansmen.[10] Nevertheless, the war tide was soon turning, and Scottish officers – both seasoned veterans (some of them Russian-born) and new arrivals – stood up to their esteem.

Several of Gordon's comrades-in-arms endured long enough to take on the Swedes, notably John Chambers, 'a Muscovite of Scots race' (in his own words.[11]). One of the chief officers with Peter's 'stableboys' (*poteshnye koniukhi*), he commanded the elite Semenovskii Guards from their foundation, avoided capture at Narva and took part in the first Russian victory over the Swedes at Erestfer, Livonia, in December 1701. His finest hour came three years later when Peter avenged the humiliation of Narva by storming the fortress. Chambers led the assault and won the rank of lieutenant-general along with Russia's highest award, the star of St Andrew.[12]

Tsar Peter entrusted senior command of the army besieging Narva to Field Marshal George Benedict Ogilvie (1644/1648–1710), as soon as the latter appeared in the Russian camp in June 1704. A baron of Austria, this hardy warrior was closely related to his clan chiefs, the Lords Airlie.[13] After the fall of Narva he led the campaign in Lithuania and disagreed with its defensive course, having to cope with contradictory instructions from Peter and King August II of Poland as well as flagrant disobedience and intrigues on the part of Russian colleagues. In such circumstances Ogilvie managed to lead Peter's army to safety in a forced march from Grodno to Kiev through almost impassable terrain. In September 1706 he had to resign from the tsar's employ, allegedly because of ill health, but really for the reasons already mentioned. Still, in just over two years of Russian service Ogilvie made a significant contribution to the reorganisation and training of Peter's soldiers, especially the infantry, which was deemed 'nothing inferior to the best disciplined troops in Europe'.[14] He introduced regular written reports for officers and mitigated military punishments in the belief that 'Russians were but in their infancy, and ought to be brought into discipline by degrees.'[15] His Grodno manoeuvre was praised as 'a classic example of the art of war'.[16] Having held supreme military rank under three different crowns (the Habsburg Empire, Russia and Poland–Saxony), he presents a unique figure in the annals of history.

Throughout the seemingly endless campaigns of Peter the Great the Scottish presence is well attested all over his dominions. Sometimes sheer luck was on their side against all odds. In the autumn of 1708 a strong Swedish corps bent on destroying St Petersburg captured a wagon with the coat of a Russian commander, Brigadier Fraser: a note in one of its pockets carried a warning of the approach of reinforcements, so that the Swedes hastily withdrew.[17] But Peter could always rely on the legendary Scottish fighting qualities. In the same year at the battle of Lesnaia 'the Czar ordered Colonel [James] Campbell with his regiment of dragoons on foot ... to march and drive the enemy off from the morass, where after a sharp dispute (the Russians attacking vigorously) the Swedes were beat from it.'[18] The official list of Russian casualties at Poltava mentions Colonel Leslie, Colonel Inglis and Major Chambers, who certainly had Scottish roots, as well as Lieutenant-Colonel Law whose name also looks suspiciously Scottish.[19] On the other hand, Swedish prisoners of war in Russia included Major-General Hamilton, officers Sinclair, Spens and two Douglases; they all stayed in Russia for many years, while Count Gustav Otto Douglas changed sides to be appointed first Russian governor of conquered Finland.

After Gordon, Peter's ablest associates of foreign descent were the Bruce brothers, born in Moscow into the family of Colonel William, a cadet of the Bruces of Clackmannan.[20] The elder brother

Robert (Roman Vilimovich) from 1704 until his death in 1720 held the post of High Commandant of St Petersburg, which rapidly grew into one of the largest ports and naval bases in northern Europe. Robert gallantly defended the capital and the nearby island stronghold of Kronstadt from the Swedes, repelling every attack on land and sea.[21] He directed the works in the SS Peter and Paul fortress, the Admiralty and other parts of the city and regularly inspected works at Kronstadt. Tsar Peter frequently resorted to Robert Bruce for reconnaissance sallies in the Gulf of Finland as well as offensive operations on Swedish soil.[22] In 1710 Bruce was present at the conquest of Viborg and seized Kexholm on the other side of the Karelian isthmus, ending his career as a lieutenant general and member of the War College. He erected the first Lutheran church in St Petersburg and was buried in the SS Peter and Paul fortress where his remarkable monument can still be seen.

His younger brother James Daniel, or Iakov Vilimovich (1669–1735), was perhaps the most widely gifted man in contemporary Russia and had something to do with almost all of Peter's enterprises. He was among the few close adherents who followed Peter to Britain in January 1698 and the only one allowed to remain there for about a year, which he spent in diligent studies. As a general James became Master of the Ordnance and commanded both Russian and allied artillery in the Great Northern War.[23] He reorganised this branch totally, setting new uniform standards of calibre, introducing a tactical distinction between regimental, field, siege and garrison pieces, and forming horse artillery over half a century before King Frederick the Great of Prussia did the same. As a statesman he was governor of Novgorod, senator and president of the College of Mines and Manufacture, in which capacity he directed the development of Russian industry and mining. Also managing the Mint, he played his part in the adoption of the first decimal coinage system in Europe. As a diplomat he led Russian delegations during Russo-Swedish congresses at Aland and Nystad and concluded the peace treaty which, Peter admitted, could not have been improved even by himself; the jubilant tsar wrote to Bruce, 'this deed of yours, celebrated in the world, can never suffer oblivion, especially since never has our Russia enjoyed such a beneficial peace'.[24] In reward Bruce received huge estates, 10 000 roubles and the title of Count of the Russian Empire. In 1724 at the coronation of Peter's wife Catherine he solemnly carried the imperial crown of Russia, and after Peter's death he retired a field marshal.

James Bruce is also remembered as a versatile scholar, one of the most enlightened men of his time. His scientific pursuits, popularly seen as sorceries, earned him a supernatural reputation, as reflected in Pushkin's description of him as the 'Russian Faust'. A man of vast knowledge, a disciple of Newton, he amassed a library of over 1500 volumes in fourteen languages on a score of disciplines spanning almost everything from astronomy to heraldry. He produced Russia's earliest printed map, founded the first observatory in the country and supervised the Moscow printing house, editing and translating a number of Western works and publishing an elaborate calendar named after him.

In scope and size Bruce's library and collection of 'curiosities' were rivalled by those of Robert Erskine (1677–1718), kinsman of the Earl of Mar and chief physician to Peter since 1704.[25] As president of the Apothecaries' (later Medical) Chancellery he reformed both civil and military medicine in the tsardom. He established hospitals, pharmacies and botanic gardens, collected the earliest surviving Russian herbal, discovered spring waters for medical treatment, planned scientific expeditions to the Caucasus and Siberia and was in charge of Peter's library and natural history museum, the *Kunstkammer*. Were it not for his untimely death, Erskine would have been the most likely candidate for first presidency of the St Petersburg Academy of Sciences, ahead of his subordinate and successor as court doctor, Lawrence Blumentrost.

Another officer active in Peter's reign was Captain Peter Henry Bruce, a cousin of Robert and James born in Westphalia, but later a farmer near Cupar in Fife. An expert engineer, he took part in descents upon Sweden, demolished the enemy fort at Helsingfors (Helsinki) and strengthened the fortifications of Reval (Tallinn) harbour after his own plan. He also made a complete survey of the shores of the Caspian and on Peter's orders taught gunnery and fortification to his grandson, the heir apparent. His thirteen years in Russia (1711–24) are covered in his memoirs.[26] The book is full of keen and sometimes unexpected observations on Russian life; for example, roads ('broad, beautiful and easy for travelling'), the Orthodox faith ('no religion in the world could be conceived to impose more severe mortification on its professors'), *maslenitsa* or Shrovetide ('extravagancies exceed almost all belief ... [they are] drinking brandy and melted butter which they pour down their throats in such amazing quantities that I would imagine the least spark of fire would set their bodies in a flame'), the new capital ('great stir is past description ... not an idle person to be seen'), women ('handsome, their features far from despicable were it not for that preposterous custom of painting their faces which they lay on so abundantly that it may be said they use it as a veil to hide their beauty') and the monarch himself ('as he is a prince that has knowledge of everything, he is not easily imposed on by others ... It was surprising to see so many great things undertaken and put in execution by one single person').

No account of Peter's innovations can be complete without considering naval matters, and here the Scots had another chance to shine. On 28 January 1694 Gordon was created Russia's first rear admiral and in May accompanied the tsar to Archangel. In order to communicate with his own ships and foreign vessels Peter devised a code of nautical signals which Gordon translated into English.[27]

The tsar took every opportunity to hire skilful specialists and craftsmen abroad. Those enlisted for Russian service in Amsterdam by the Grand Embassy were mostly Dutch, but there were ten Scots among them: Commodore George Walker, two 'constables' (naval artillery officers) and seven sailors.[28] Those engaged in England, probably through Vice-Admiral Sir David Mitchell, an Aberdonian who escorted the tsar during his visit, included blacksmith John Lindsay, bombardier Luke Kennedy and Henry Farquharson, lecturer in mathematics from Marischal College, Aberdeen. Farquharson (ca. 1675–1739), perhaps Peter's luckiest signing, was soon running the first special educational institution in Russia, the Moscow School of Mathematics and Navigation, transferred to St Petersburg in 1715 as the Naval Academy.[29] In forty years as a professor he educated hundreds of cadets who served with distinction in the Baltic and elsewhere. Moreover, he published the earliest Russian works on mathematics and astronomy ('Tables of Logarithms', 'Euclid's Elements', etc.), helped to substitute Arabic numerals for Cyrillic and laid out a new straight road between Moscow and St Petersburg which is still in use today. Another important commission from Peter was to keep an eye on the skies, especially 'to calculate all the Eclipses how they will appear, that happen to be visible in his Countrey, which [Farquharson] has always done with very great Satisfaction to the Czar.'[30]

In this period many Scots in Russia remain shadowy figures, but their qualities are readily apparent from the start: valour, endurance, loyalty, smooth integration into an alien, often unfriendly, environment and an amazing range of activity in time and space. Usually added to professional experience, all these ensured their worth and high reputation. The clannish principle and ethnic solidarity were also very much apparent. A thriving Scotsman seldom stands alone. Among the men invited to Russia by Robert Erskine, for instance, were Commodore Thomas Gordon, Captains Robert Little and William Hay and Lieutenant Adam Urquhart,[31] all Jacobite exiles dismissed from the royal Navy. They came to Russia in time to take part in the final phase of the Northern War, but their lots fell differently.[32] Hay, who had commanded British warships for thirteen years, quit his Russian post in less than six, although he saw some action and captured a trophy near Stockholm. In 1719 Little and Urquhart suffered an accident when their ships ran onto a sand bar off Kotlin island.[33] Urquhart lost his life trying to get free, while Little was arrested and demoted, but soon restored to captaincy; he carried on as canal-builder in Kronstadt and died a commodore in 1735. No such troubles afflicted Thomas Gordon, Patrick's cousin or nephew, always highly favoured by Tsar Peter and his heirs. At the head of a large squadron Gordon quickly advanced to vice-admiral (the patent can be seen at the Scottish Record Office), commander-in-chief of Kronstadt and knight of the order of St Alexander Nevskii. He contributed to the Naval Statute of 1720, Russia's oldest, and became the first Briton to achieve full admiralship of the Russian Empire in 1727.

The last reinforcement of Peter's marine staff was Kenneth, 3rd Lord Duffus, who was 'oot' in the Jacobite rising of 1715, and on his forfeiture and release from the Tower of London settled in Holland. He applied to the Russian ambassador at The Hague, offering to become Inspector General or Superintendent of the imperial navy, and supported his claim with a complete written account of British naval regulations and ranks. Impressed, the Russian government hired him in 1722 as rear admiral and member of the Admiralty College with a year's pay in advance.[34]

All told, I have come across thirty Scots recorded in the Russian navy during the reign of Peter I. They were mostly officers, including three admirals (the two Gordons and Duffus). However, it was also the lesser men like Lieutenant Peter Hamilton, translator to the Admiralty, or skipper and rigging master William Caithness who faithfully served the fleet which became the mightiest in the Baltic: 34 ships of the line, 15 frigates and hundreds of smaller vessels. Admiral Thomas Gordon confidently declared that these men-of-war were as good as the English.[35]

The most obvious sign of Scottish legacy is the Russian naval flag, introduced by Peter the Great, discarded by the Bolsheviks and recently restored by the Russian government: a blue saltire on white, a precise mirror image of the Scottish national banner. A chance resemblance? St Andrew, of course, is our common Patron, and the opening passage in the Declaration of Arbroath affirms that the Scots originally came from Greater Scythia, that is the steppes of southern Russia, or Ukraine, where that Apostle allegedly preached. From the days of Kievan Rus' St Andrew was revered as the baptiser of the Slavs, although, contrary to nationalistic claims, Orthodox tradition hardly ever depicted him with a diagonal cross until the very end of the seventeenth century, when the emblem was evidently borrowed from the West. There can be little doubt that the adoption of St Andrew's banner was subsequent to, and closely connected with, the establishment of Russia's first and highest Order dedicated to that saint. I have recently edited for publication the oldest existing Statutes of the Order, dated 1720, but probably going back to its foundation by Peter the Great in 1698. This text contains a straightforward reference to 'the Scottish Order of St Andrew', clearly meaning the Most Ancient and Most Noble Order of the Thistle. The argument goes that since the Scottish Order was suspended on the deposition of the Stuarts – and, when revived in the United Kingdom, it was considered secondary to the English Garter – Russia must restore the prestige of the saint.[36] Curiously, the Russian Statute of the Order retained some features of its Scottish predecessor, that is green mantle, black hat with white plume, the initial number of knights (twelve) and, naturally, the saltire as its main symbol. The question is not *whether* it was a Scottish influence, but rather *who* was the instrument of that influence when the cross of St Andrew became a national device in

Russia. Among the circle of important Scots surrounding Peter, I would suggest James Bruce, who was expert in armorial matters; besides, the saltire is the main charge of the Bruce shield which he proudly bore.

For all the dominance of military and naval issues, Russia's contacts with Europe also flourished in other fields, such as trade. Scottish merchantmen were a common sight in Archangel around 1700,[37] and they quickly appreciated the advantages of Baltic ports newly acquired by the tsar, who once personally 'went on board a small Scots ship, drank a mug of flip with the master and made him a present of a cable'.[38] Links of a different sort are manifest in the macabre story of Mary Hamilton, lady-in-waiting to Tsaritsa Catherine and, by some accounts, mistress to the tsar. In 1719 she was executed in St Petersburg for murdering her child. Peter is said to have supported her to the scaffold and kissed her severed head which he then put on display in a crystal vessel in the *Kunstkammer*; where after many years visitors were still struck by the beauty of the face. The fate of Mary Hamilton strangely resembles a medieval Scots ballad, 'Queen's Marie', which, scholars believe, was revitalised by the tragedy at Russian court.[39]

To conclude, the Scottish impact on Petrine Russia and on its ruler was unsurpassed by any other foreign party, not even the Dutch. This relationship, largely of a personal nature, had the most direct and immediate bearing on the course of events. As long as the greatness of Peter and his age is generally and rightly acknowledged, we must also do justice to the astonishing contribution made to Russian history by one of the most distinguished small nations in the world.

NOTES

1 *Vedomosti vremeni Petra Velikago*, I, Moscow, 1903, pp. 11–12, 395.
2 Russian State Historical Archive (RGIA), St Petersburg, f. 1343, op. 31, no. 2852; *Dvorianskii Adres-Kalendar'*, St Petersburg., 1898, pp. 197–201. See also a birth-brief of Lieutenant-Colonel Alexander Hamilton of the tsar's service (*Register of the Privy Council of Scotland*, dated 1 March 1670). A huge and elaborate family tree of the Hamiltons was ordered by

Matveev from Britain, for a copy of which I am obliged to Mr Igor A. Khomutov.

3   N.V. Charykov, *Posol'stvo v Rim i sluzhba v Moskve Pavla Meneziia.* St Petersburg, 1906.

4   *Rossiia XV–XVII vv. glazami inostrantsev*, Moscow, 1986, pp. 476–8. See also Foy de la Neuville, *A Curious and New Account of Muscovy in the Year 1689*, ed. L. Hughes, London, 1994, pp. 6–8.

5   MS in 6 vols in Russian State Archive of Military History (RGVIA), Moscow, f. 846, op. 15, nos 1–6. All editions to date are faulty and far from complete. See *Passages from the Diary of General Patrick Gordon of Auchleuchries*, Aberdeen, 1859; *Tagebuch des Generals Patrick Gordon*, Bd 1–3, Moscow–St Petersburg, 1849–53.

6   P. Gordon, *Diary*, IV, f. 254.

7   *Ibid.*, 5, f. 11.

8   *Ibid.*, 6, ff. 196v.–201.

9   Gordon's son James, who also served in the Russian army and attained the rank of brigadier, was wounded at the battle of Killiecrankie. On Patrick Gordon's possible contributions to the *London Gazette*, see G. Herd, 'General Patrick Gordon of Auchleuchries: a Scot in Seventeenth-Century Russian Service', unpublished PhD thesis, Aberdeen, 1994.

10 Colonel Alexander, Lieutenant-Colonel Andrew (or Henry) and Captain James Gordon: see N. Ustrialov, *Istoriia tsarstvovaniia Petra Velikago*, 6 vols, St Petersburg, IV, pt 1, 1863, p. 50.

11 *Ibid.*, II, St Petersburg, 1858, p. 127.

12 In 1708 Chambers was made a scapegoat for the unlucky, though not disastrous, Russian defeat at Holowczyn and disappeared from sight; but a Major Chambers, probably his son, served on and was wounded at Poltava.

13 On Ogilvie, see A.F. Steuart, *Scottish Influences in Russian History*, Glasgow, 1913, pp. 73–4; Ustrialov, IV; D.N. Bantysh-Kamenskii, *Biografii Rossiiskikh Generalissimusov i General-Feldmarshalov*, I, Moscow, 1991, pp. 61–8.

14 A. Gordon, *The History of Peter the Great, Emperor of Russia*, 2 vols, Aberdeen, 1755, II, p. 28.

15 Steuart, *Scottish Influences*, p. 74.

16 D.F. Maslovskii, *Zapiski po istorii voennago iskusstva v Rossii*, St Petersburg, 1891, I, p. 105.

17 *Sbornik Imperatorskago Russkago Istoricheskago Obshchestva*, 50, St Petersburg, 1886, pp. 106–7.

18 A. Gordon, *History of Peter the Great*, I, pp. 274–5. After Lesnaia Campbell was promoted to brigadier.

19 *Zhurnal ili Podennaia Zapiska ... Petra Velikago*, 2 vols, St Petersburg, 1770, I, pp. 220–1.
20 See my article on Russian Bruces in *The Scottish Soldier Abroad*, ed. G.G. Simpson, Edinburgh, 1992, pp. 55–66.
21 Ustrialov, IV, pt 2, pp. 317–20, 335–56. Two colonels under Robert's command were named Hamilton and Sharp.
22 *Materialy dlia istorii russkago flota*, I, St Petersburg, 1865, *passim*.
23 A large part of James Bruce's vast correspondence is preserved in the Archive of the Artillery Museum, St Petersburg, f. 2, op. 1.
24 *Zhurnal ili Podennaia Zapiska ... Petra Velikago*, II, p. 177.
25 See R. Paul, 'Letters and Documents relating to Robert Erskine', *Miscellany of the Scottish Historical Society*, XLIV, no. 2, 1904, pp. 373–430; J.H. Appleby, 'Robert Erskine: Scottish Pioneer of Russian Natural History', *Archives of Natural History*, I, no. 3, 1982, pp. 377–98.
26 *Memoirs of Peter Henry Bruce, Esq., a Military Officer in the Services of Prussia, Russia and Great Britain*, London, 1782.
27 Gordon, *Diary*, V, ff. 356v., 369–94.
28 Ustrialov, III, St Petersburg, 1858, pp. 576–81. Walker was recommended to Patrick Gordon by a John Drummond of Amsterdam.
29 See my article 'A Scottish Mathematician in Russia: Henry Farquharson', in *The Universities of Aberdeen and Europe: The First Three Centuries*, ed. P. Dukes, Aberdeen, 1995, pp. 102–18.
30 J. Perry, *The State of Russia under the Present Czar*, London, 1716, p. 212; *Pis'ma i bumagi Imperatora Petra Velikogo*, IX, pt 2, Moscow, 1952, no. 3045 and p. 665.
31 *Materialy dlia istorii russkago flota*, III, pp. 164, 177–80.
32 For their careers and those of other Scots see *Obshchii Morskoi Spisok*, I, St Petersburg, 1885, and *Materialy dlia istorii russkago flota*.
33 C.A.G. Bridge (J. Deane), *History of the Russian Fleet during the Reign of Peter the Great*, London, 1899, p. 71.
34 *Ibid.*, p. 92; *Materialy dlia istorii russkago flota*, III, pp. 218–9.
35 *Dnevinik kammer-iunkera Berkhgoltsa*, III, Moscow, 1860, p. 59.
36 Original document in RGIA, f. 496, op. 3, no. 1, f. 6v.
37 *Trevozhynye gody Arkhangelska, 1700–1721*, Archangel, 1993, pp. 109, 113–4, 130–1, 142.
38 A. Gordon, *History of Peter the Great*, II, p. 63.
39 M.I. Semevskii, 'Kamer-freilina M.D. Gamilton' in *Slovo i delo. Ocherki i rasskazy iz russkoi istorii XVIII v.*, St Petersburg, 1884, pp. 185–268; Steuart, *Scottish Influences*, pp. 90–2.

Part IV

Maritime History

7 British Merchants and Russian Men-of-War: the Rise of the Russian Baltic Fleet

Richard Warner

On 26 June, 1712, the Swedish ambassador, Count Gyllenborg, wrote to Lord Bolingbroke, Secretary of State for the Northern Department, that he had been 'credibly informed that one Count Golovin, a Muscovite gentleman, is fitting out a ship called the *Tyger* now lying in Hungroad by Bristol'. He reported that 'a number of English subjects have entered themselves on board, including one Robert Morley as master, who has secured a protection from the press for one hundred and fifty men.'[1] The *Tyger* had been built by the Dutch East India Company in 1706, but had been taken by the French and was refitted as the *Vanqueur*. The *HMS Plymouth*, Captain Hanway commanding, captured her off the Island of Scilly in January of 1710 and took her to Bristol.[2] There she was purchased at an inch and candle sale by Ralph Robinson, a London merchant and a member of the Board of Assistants of the Russia Company.[3] Pointing out that the ship had been renamed the *Victory* and that it had secured a pass 'pretending to be bound for the Mediterranean', the ambassador demanded an inquiry, warning that one could 'not doubt, but all this will be found a sham, the easier to carry the ship off and to man her with English seamen'. Gyllenborg reminded Bolingbroke that 'this is directly opposite treaties concluded between our two crowns against the sale of any ship to the Czar, or his subjects, that may afterwards be fitted out as a man-of-war'.[4]

Bolingbroke transmitted the complaint to the Admiralty, which made an inquiry through its port admiral in Bristol, Sir William Wyndham. The investigation brought forth a number of interesting details, but no action. It revealed that Robinson, Morley and two other London merchants claimed ownership, that the mayor of Bristol, Abraham Elton, had been employed to fit the ship out, and that they planned to add twenty cannon to her armament in the Downs.[5] In the final report, Wyndham admitted that 'the whole country agrees that she is intended ... as a man-of-war for the Czar, tho' no certainty can be come at, for want of a power to examine upon oath'.[6]

There it was: the technicality that the merchants needed to allow the *Tyger* to slip out of Bristol. After a cruise to Lisbon, she returned to the Downs, took on her cannon and additional crew. She then joined a British naval convoy and set sail for Copenhagen with other vessels masquerading as merchantmen but in truth destined for Russian naval service. In 1713, the *Tyger* joined the Russian fleet as the *Victoria*.[7]

The watchful, but powerless, Gyllenborg wrote in December that two other ships were involved in the same charade and that one had been renamed the *Bolingbroke*! 'These three ships all belong to one owner, and the pretence of their voyage is to Lisbon and from there to Copenhagen.' Ironically, the *Bolingbroke* was captured by the Swedes off Reval (Tallinn) just before delivery to the Russians. The report described Robinson as 'of the Muscovy Company ... used to sell arms and ships to the Muscovites' and as an owner, who urged the captain to make a 'timely delivery to the designed harbour', where he would receive 'a good reward and great commendation for his pains'. The *Bolingbroke*'s captain was Robert Morley, the owner was Robinson, and the 'designed harbour' was Reval.[8]

In 1712 Peter had only a fleet in miniature, mostly smaller vessels built on Lake Ladoga. Unable to supply sufficient timber of quality to his fledgling yard at St Petersburg, the tsar launched his first warship there at the end of 1714.[9] To compensate, he began an energetic search for vessels abroad, dispatching a special agent,

Fedor Saltykov, to co-operate with Prince Kurakin, the ambassador in The Hague and London.[10] A shipwright himself, Saltykov was instructed to conduct inspections and to arrange financial transactions. Though the first ships were bought in Holland, Hamburg and Dunkirk, the tsar urged his agent to transfer operations to England and stipulated that negotiations there be conducted by Russia Company merchants.[11] From London, Saltykov reported enthusiastically about the purchase of the *Tyger*. It had cost only £1200 and an additional £4880 to refit and supply 'like a new ship'. The price of 1220 pounds sterling included thirty-six cannon, all supplies, anchors, sails, masts and cordage. He gloated that the price was only 40 per cent of the cost of a comparable new vessel and was 'cheaper than ships built in St Petersburg'.[12] Unaware of the vigilance of Gyllenborg, he wrote, 'it is possible to purchase ships here without revealing the Muscovite name'. Saltykov complimented what he described as 'the good work of our local merchant friends' but, once discovered, he confidently declared, 'it will be impossible to block the enterprise, because all is done in Robinson's name.'[13]

In 1713 the tsar's agents enjoyed great success, locating ships in good condition at prices ranging from 3000 to 6000 pounds, which were quickly acquired and fitted out for delivery to the Baltic fleet. The ill-starred *Bolingbroke* 48 (guns), the *Landsdown* 50, the *Strafford* 45, the *Oxford* 50, and the *Randolph* 50 joined the *Tyger/Victoria* and four vessels purchased elsewhere – the *Esperance* 46 from Dunkirk, the *Pearl* 52 from Rotterdam, and the *Saint Antonio* 50 and the *Saint Nicholas* 50 from Hamburg – in convoy to Copenhagen, where they were to be escorted by a Russian squadron to the Gulf of Finland.[14] The tsar fussed over the security, logistical and manning problems associated with the delivery of this first cohort of ships, for he was acutely aware that a successful delivery would change the naval balance of power between Russia and Sweden. Indeed, writing to Prince Dolgorukov, his ambassador in Denmark, Peter described the arrival of the ships as 'the most important moment of the war'.[15] As the Russians took delivery, Count Gyllenborg repeatedly registered protests to the British government, citing treaty agreements which prohibited the sale of ships that might be fitted out as men-of-war. He argued that 'Sweden's best friends and allies have contributed to her ruin ... by yielding to the avarice of their subjects' and that 'Muscovy soon will be able to mount a fleet of 20–30 ships'.[16]

What the Swedish ambassador did not discover was an offer made by another Russia Company merchant, a Mr Charles Goodfellow, commercial consul in St Petersburg and business partner of Ralph Robinson. While the sale of the *Tyger* was under investigation in 1712, Goodfellow sent a proposal to Count Apraksin, the head of the Russian Admiralty, offering to build ships in England for the tsar's fleet. Writing that he could construct fifty- and sixty-gun vessels fully ready for sea with crews and captains for £8000, Goodfellow promised that they would take only one year to build and that they would be 'constructed as well as English men-of-war ... with great secrecy ... under his name', and that he could deliver the ships 'under a British trade flag wherever His Majesty directs'. Half of the cost would be required when construction was begun and half when a ship was ready to sail.[17] Other imaginative plans abounded to build ships in England and to provide English builders in Holland with materials from Russia for construction. The tsar's agents were not attracted to Goodfellow's offer or others, for prizes and other ships were plentiful and it was easier, cheaper, quicker and less visible to purchase ships like the *Tyger*. Prince Kurakin regarded it 'dangerous' to contract construction in England where supplies might be confiscated in accord with a recent prohibition against using naval stores for private construction and he dismissed the notion of employing English builders in Holland as 'too complex'.[18] The tsar and his agents were impatient and realised that a window of opportunity that had been opened by the peace of Utrecht and that it might soon close.

The sales continued. In 1714 Russian agents purchased the *Arundel* 46, the *Armont* 50, the *Fortune* 48, the *Saint Michael* 50, and *le Firme* 70 and, the following year, the *Richmond* 44, the *London* 54 and the *Britannia* 25. Masquerading as merchant vessels, they were escorted into the Baltic by British naval convoys in 1715 and 1716. They were even joined by three other ships, built by Dutch shipwrights at Archangel, which sailed around the North

Cape to enter the Baltic in the security of the convoy.[19] As the size of the Russian fleet grew, Gyllenborg wrote: 'It is certain that when all of Finland is taken, the Muscovites will then be able to attack Sweden by sea, because of the ships supplied by the British and the Dutch.' He lamented that, 'without a miracle, they will descend upon us this summer' and warned that 'this savage, cruel, and barbarous people design to become masters of the Baltic'.[20] After the great victory of the Russian galley fleet at Hangö Head in 1714, Gyllenborg transmitted a memorial from Queen Ulrica Eleanora and the Swedish Senate to Queen Anne, which described 'the terrible preparations made by the Czar, which has produced this force so superior to ours that it will, with the first wind, easily fall upon our little squadron.'[21]

The ambassador became bolder and more public in his criticism after George I came to the throne. It seems that he may have coined or at least gave broad currency to the term 'Northern Crisis', when he anonymously published a pamphlet entitled 'The Northern Crisis or Impartial Reflections on the Policies of the Tsar', in which he posed as a 'concerned English citizen', writing:

> [T]he Tsar went over to Great Britain, where his vast nation ... lay neglected, unconsidered, and overlooked and he gained a ship or two for his diversion and then two or three more, and after that two or three more. So he also insinuated himself into the good will of many of our best workmen and later sent some private men and some officers to negotiate for more workmen and good seamen, who might be advanced and promoted.
>
> The Tsar then did use this assistance to take possession of Swedish territory ... The Tsar's fleet will soon outnumber the Swedish and Danish put together ... and will be the master of the Baltick. We shall wonder then at our blindness that we did not suspect his great designs.[22]

Arguing that the maritime powers had been 'entirely neglectful in the North', Gyllenborg pressed them to realise that 'things have now come to such crisis that peace should be, as soon as possible, procured to the Swede with all the possessions he formerly held in his Empire.' He urged intervention to smash what he called the Muscovite 'cockatrice'.[23]

After the peace of Utrecht, the Maritime Powers – England and Holland – took a keener interest in the emerging crisis in the north. Both were utterly dependent on the naval stores and maritime supplies originally traded through the Swedish lands in the eastern Baltic. Finland was the producer of pine tar and pitch and Riga was the source of crucial hemp and timber products mainly grown in Russia and northern Ukraine. When he went to war against Sweden, the tsar required Russian merchants to transfer their operations to Archangel.[24] At the end of 1713, the tsar abruptly closed Archangel and redirected the trade to his newly won ports on the Baltic, particularly St Petersburg.[25] The closure of Archangel was a masterful diplomatic stroke. Confident that it would provoke a hostile response from Sweden, the tsar effectively poisoned Swedish relations with the Maritime Powers. Infuriated by the part the merchants had played in Russian purchases of men-of-war, the Swedes responded as expected, by proclaiming a privateering campaign against all shipping headed for Danish and Russian ports.[26] The losses suffered by British merchants in 1714 were staggering and they petitioned the government for convoy protection from 'the great hazards presented by Swedish men-of-war and privateers'.[27] Lord Townshend warned that a scarcity of naval stores 'would disable His Majesty from fitting out a fleet next spring'.[28] Townshend urged ambassador George Mackenzie, who had recently returned from St Petersburg, to analyse the Russian situation, which he did in a remarkably reflective report.[29] Tellingly, he argued: 'Just, as Moscow is forsaken [as the capital], so Archangel is stripped of its staple [as the entrepôt].' Describing 1714 as 'the dead time of trade', he predicted that the Dutch would return to dominance at Riga and that the British would be the losers. This he linked with Britain's failure to prevent the sale of ships to the tsar. Echoing Count Gyllenborg, he wrote, 'I am credibly informed that a great many other ships already sent the Czar from hence, contrary to our treaties with Sweden, that more are now in the river ready to be sent to him!'[30]

In 1715, Admiral Hamilton took command of a fleet to convoy the trade, establishing an English naval presence in the Baltic that lasted for a decade. It was a decisive action designed to protect the Baltic trade, which was almost exclusively naval stores. At the same time, the government seemingly yielded to Swedish diplomatic pressure and affirmed its prohibition against the sale to or construction of men-of-war for foreign powers.[31] The action was, in truth, considerably less decisive than it appeared, for the sale of warships continued in 1715 and the contraband vessels were delivered again in 1716, protected by a British naval convoy.[32] Undaunted, the mayor of Bristol and member of parliament, Abraham Elton, advised Prince Kurakin that he could supply the Russians with new or refitted vessels, offering to build several 60–70 gun ships in eight months time, as he said, 'even in violation of the British Admiralty ... [and] without danger of sanction from acts of parliament'.[33]

The position of the arms-dealing merchants was equivocal. Indeed, Robinson, who held the contract to supply the Admiralty with pine tar and pitch, was the largest loser in the Swedish privateering campaign of 1714 and with other Russia Company merchants he petitioned the government and parliament for compensation and for convoy protection.[34] Of course, these were the same merchants who continued to purchase English ships and to attend to their delivery to the tsar's Baltic fleet.

Robinson and his associates sought advantage in every aspect of trade in and out of both countries and they were intimately aware of the tsar's desire to acquire naval and maritime technology. This is reflected well in a fanciful and outrageous project presented by a young factor named Samuel Garthside. In the spring of 1712, he petitioned the Russian government to grant his firm, Garthside and Company of London, a thirty-year monopoly over most of Russia's foreign trade at the port of Archangel, then Russia's only viable entrepôt.[35] It promised the tsar huge profits, but the major feature was the company's pledge to create an infrastructure for the support of the tsar's budding maritime and naval ambitions. An imaginative scheme, it proposed to integrate all company operations and enterprises with a large investment in education and training in order to facilitate a massive transfer of maritime technology.[36]

The first essential infrastructural element of the proposal called for the establishment of a monopoly over fishing, sealing and whaling in an area stretching 'from the river Pechinka to the straits of Weygate'. Aiming 'to train young Russians in the art of seafaring', the company proposed to contract eight hundred young men per year to go to sea for periods of three years. Afterwards, they might be selected to continue employment aboard company ships or to be trained and utilised in other company enterprises. One hundred were to be selected each year to be sent to England to continue training under company supervision. Others might attend schools and apprentice in enterprises ashore for careers in shipbuilding and maintenance. The whole task was to be accomplished by 'foreign masters and workmen' who were to 'instruct the Russians in all the arts belonging to the building and navigating [of] ships'.[37]

The proposal committed the company to the development of Russia's material resources as well as its human ones. There were two basic objectives: the construction of maritime support facilities at the port and the construction of enterprises to process goods for exportation. For this purpose the project requested that the government assign one thousand peasants per year to provide the necessary labour force. The company agreed to pay them wages and asked that they be exempted from military service. They would be employed first in the building of docks and yards for the service of the fishing and commercial fleets. Next, factories, foundries and forges were to be set up to provide finished materials for the company's use at Archangel in the construction and fitting out of ships and eventually for export as trade goods.[38]

The plan envisioned the domestic manufacture of naval stores such as rope, sail cloth and canvas. Archangel had become a major centre for the export of naval stores, particularly raw hemp and flax, but had not yet developed the industry to increase their value. The Garthside project also recognised the potential of the port to become a larger supplier of pine tar and pitch and that it was rapidly developing as an important source for oaken plank boards and fir mast timber. It even promoted the development of other enterprises, less related to the dominant trade in naval stores, such as the manufacture of soap, refined sugar and beer. Russia's exports were at the time almost exclusively raw materials and the company saw an opportunity to use cheap and available Russian labour to produce finished goods such as cordage, sail cloth, flax products, fish and whale oil and soap, to add value to the merchandise they could offer for sale abroad.[39]

In order to facilitate commerce, the company planned to establish banking, credit, exchange and insurance facilities in Archangel and in Amsterdam. The proposal stipulated that the company would 'control the trade at the port, *of all nations*' and that it would monopolise the trade coming to Archangel from the Russian interior, China and Persia. It would service all transhipment and have exclusive rights to trade in caviar and linens. The Garthside merchants wanted control over the huge Russian importation of British woollens, other textiles, colonial products and goods traded from other countries. The proposal was designed to place the company in a position to regulate nearly all commerce coming to Archangel. The company asked the government for a seven year reduction of customs duties, while promising to increase the tsar's yearly profit to £357 000 in hard currency.[40]

When it was delivered to the Russian Senate, Garthside's project aroused immediate concern in the merchant community and drew the ire of the British ambassador, Charles Whitworth. Reporting to London, he characterised it as 'ridiculous', 'extravagant' and 'impracticable', and reported that he had 'reprimanded the factor very severely'.[41] Though Garthside agreed to withdraw the proposal, Whitworth lodged an angry protest to the Russian minister, Count Golovkin, calling it 'a piece of nonsense intended to increase monopolies'.[42] The Count assured him that 'no notice would be taken of it'. Still suspicious, Whitworth warned his superiors that the plan might be 'ruinous to the nation'. The ambassador was suspicious of Garthside's youth and demeanour, remarking that he was at first 'very shy of declaring who were concerned with him' and that the project seemed to be 'too much laboured and digested for a young factor [and] the design too vast to be thought on by men of ordinary interest and purses'. His anxiety was confirmed when Garthside revealed that he had been encouraged by 'leading men in Bristol and Liverpool' and that 'one Robinson in London' was his partner and chief correspondent. In cipher, the ambassador warily concluded that 'though [the Russians] have not yet knowledge enough to pick the corn from the chaff, there are several hints which ought not to be given by Englishmen.'[43]

After the third cohort of vessels was delivered in 1716, the window of opportunity for purchasing ships in England closed. Even so, the tsar's agents still found occasional ships on the other side of the North Sea, particularly in Holland where Prince Kurakin negotiated the construction of several frigates. Indeed, the English builder Davenport was sent from Russia to supervise construction in a Dutch yard with materials that the Russians themselves imported from Archangel.[44]

Between 1714 and 1716, Peter took possession of eighteen foreign men-of-war, which when added to those brought from Ladoga yards and constructed in his new facilities in St Petersburg gave him twenty-eight men-of-war: a fleet decidedly superior to that of his Swedish adversary.[45] In July of 1719, James Jefferyes, the British ambassador in St Petersburg, reported home that:

> the Czar hath lately said in full company that his fleet and that of Great Britain are the two best in the world. If then at present he looks upon his fleet to be preferable to that of Holland or France, may it not be supposed that in some years time he will look upon it to be equal if not preferable to ours likewise ... My Lord, the Ships that are built here are as good as any in Europe.[46]

Jefferyes was aware of the crucial role played by the English in the massive transfer of technology to the tsar's fleet in the Baltic. His dispatches fully describe the contributions of British mercenary officers, shipbuilders, merchants and others. Indeed, he recommend their recall as the only way to check the Russians in their pursuit of maritime power.[47] What he overlooked was that most of the ships in the tsar's fleet were not built in Russia, that Peter the Great bought most of his fleet abroad between 1712 and 1716, when he masterfully exploited the window of opportunity available to him. The tsar's own shipbuilding program, as impressive as it was, would not have allowed him to develop a competitive fleet during his war with Sweden. That he understood the dilemma, that he found a solution and that he applied it so successfully is a mark of his greatness.

NOTES

1 Gyllenborg to Bolingbroke, 26 June 1712, PRO SP100/61.
2 Captain Jonas Hanway to the Admiralty, 16 February 1711, PRO Admiralty Papers 1/1878, Captain's Letters 'H'.
3 Report of Francis Webber dated 26 July 1712, located in Lords of the Admiralty to Lord Bolingbroke, 8 August 1712. PRO SP 42/11. The sale is described by Fedor Saltykov in Saltykov to Peter I, London, 8 April 1712, in *Materialy dlia istorii russkago flota* (*MIRF*), I, pp. 279–80.
4 Gyllenborg to Bolingbroke, 26 June 1712, PRO SP 100/61. He also complained bitterly about a fourth-rate naval vessel 'still in the dock at Blackwall, that was designated for Her Majesties service, but [was] afterwards sold to one Mr. Styles, a Russia Company merchant ... to dispose of her to the Moscovites.'
5 Lords of the Admiralty to Lord Bolingbroke, 8 August 1712. PRO SP 42/11.
6 Sir William Wyndham to Lord Bolingbroke, 20 August 1712. PRO SP 42/11.
7 Saltykov to Peter I, London, 6 December 1712, *MIRF*, I, pp. 335–6. He wrote that the Robinson would take several purchased vessels to Lisbon with trade goods in December and would deliver them to Copenhagen in March. *MIRF*, I, p. 383, notes the *Victoria*'s arrival in Reval (Tallinn) on 23 March 1712, delivered by a Captain Parnell.
8 Gyllenborg to Bolingbroke, 12 April 1713, PRO SP 100/61.
9 In June 1711 Alexander Menshikov advised the tsar that timber was so scarce in St Petersburg that 'with God's help we might produce one ship next year'. Menshikov to Peter I, St Petersburg, 30 June 1711, *MIRF*, I, pp. 245–6.
10 The instructions given to Prince Kurakin are contained in 'Punkty dannye Gosudarem Kniaziu Borisu Kurakinu, October 1711' in *MIRF*, I, p. 259. This volume is filled with detailed instructions on ship purchases addressed to Kurakin and Saltykov.
11 Kurakin to Peter I, The Hague, March 1712, *MIRF*, I, pp. 275–6.
12 Saltykov to Peter I, London, 8 April 1712, *MIRF*, I, pp. 279–80.
13 He warned that it was necessary to have money on account 'in order not to miss good opportunities'. Saltykov to Peter I, London, 7 July 1712, *MIRF*, I, pp. 292–3.
14 Reports on vessels purchased in 1712 and 1713 are included in: Kurakin to Peter I, The Hague, 4 November 1712 and 25 July 1713, *MIRF*, I, pp. 328–34, 417–18.

15 'Sie delo samoe glavnoe v sei voine', Peter I to Dolgorukov, Gribswald, 27 September 1712, *MIRF*, I, p. 322.
16 Expressed here in Gyllenborg to Bromley, London, 24 March 1714, PRO SP 100/61.
17 The proposal was communicated to the head of the Admiralty, Count Fedor Apraksin, in a document dated 19 August 1712, *MIRF*, I, pp. 307–9.
18 Kurakin to Peter I, The Hague, 9 March 1714, *MIRF*, I, p. 466. See also Saltykov to Peter I, London, 23 March 1714, *MIRF*, I, p. 472.
19 Saltykov to Peter I, London, 31 May 1715, MIRF, I, p. 631. Kurakin to Peter I , The Hague, 17 May 1715, *MIRF*, I, p. 624.
20 Gyllenborg to Bromley, London, 28 July 1714, PRO SP 100/61.
21 Memorial of Her Majesty the Queen and the Senate of Sweden, 8 May 1714, PRO SP 100/61.
22 Count Carl Gyllenborg, *The Northern Crisis or Impartial Reflections on the Policies of the Czar*, London, 1716.
23 *Ibid.*
24 *Ukazy* of August 18 and October 25, 1701 in *Polnoe sobranie zakonov rossiiskoi imperii* (hereafter *PSZ*), IV, pp. 172, 174.
25 *PSZ*, V, p. 66.
26 The Swedish privateering ordinance is located in PRO SP 95/20, 19 February 1714.
27 Petition of the Muscovy Company to the Queen, 13 May 1714, PRO SP 91/107. The Muscovy Company merchants kept petitioning; see: Benjamin Aylosse, Grievances of the Muscovy Company Merchants, 26 May 1714, PRO SP 91/107; Memorial of the Muscovy Company to Secretary of State Bromley, 5 May 1714, PRO SP 91/107; Petition of the Muscovy Company to the King, 28 October 1714, Russia Company, General Court of Assistants, Minute Books, IV, Guildhall, MS, 11, 714/4, pp. 324–6.
28 Lord Townshend to Admiral Norris, 2 August 1714, British Library, Add. MSS 28, 154, 248–51.
29 Ambassador George Mackenzie's Report to Lord Townshend, London, August 31, 1715. PRO SP 91/107.
30 *Ibid.*
31 The Russian reaction to the impending prohibition is well expressed by Kurakin, who charged 'the Tory Party is against Your Majesty's interest in preparing men-of-war here for Your service. They are friends of the Swedes.' He wrote of plans to deliver three more ships and expressed the opinion that parliamentary action 'might complicate matters'. Kurakin to Peter I, London, 5 April 1715. *MIRF*, I, pp. 607–8.

32 Lords of the Admiralty to Secretary Stanhope, London, 23 April 1715. PRO SP 42/14. Lords of the Admiralty to Lord Townshend, London, 2 May 1715. PRO SP 42/14.
33 Kurakin to Peter I, London, 4 January 1715. *MIRF*, I, p. 586.
34 Robinson reported losses of £22 976, which included £13 300 for the *Bollingbroke*. There were thirty-seven other claimants for a total of £45 698. Moscovy Company Petition to the King, 14 November 1714. Benjamin Aylosse of the Moscovy Company was presented another petition for reimbursement in 1717. Moscovy Company Petition to the King, 14 November 1714. Guildhall, MS 11, 741/4, pp. 326–7, 437–8.
35 This is enclosed with a report from Ambassador Charles Whitworth, St Petersburg, 28 September 1712. PRO SP 91/7, pp. 310–12. In some sources the name appears as Gartside.
36 *Ibid.*
37 *Ibid.*
38 *Ibid.*
39 *Ibid.*
40 *Ibid.*
41 Whitworth to St John, St Petersburg, 19 June 1712, PRO SP 91/7. Conveniently published in English and Russian translation in *Sbornik imperatorskago russkago istoricheskago obshchestva* (*Collections of the Imperial Russian Historical Society*) (*SIRIO*), LXI, pp. 212–13.
42 Whitworth to St John, St Petersburg, 28 June 1712, PRO SP 91/7. *SIRIO*, LXI, pp. 220–30.
43 *Ibid.*
44 *Ibid.*
45 For the delivery of men-of-war, see Captain John Deane's *A History of the Russian Fleet during the Reign of Peter the Great by a Contemporary Englishman*, 1724, Navy Records Society, London, 1899. P.A. Krotov in E.D. Spasskii, *Istoriia otechestvennogo sudostroeniia*, I, St Petersburg, 1994, p. 131. Krotov, the author of the chapters on Peter the Great, has made an important contribution to the study of the foundation of the Russian fleet in the Baltic.
46 Jefferyes to Craggs, St Petersburg, 15 May 1719. PRO SP 91/9.
47 Jefferyes to Stanhope, St Petersburg, 3 April 1719. PRO SP 91/9. Jefferyes to Craggs, St Petersburg, 16 July 1719. PRO SP 91/9.

8 State, Navy and the Origin of the Petrine Forest Cadastral Survey

Aleksei Karimov

The era of Peter the Great is a controversial one. On the one hand, the system of feudal representation and the traditional medieval state and social institutions were replaced by the bureaucratic authoritarian empire. On the other hand, the country became more open to foreign influence, overcoming its tradition of introspection and isolation. It was not only the state administration, economy and technology which changed. Modern Western science developed in Petrine Russia, bringing with it social institutions and regulations which required autonomy of thought, intellectual freedom and a whole new environment for the development of pure science and education. It was in this environment that the educated elite was brought up: statesmen, army officers, diplomats, architects, geodesists.

At the beginning of the reforms the introduction of Western state and economic institutions was determined by the practical need for efficient state management and army and navy reform.[1] The history of forest surveys shows that the state institutions of early Petrine Russia continued to be based on forms of government and economy inherited from the preceding medieval period. Changing in response to current needs, they developed away from their medieval successors and closer to their Western counterparts. The middle of the century saw the total transformation of these institutions. In addition to their practical application, they began to play an important role in the development of academic science, the collection of geographical information and in professional training. They, thus, contributed to the introduction of a Western-style scientific community and the social regulations associated with it. This reflects the dualism of Petrine intellectual history.

Petrine forest surveys and the whole system of forest cadastral surveys demonstrate the rise of the power and influence of the centralised bureaucratic empire. A comparison of forest surveys in Russia and in England underlines even more the role of the total transformation of the character of the Russian state under the Petrine regime. On the other hand, the history of forest surveys illustrates a different trend: the links and influence of Russian medieval state and economic institutions on Petrine ones. It shows the basis on which the Western approach to the state, economy and science was transplanted and illustrates how academic geographical science developed from various kinds of geographical practice.

Medieval forest descriptions are found in the survey books (*pistsovye knigi*) of the Chancellery of Landed Estates (*Pomestnyi prikaz*). Since the end of the fifteenth century this chancellery had carried out regular surveys of the territories of the Muscovite state. Descriptions of the whole state and its separate provinces were thus created; the descriptions included the number of peasants in each village on an estate, the quantity of arable lands, areas of slash-and-burn farming and meadowlands, and approximate data on forests. As one survey superseded its predecessor, by the late seventeenth century these descriptions provided reliable and complex feudal cadastral surveys.

The cadastral surveys of this period were produced for tax purposes, evaluating settled and exploited lands. They also sometimes dealt with fisheries, apiaries and the hunting estates of the tsars. Virgin forests, 'empty' lands and marshes did not attract the attention of the surveyors. This situation reflected the abundance of agricultural resources and the low density of the peasant population. This in turn reflected the level of geographical knowledge of the period: major waterways and highways may have been described and well known, but contemporaries of Ivan the Terrible and Boris Godunov seem to have been unaware of the endless Russian forests, as ambassadors and merchants had been on their way to the capital of Muscovy. Contemporary documents show that it was a commonplace event for even wealthy Russian nobles to lose their way while travelling in the forests of Central Russia. Sometimes they even used this as an excuse in unsuccessful attempts to escape from Russian service by fleeing abroad.[2]

The Petrine reforms spelled the end of the old order. The state economy, urgently in need of changes, increased day by day. Practically all economic projects (including military ones) were based on the rich resources belonging to the state or quasi-state enterprises containing forests, mines and serfs, such as Baron Stroganov's vast estates in Siberia or, some time later, Nikita Demidov's iron works in the Urals. The demand for natural resources was constantly growing. Forests had to satisfy the needs of the navy and metallurgical industry and the peasantry also provided the resources for state building projects on a grand scale. The rights of the various classes were severely restricted and the basis of common rights regulating the relations between vassals and the supreme power decreased. The development of serfdom in Petrine Russia, for example, is regarded by the historian P.N. Miliukov as a result of fiscal reform and the state's growing demand for taxes.[3]

The first steps in the Petrine reforms were brought about by the urgent needs of the war. The beginning of the eighteenth century saw a search for new ways to manage forest supplies. The first experiment in forest cadastral surveying took place in 1698–1701, when the first men-of-war were built at Voronezh dockyards. In these years the tsar ordered surveys of the Voronezh forests to be carried out in an attempt to find timber for shipbuilding.[4] Documents from these surveys are stored among the paper of the *tsarskii shater* in the Naval History Archive (RGA VMF) in St Petersburg. They demonstrate survey techniques very similar to the medieval surveys found in the *pistsovye knigi*, the only difference being that these detailed and explicit descriptions were devoted to forests rather than agricultural lands.

A clear analogy with medieval traditions of natural resource management can be observed. The first experiments in forest management show that the young Petrine administration used the experience of the Chancellery of Landed Estates surveys and the whole tradition of taxation for a new purpose: the survey and management of navy forests. Naval offices and clerks seem to have had just the same functions as the secretaries (*d'iaki*) and scribes (*pistsy*) of the Estates Chancellery. In one case, the officials sent to Voronezh district to survey ash forests are called clerks (*pod'iachie*), in the old manner.[5] They received special instructions from the tsar and were vested with power to issue orders to local landlords and clergy, to check property rights and to put in requisitions. The context of these descriptions is similar to those in the *pistsovye knigi*, except for the fact that, in contrast to the latter, forest statistics were set out according to river basins, while *pistsovye knigi* were set out according to local proprietors, listed name by name. But the terminology, measurements and technical language seem to be just the same. The first forest surveys were fragmentary descriptions for the purpose of building just a few war ships. Only the most suitable forests along the main rivers near the town were described. No systematic, regular cadastral surveys were planned and implemented at that time.

The survey documents of the 1720s – the period of naval activity in the Baltic – are much more detailed and complete. They show the first attempts to develop the regular forest cadastral survey which was required to ensure timber supplies for the Baltic fleet . A decade later they resulted in a regular cadastral survey. In the 1720s a series of surveys organised according to identical plans was carried out around St Petersburg, on the islands of the Neva delta and along the rivers of Novgorod *guberniia* (province).[6] These were the first attempt at a systematic, regular survey of Russian forests. Admiralty records contain correspondence on the copying and distribution among district military offices (*voevodskie kantseliarii*) of 'forest ranger [*val'dmeistr*] books for the years 1722 and 1723', which contained descriptions of protected forests.[7] Probably a large part of Russian forests were described by this time.

It is a significant fact that Admiralty surveys were among the earliest regular geographical surveys carried out in Russia. Naval geodesists laid the foundations for map-making in the whole country. A Senate decree 'on the dispatch of St Petersburg [Naval] Academy pupils for mapmaking' (*O posylke uchenikov S. Peterburgskoi [Morskoi] Akademii dlia sochineniia landkart*), issued in 1720, shows that the navy was deemed to possess the approved 'know-how' for making geographical surveys and descriptions of the country. Henry Farquharson, professor of the Naval Academy, prepared the official instructions for the geodesists, who carried out surveys under the general supervision of State Secretary Kirillov.[8] Together with the navy's other geographical activities, these forest surveys played a key role in the development of geographical practice in Russia.

The decade of the 1720s saw the emergence of a general programme of mapping and geographical exploration in Russia aimed at raising the efficiency of the central government and establishing stricter control over the regions. The forest surveys of the 1720s coincided with Peter's General Regulation (*General'nyi reglament*), in which the effective administration of the state was cited as the main purpose of the mapping and exploration of the empire.[9] They began on 14 March, 1720, just fourteen days after the publication of the General Regulation.[10] A large number of geographical activities took place under this programme, of which forest surveys were the earliest and most important.

In the 1720s the special regulations on forest management (established by a decree of 1703) was finally put into practice. It restricted forest owners and in fact signalled the nationalisation of forests. From that time the Admiralty became *de facto* the supreme proprietor of high-quality timber. We have studied documents devoted to the building of the road from Moscow to St Petersburg.[11] They include special orders allowing the cutting of suitable timber for this purpose, regardless of who owned the land. The correspondence of the Admiralty with the Holy Synod include the Synod's instructions to monastery peasants in Novgorod *guberniia* to obey the orders of naval officers surveying the Novgorod forests.[12] At this time and later people were forbidden to cut forests suitable for naval supplies lying at a fixed distance of 50 versts from big rivers and 20 versts from smaller ones. These restrictions were not only applied to state, monastery and common forests; private owners were also banned from cutting high-quality timber without a special permit from an Admiralty officer stating that this timber was not suitable for use by the navy. L. Zakharov, historian of the Ministry of State Property, established that rights were restored to private owners only in 1782, by order of Catherine the Great.[13]

In the 1730s, forest surveys and forest management had developed into a mature and stable system. This was a period of systematic exploration of Russian forests and of countrywide cadastral surveys, according to the programme worked out in the previous decade. In 1732 the first countrywide instructions on forest preservation were issued. At that time the forest cadastral survey was regarded not only as a source of naval supplies but also as an institution at the service of the state. The mapping of forests began. We have studied Admiralty forest statistics in the Naval History archive and found that in some cases they correspond to the forest maps stored in the Department of Manuscripts of the Academy of Sciences Library (OR BAN). In fact, the statistics from the Naval History archive and the corresponding maps from OR BAN come from the same survey. The titles of Admiralty files from RGA VMF mention mapping and statistical descriptions as two components of the survey.[14] Navy geodesists and Senate officials, whose activities were closely connected with the Geography Department of the Academy of Sciences, worked hand in hand with common aims.

Forest maps were not included in the most important geographical atlases (the Kirillov Atlas and the Big Academy Atlas) because they did not cover a large territory. But they were kept in the same map collections as the maps that Petrine geodesists used for the compilation of these atlases. The Academy of Sciences participated in devising a programme for mapping navy forests. Directives instructing the commencement of Admiralty forest surveys were issued by the Senate.[15] In many cases, forest maps and statistics covered the areas where general topographic mapping had taken place several years earlier.[16] All this demonstrates the common interests of the Senate, the Geography Department and the Admiralty and the existence of a unified and co-ordinated programme for mapping the country.

The fact that the forest surveys are surprisingly detailed and exact deserves special attention. Also surprising is the large quantity of forest maps and statistics to be found in various archives. If we take into consideration the fact that large-scale mapping was something new for Russian state management, we can appreciate the importance of forest surveys for the Petrine administration. It makes clear the scale of the shipbuilding plans both of the Admiralty and also of Peter himself, that 'Sailor and Carpenter', as Pushkin called him. The mapped resources of timber forests were many times greater than actual timber consumption and shipbuilding had ever been, at that time or later.

The technology of forest mapping is well known.[17] It was borrowed largely from Western map-making practice. The aim of the Petrine cadastral survey and the general style of forest management are similar to Colbert's forest cadastral survey and the management of the French crown estates.[18] But while the Colbert cadastral survey managed only forests belonging to the crown, all the Russian forests in practice belonged to the crown for almost a century after the implementation of the Petrine cadastral survey. This nationalisation seems to have nothing in common with European management of natural resources.

In the middle of the eighteenth century forest mapping became an obligatory part of forest cadastral surveys. A series of surveys was carried out in the 1740s, and at the same time countrywide regulations on the preservation of forests were issued. In the middle of the eighteenth century all state forests were divided into three categories:

- naval forests (Plate 6);
- forest defence lines, a category which soon lost its importance when the frontier moved southwards (Plate 7); and
- the forests of the College of Mines (*Berg-kollegiia*), linked to mines and factories (Plate 8).[19]

Rules for the exploitation of forests were introduced. Some of the College of Mines' maps show plans for forest rotation. But most of the forests remained under the ownership of the Admiralty, which continued to map and survey them.

All the timber forests were examined and mapped by naval officers. All oaks, pines, limes and firs were counted and measured. The last thirty years of the century saw a veritable forest Doomsday. Hundreds of large-scale maps and charts, accompanied by statistics, were prepared. Later these documents served as the source for general forest atlases such as the 'General Atlas ... of various kinds of forests'.[20] It reflects in particular the 1734 plan of the first Russian forest plantation, the Lindulovskaia plantation outside St Petersburg.

At the end of the eighteenth century forests were placed under the jurisdiction of the Ministry of Finances. At this time, the map collection of its Forest Department contained 4549 district (*uezd*) and province (*guberniia*) Admiralty maps and eight atlases of the provinces of St Petersburg, Kherson, Taurida (Crimea), Novgorod, Iaroslavl', Kazan', Vologda and Olonets.[21] At the same time forest cadastral surveying becomes a stable institution and normal form of geographical practice in Russia. The form of surveying which had been worked out existed until the Revolution of 1917 and even to the present day.

The fact that the Petrine cadastral survey illustrates changes in the character of the state and the development of an authoritarian bureaucratic empire becomes especially clear if one makes a comparison with the English experience of forest surveys and management. The English cadastral tradition assumes the leading role of local initiative in surveying territory. This is especially true for land cadastral survey and evaluation. Regulations on land use, land evaluation and tax distribution were the duty of the local community, not state officials. The numerous land maps of Parliament Enclosure and Tithe Commutation include maps of separate landholdings and parishes. In the history of English land mapping there were no centralised surveys (with very few exceptions) similar to the Russian General Boundary Survey of the eighteenth century.

Great Britain was much more dependent on forest supplies than Russia owing to the importance of its navy. However, despite that, the central authorities responsible for forest supplies did not suggest any restrictions on property rights, nor was there any mention of nationalisation. There were three basic sources of timber supplies: imports from Central and Northern Europe, purchase of private timber at home and timber supplies from the Crown forests and plantations.[22] Internal forestry was therefore only one of the sources of timber supplies. Special attention was paid to English forests at times when military conflicts on the Continent threatened overseas timber outlets.

During the Napoleonic wars the British Parliament, the British navy and the Forestry Commissioners were anxious to find an adequate replacement for imported timber.[23] The continental blockade threatened the building of new vessels. An Act of Parliament on the New Forest proposed a policy of forest preservation, stating that:

the wood and timber, not only in the New Forest but in this kingdom in general, had of late years been much wasted and impaired, and the said Forest, that might be of much use and convenience for supply of His Majesty's Royal Navy was in danger of being destroyed if some speedy course were not taken to restore and preserve the growth of timber there.[24]

The Act of 1812 on Alice Holt forest[25] stressed the obstacles for timber import and lack of private forests. It suggested implementing a policy of planting forests for timber supplies in the future. Some other Acts also proposed planting forests. As a result, some plantations were established; in the New Forest, for example, artificial forests are known from 1700, 1756, 1775, 1808–17, 1830, 1847–62, 1852–62, corresponding to contemporary parliamentary acts.[26] However, in general, these efforts failed to produce a stable and co-ordinated programme of forest planting, preservation and mapping, for a common approach to the management of lands and forests was not based on state initiatives but on local initiative and trade. Britain and Russia developed contradictory but nevertheless effective ways of satisfying the demands of their respective navies.

*****

The Russian forest cadastral survey of the eighteenth century and its evolution provide an example of the evolution of the methods and organisation of medieval tax surveys. It shows the influence of the practical needs of the state and the development of the navy and industry. The Petrine forest cadastral survey developed into a separate state institution, with stable organisation, regular updates and a scientific basis.

The general style of forest management which began under Peter the Great reflects the rise of state influence and the emergence of an authoritarian bureaucratic empire. This is especially clear when one compares the Russian example with the English tradition of land and forest management. The supreme authorities in Russia regarded the country's rich natural resources (including the population) as an immense source of power and strength, which gave them an opportunity to implement their political, economic and social plans. Property rights and other traditional rights were restricted and allowed only in so far as they complied with the interests of the state.

The development of a scientific basis for forest surveys illustrates the introduction of Western science in Russia in general. It shows that the introduction of Western science was based on the demand for state reforms and the improvement of the efficiency of state administration and the economy. But once they were introduced, the forest cadastral survey became a means for the geographical exploration of the country, not only for practical needs but also in the interests of knowledge.

NOTES

The author is grateful to the Organising Committee of the Conference for providing financial support for his participation at Greenwich and to Prof. Lindsey Hughes for her kind encouragement and practical help. I would also like to acknowledge the financial support of the Russian Humanities Foundation for this research project (no. 98–03–04093). I am grateful to the staff of the Manuscript Department of the Academy of Sciences Library, the Russian State Historical Archive (RGIA) and Naval History Archive, St Petersburg. My colleagues, Prof. A.V. Postnikov, Prof. V.K. Rakhilin and Dr O.A. Aleksandrovskaia, gave important advice for which I am grateful. I also wish to thank Dr I.A. Merliakova, who was my first reader and critic.

1 On the reforms in general, see L. Hughes, *Russia in the Age of Peter the Great*, New Haven, CT, 1998.
2 See L. Alekseev, 'Okovskoi les "Povesti vremennykh let"' in *Kul'tura srednevekovoi Rusi*, Leningrad, 1974, p. 8.
3 P.N. Miliukov, *Ocherki po istorii russkoi kul'tury*, I, St Petersburg, 1896, p. 198.
4 Probably the first Petrine forest survey is 'Knigi lesov: opisannykh kapitanom Ivanom Verkhovskim po Severnomu Dontsu, 1698–1701', Naval History Archive (RGA VMF), f. 177, op. 1, d. 7, l. 88.
5 RGA VMF, f. 175, op. 1, d. 13, ll. 37–54: 'O posylke pod'iachikh v Voronezhskii uezd dlia osmotra i opisi iasenevykh lesov'.
6 See, for example, RGA VMF, f. 223, op. 1, d. 234, l. 304: 'Opis' sosnovym i berezovym lesam, osmotrennym v 1723 g. na ostrove Dago s oznacheniem razmerov derev i sortov lesa'.

7 RGA VMF f. 138, op. 1, d. 280: 'Ob otpravke v Borovskuiu voevodskuiu kantseliariiu kopii s opisnykh val'dmeisterskikh knig 1722 i 1723 godov ob okhrane zapovednykh lesov dlia rukovodstva v voprose sokhraneniia lesov'. The local office of forest ranger (*val'dmeistr*) was created by Peter in 1718.
8 O.A. Aleksandrovskaia, *Stanovleniie geograficheskoi nauki v Rossii v XVIII veke*, Moscow, 1989, p. 30. On Farqharson, see Chapter 9 in this volume.
9 V.F. Gnucheva, *Geograficheskii departament Akademii nauk XVIII veka*, Moscow–Leningrad, 1946, pp. 20–1.
10 *Ibid.*, p. 21.
11 RGA VMF, f. 212, ukazy III otdelenie, d. 5, l. 52ob.: 'O pozvolenii rubit' les dlia pochinki i postroiki Moskovskoi preshpektivnoi dorogi vo vsekh dachakh, ch'i by oni ne byli'.
12 *Ibid.*, d. 74, l. 27: 'Po isprosheniiu u Dukhovnogo Sinoda Poslushnogo ukaza v Novgorod, v Arkhiereiskii prikaz: o podchinenii krest'ian v votchinakh arkhiereiskikh, monastyrskikh i tserkovnykh kapitanu Dubrovinu, komandirovannomu dlia osmotra i opisi korabel'nykh lesov'.
13 Rossiiskii Gosudarstvennyi Istoricheskii Arkhiv (RGIA), f. 381, op. 47, d. 526, Zakharov Lev. 'Istoricheskii ocherk po upravelniiu gosudarstvennymi imushestvami za stoletnee sushestvovanie'.
14 See RGA VMF, f. 138. op. 1, d. 68: 'Ob otpravke geodezista Zubova dlia opisaniia kedrovogo lesa i sostavleniia karty Iarenskogo uezda Vologodskoi gubernii'.
15 For an example, see *ibid.*, l. 3.
16 See illustrations from f. 35 OR BAN: Landkarta Nizhegorodskogo uezdu chast' (no. 496; see Plate 5); and Spetsial'naia karta lesov s ukazaniem khoroshikh dubovykh uchastkov (no. 583; see Plate 6), which was prepared soon after the first one, as could be seen from its design. All illustrations in this paper are by courtesy of the Academy of Sciences Library, St Petersburg.
17 S.M. Gul', 'Istoricheskii ocherk lesnoi geodezicheskoi s'emki', in *Trudy Lesotekhnicheskoi akademii imeni S.M. Kirova*, 69, 1950; A.V. Postnikov, *Razvitie krupnomasshtabnoi kartografii v Rossii*, Moscow, 1989.
18 See R.J.P. Kain, E. Baigent, *The Cadastral Map in the Service of the State*, Chicago, IL and London, 1992, pp. 210–12.
19 Plate 7, a map of the forest defence line, contains an amusing mistake: it confuses the points of the compass. North (*nord*) is written at the bottom and south (*zuid*) at the top, although the geographical situation is shown correctly. This may indicate that an Old Russian geographical seventeenth-century drawing (*chertezh*) was the source for this map; Plate 8, a map of

the Novopavlovskii works forest, shows a plan for annual forest rotation (parcels under letters A, B, C, D).
20 Russian National Library, St Petersburg, Department of Manuscripts, Ermitazh collection, d. 610.
21 RGIA, f. 387, op. 47, d. 454, ll. 44–45ob. Sluzhebnye bumagi Lesnogo Departamenta, 1806.
22 See R.G. Albion, *Forests and Sea Power: The Timber Problem of the Royal Navy*, Cambridge, 1926.
23 See Public Records Office, class CRES 60/2, first report of the Surveyor General of His Majesty's Land Revenue, 1 December 1796, p. 6, and the Fourth report of the Surveyor General, April 1809, p. 186.
24 Acts of Parliament, 9 & 10, Will. III, c. 36, 48.
25 Act of Parliament, 52, Geo. III, c. 72.
26 PRO, class F3/1167.

9 Peter the Great and English Maritime Technology

W.F. Ryan

We have little hard information on what Peter the Great's real intentions might have been in embarking on his Grand Embassy in March 1697 or on his intended itinerary. One official reason given for the Embassy was that it was an attempt to expand support for the alliance against the Turks (which at the time included Poland, Venice and the Empire) but, as Molchanov has pointed out, there was no likelihood of such a mission being met with any great enthusiasm at any of the other major European courts at that particular time when most were concerned with the War of the Spanish Succession. Perhaps the intention was rather, as recent Russian historians of Peter's reign such as Molchanov and Anisimov would have it, to study Western countries at first hand with a view to adopting new methods of government and military organisation and acquiring western technology; perhaps, as Lindsey Hughes has suggested in her recent book, Peter was already moving towards an attempt to form an anti-Swedish alliance; perhaps it was simply that Peter was excited by all the talk of his friends in the Foreign Quarter and just wanted to see it all for himself on a kind of Grand Tour.[1] Anisimov vigorously denies the 'Grand Tour' explanation and suggests that, judging from the charters sent out before the Grand Embassy, Peter intended visiting Austria, Brandenburg, Rome, Venice, Holland and England. I have seen no document confirming that Peter intended from the outset to visit England, but several which suggest that he was persuaded to do so while in Holland. Several of Peter's older biographers – from Ustrialov in the nineteenth century to Bogoslovskii in the Soviet period – are of the opinion that Peter's main aim was to acquire maritime technology; hence the subject of this chapter.

Before Peter, Russia had little opportunity to foster maritime ambitions, although there is a long history of fishing and river and coastal shipborne trade in Russia's northern waters, using relatively small ships built by traditional shipbuilding methods. There had been abortive attempts at Western-style shipbuilding: the *Frederick* was built by Holsteiners with Russian craftsmen in 1636, and Peter's father, Tsar Alexis Mikhailovich, had ordered the construction of another ship, the *Orel*, with Dutch involvement, but this too led to nothing.[2] Peter's early enthusiasm both for warfare and for boats, for which there is ample historical and anecdotal evidence,[3] was reinforced by several political factors: conflict with the Turks in the south, a desire to expand into the Baltic area to usable ports in the north, and the inevitable conflict with Sweden that this entailed. Very early in his reign Peter had decided that naval strength was the key to controlling the sea of Azov and establishing a presence in the Black sea. He built a southern fleet at Voronezh on the Don with Dutch and Venetian help, but the political outcome of the struggle with the Turks meant that the Voronezh fleet, though it continued to be augmented, was not seriously used, and most of Peter's naval ambitions were realised in the north, where Sweden was already a substantial naval power.

Whatever Peter's original intentions might have been in embarking on his Grand Embassy, in the event the acquisition of technology and technical specialists (in particular, but by no means exclusively, those connected with the sea), turned out to be his major preoccupation and perhaps his greatest success. Peter was quite happy to buy technology abroad wherever he could get it and to employ foreign personnel from any quarter, from Norway to Greece, but Britain and Holland were in the event the main sources.[4] Although Peter spent some time in Holland engaged mainly in shipbuilding, which is a large topic in itself, and had many Dutchmen working for him, and a large volume of Dutch trade, England arguably played a more important role in the creation of a modern Russian navy, first at the time of the Grand Embassy and its immediate aftermath, and in varying degrees thereafter. Many of the documents which illustrate this may now be consulted in *Britain and Russia in the Age of Peter the Great: Historical Documents* which was published to mark the tercentenary of Peter's visit to England.[5] I shall discuss what Peter acquired in England as six topics:

- advice on naval affairs;
- hands-on experience of ship-handling;
- ships;
- shipbuilding and shipbuilders;
- scientific instruments; and
- navigation.

Most of these topics involve the figure of a now largely forgotten aristocratic admiral, Peregrine Osborne, Marquess of Carmarthen,[6] and interwoven commercial and political interests are ever present.

But before looking at these specific points, a brief outline of Peter's visit to England from the naval standpoint is necessary. Peter's knowledge of England and English maritime matters begins with the famous story of the *botik*, the small English boat about 19 feet in length, designed to be sailed or rowed, later called the 'Grandfather of the Russian Fleet'. This story is enshrined in the preamble to Peter's *Morskoi Ustav* (Naval Statute) of 1720, Peter's enactment of which finally established the administration of a serious Russian navy, and was known in England from Thomas Consett's *The Present State of Russia*, published in 1729.[7] It tells how Peter as a boy had found an old English boat in a warehouse at Izmailovo and had it restored. His Dutch mentor Franz Timmerman is said to have told him that its great advantage was that it could sail both with and against the wind. Naval terminology was not well established at the time, and '*protiv vetra*' must be taken in the sense 'close to the wind'. Fore-and-aft rigged ships, which could sail closer to the wind than square-rigged ships, were not, of course, an English invention or even a novelty (except in the navy), but it is a point which impressed Peter and is one to remember in what follows.

There is evidence that English merchants in the Russia trade – both those in the Muscovy Company, and those who were seeking through Parliament to abolish the Muscovy Company's monopoly at home – were aware of Peter's travel plans in advance and made quite elaborate expensive plans to influence him. A report from the Board of Trade and Plantations[8] expressly urged the King to attempt during Peter's visit to Holland to regain the former privileges of English merchants in Russia, a reference to the decayed fortunes of the Muscovy Company which had lost its earlier importance after its privileges had been withdrawn by the Russians following the execution of Charles I. It was at that time the subject of a bill in Parliament to remove its monopoly in England,[9] a movement led by some of the newer City merchants. Luttrell in his *Brief Historical Relation of State Affairs* records that in December 1696 the Muscovy merchants had heard that Peter was to visit the English and Dutch factories near Archangel and had sent funds to entertain him splendidly.[10] Some records suggest that they later (1715) presented him with a magnificent planetarium made by John Rowley.[11] The Muscovy Company's grievances had first been raised by Sir John Hebdon in 1676 and then, and thereafter, were regularly linked with attempts to obtain a monopoly on the import of tobacco into Russia, attempts strongly supported by the Virginia tobacco interests.[12] The other crucial Russian interest of both the administration and the merchants was the supply of shipbuilding materials from Russia and the Baltic, and it is not without interest that Peter in London twice dined with Henry (Andrew) Stiles, a monopolist of Russian tar, pitch and potash, all of them dockyard materials. Henry Stiles was one of Peter's intimates and acted in effect as his banker and agent in London; he was one of the party that accompanied Peter on his visits to the Greenwich Observatory.[13] He and his brother Thomas, a member of the Muscovy Company, were for several years thereafter the main English agents to whom Peter turned when he wished to acquire ships, scientific instruments or hire technicians.

Lobbying in those days was powerful and relatively uninhibited. The efforts of the merchant interests were not in vain: William III certainly did exert himself on behalf of the English merchants and their backers, to the detriment indeed of the commercial interests of his Dutch subjects who were keen rivals (and, indeed, at this time more successful rivals) in the Russia trade.[14] The expansion of the market for tobacco from England's American colonies was always one of the main objectives. The King's secretary William Blathwayt – who had formerly been under-secretary to the Earl of Conway, the Secretary of State for the Northern Department, which dealt with Muscovite affairs – wrote to Sir William Trumbull, secretary of state, on 4 August 1697, that the king – who was also the Stadtholder of the United Provinces – intended to meet Peter to show him the army, and suggests that the English might 'obtain some advantage in Trade or at least the Restoring Our former Priviledges from the good Nature of the Czar when we shall have made much of him'.[15] He further wrote on 8 October 1697: 'Our Ambassadors at the Hague have full instructions to treat with the Czar and his ambassadors for the restoring of our privileges in Muscovy and sending our tobacco throughout their vast dominions.'[16]

As to what 'making much of' the Tsar might mean, on 12 October a letter from George Follet to Robert Harley states that the King had given a ship called the *Royal Transport* to the Tsar and that the trade treaty was almost completed.[17] Another letter dated 12 October from Blathwayt reads:

> His Majesty being desirous to gratify the Czar of Muscovy in what may be most acceptable to him, has thought fit to present him with the Royall Transport ... His Majesty has sent her to Greenwich and commanded me hereby to signify his pleasure to their Excellencies that she be there be put into the most compleat order and condition in all respects and sent back to Roterdam as soon as possible in order to be presented to the Czar.[18]

This seems to indicate that Peter was not, at that time, expected to visit England in person. Admiralty records for the next few months are full of references to the *Royal Transport*, to her designer Admiral Lord Carmarthen and to the various activities of 'His Czarish Majesty'. From these records a picture emerges which is a good deal more interesting than the received history which usually refers to the *Royal Transport* simply as a yacht, and to Carmarthen, if at all, as one of Peter's drinking companions. The offer of the *Royal Transport* clearly did intrigue Peter, who was busy working in the shipyards at Saandam, and being courted no less assiduously and expensively by Dutch trading interests. He sent his aide Adam Weide[19] to England, under pretext of announcing a Russian victory, to inspect the ship.[20] Weide duly reported back that the ship was very good, with twenty brass cannon, that he had seen ships being built which were in every respect cleaner and more imposing than the Dutch ships and that London was a town well worth seeing.[21] It is hard to know how far this comparative assessment of English and Dutch shipbuilding really corresponds to reality, but it is certainly true that in this period in England the promotion of mathematics, mathematical instruments and the teaching of mathematics, in particular for maritime purposes, was a matter of national policy; and it is largely true that English ship design and construction had become more mathematical in method than the Dutch. Peter's reported disappointment with what he was learning in Holland and his statement that in England they build ships using mathematical methods (as opposed to alleged Dutch traditional rule-of-thumb methods) – and that if he had stayed in Holland he would have remained 'ignorant of that art'[22] – is worth taking seriously: Peter after all had a great affection and admiration for things Dutch, spoke a little Dutch, had many Dutchmen in his service and had strong Dutch trading and technical links. A strong incentive was needed for Peter to listen to blandishments from the English. Bogoslovskii, Peter's Soviet biographer, was sure that Peter's desire to visit England was due to the gift of the *Royal Transport*.[23]

Certainly no expense was spared, and no aspect of technology ignored in the attempt to secure commercial advantages for England.

- Peter was lent a house next to Deptford dockyard (it belonged to John Evelyn the diarist, but had been let to Admiral Benbow);
- he had the almost constant companionship of Admirals Lord Carmarthen and Sir David Mitchell (and, according to one source, Sir Anthony Deane,[24] one of the outstanding shipwrights of the time);
- he was introduced to the design methods of the mould loft;
- he was introduced to mathematicians with whom he took lessons;
- he was taken to the Royal Observatory at Greenwich, which played a key role in developing English mathematical navigation;
- he was given a considerable collection of ship models of recent ships;
- he purchased scientific instruments;

- he sailed ships in the Thames and observed the testing of mortars on bomb-vessels at Woolwich; and
- he took part in a mock sea battle near Portsmouth.

Considerable numbers of specialists and craftsmen were found to enter his service. Considerable numbers of ships were sold to him. The outflow of technology was unprecedented and possible considerations of national security were at first ignored. The London merchants, attempting to wrest some of the potential trade from the Muscovy Company's monopoly, wrote in their 1697 Memorial to the Council of Trade: 'the Russes can never be in a capacity to make a Sea War with us, having no ships of their own.'[25] Since they were soon to be selling ships to the Russians this argument could not be maintained for long. In fact, as Janet Hartley observes in Chapter 4 of this volume, the general perception of the situation changed markedly within a few years; apprehensions were aroused, and eventually there would be a reaction in the City and in Parliament and an act to restrict such activity.[26] When Peter left England at the end of April 1698 he had acquired a great deal, and if the later flow of technology was smaller, this one burst of activity was enough to leave its mark on the Russian navy for several decades.

*****

I should like to look now in a little more detail at the categories of technological assistance which I outlined above.

First, advice on naval affairs. As already mentioned Admiral Lord Carmarthen had drawn up a short prospectus for Peter on the establishing of a navy[27] and was almost constantly in the tsar's company to explain to Peter the significance of what he was seeing. He had himself considerable experience both of ship design, construction and management, and the command of ships at sea in time of war (specifically the disastrous attack at Camaret Bay in the expedition against Brest in 1694). Though perhaps slightly eccentric and certainly headstrong in private life, in naval matters he was far from being the aristocratic amateur who occasionally plagued the navy in the seventeenth century. He was certainly conscious of the importance of the navy in affairs of state, and was no stranger to politics: he and his

1 The actress Letitia Cross as St Catherine. Engraved by John Smith after Kneller (1699?).

2 Peter I by Sir Godfrey Kneller (1698).

3 Engraving of Peter I by John Smith after Kneller (1698).

4 'Peter I in Deptford, 1698' by Daniel Maclise (1857).

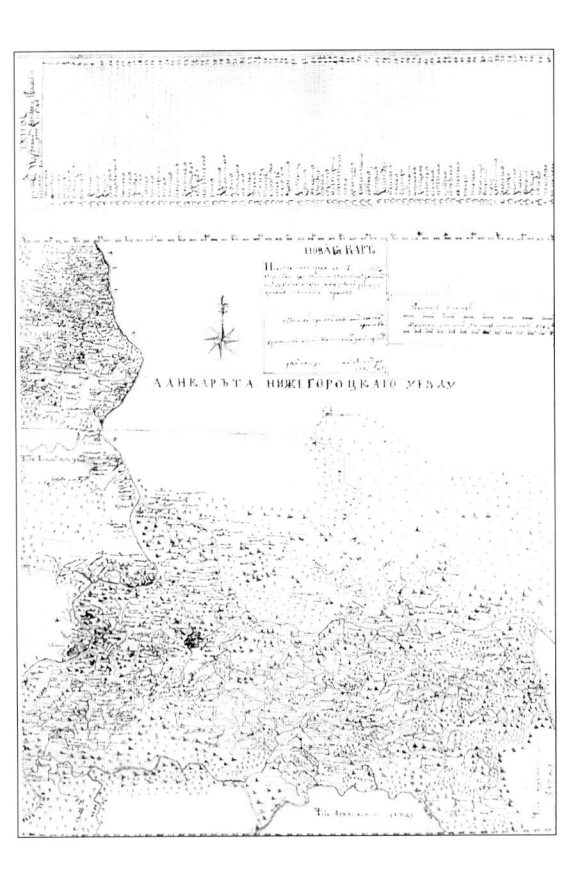

5 Topographic drawing of Nizhegorodskii uezd (*ca.* 1733).

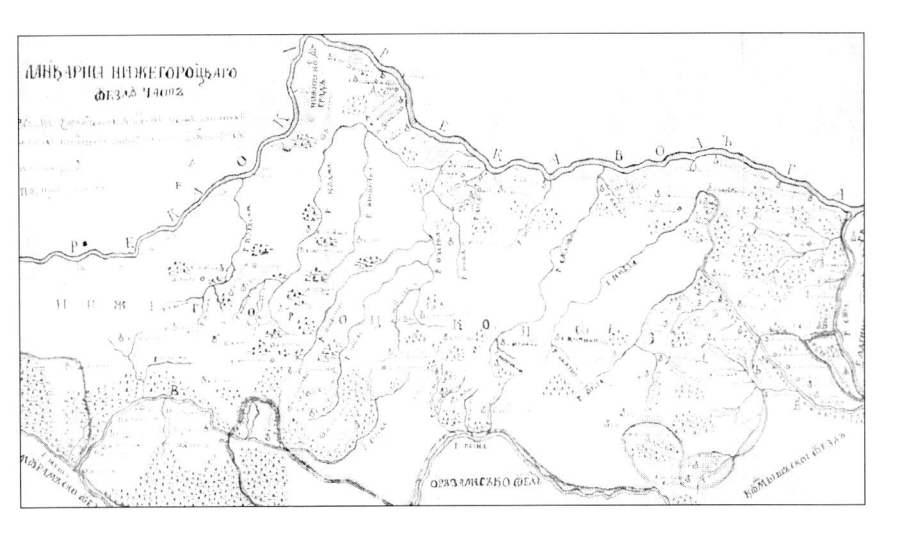

6 Map of pine forests for navy, Nizhegorodskii uezd (*ca.* 1736).

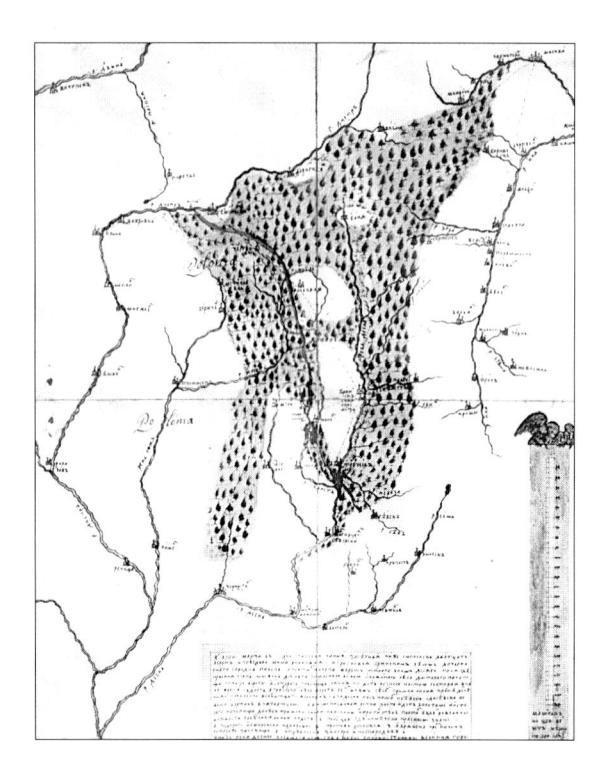

7 Forest defence line (founded 1706) from Smolensk to Chernigov (early 18th c.).

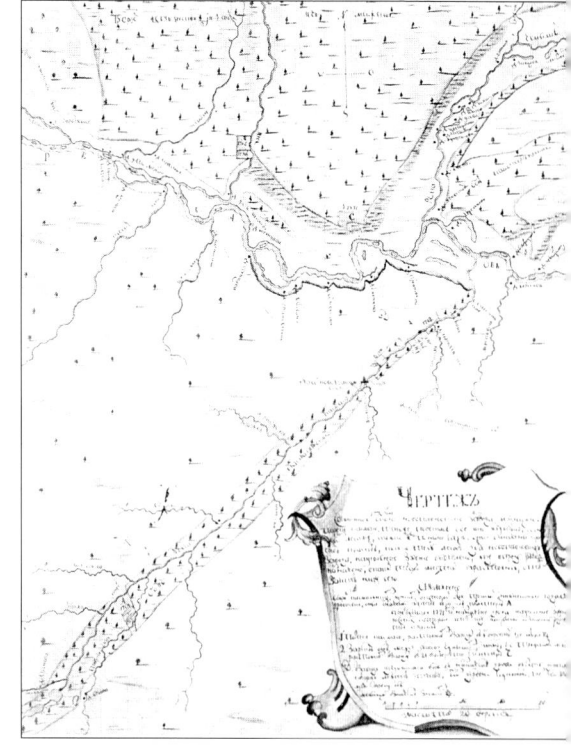

8 Forests of Novopavlovskii plantation.

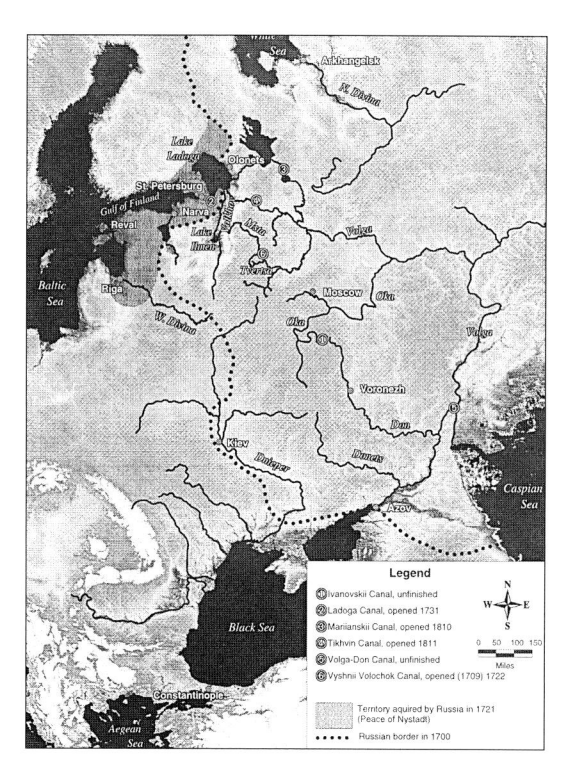

9 Canals and waterways of European Russia.

10 Portrait of Catherine I by A. F. Zubov (1726).

11 Print marking the coronation of Catherine as consort by A. F. Zubov (1724).

12 Coronation portrait of Peter I. Anon. (1682).

13 Peter I by Jan Kupetsky (1711).

14 Peter I crowned by Victory at Poltava by J. G. Dannhauer (1710s).

15 Round portrait of Peter I, attributed to Ivan Nikitin (1720s).

16 Peter I on his deathbed, attributed to Ivan Nikitin (1725).

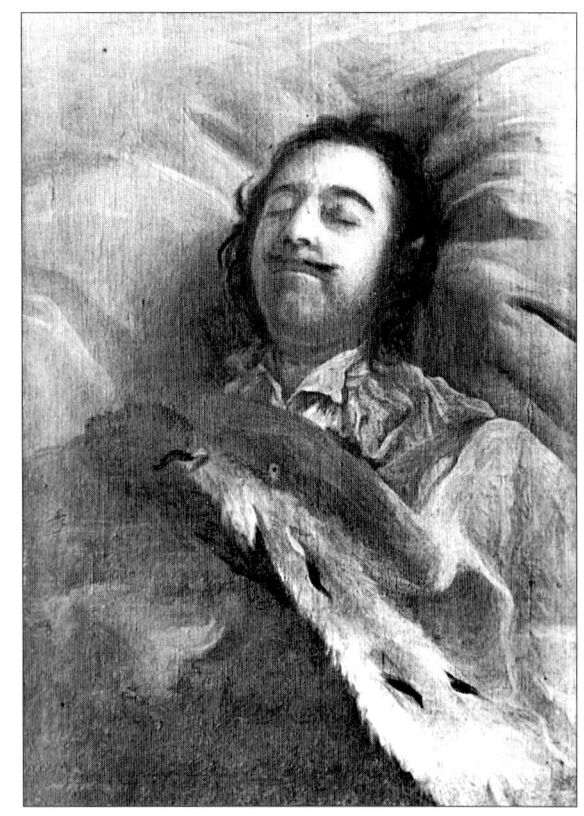

father (best known as Lord Danby, but by this time the first Duke of Leeds, Lord President of the Council and sometime Treasurer of the Navy), though related by marriage to James II, had been among those who brought over Dutch William (although Carmarthen later defected to the Jacobite cause). Since most of the points in Carmarthen's prospectus were realised, we may assume that Peter did in fact take his advice. A letter to Carmarthen from one of the English specialists sent to Russia, John Deane (son of Sir Anthony Deane mentioned above), was published as a pamphlet in London in 1699. Its title – *A letter from Moscow to the Marquess of Carmarthen relating to the Czar of Muscovy's forwardness in his great navy etc., since his return* – suggests that Carmarthen's role was well understood at the time, and it includes a remark about a ship being built by Peter: 'One may, methinks, call her an abstract of his own private observations while abroad, strengthned by Your Lordship's improving discourses to him on that subject, and his own extraordinary notion of sailing.' Peter also spent time with Vice-Admiral Mitchell, who had been charged jointly with Carmarthen to be in waiting on Peter in England. Mitchell had been entrusted with bringing Peter from Holland by sea, and with organising the naval manoeuvres at Portsmouth for his instruction. He was a professional officer held in high regard and he had been specifically asked for by Peter because of his knowledge of Dutch. Since Peter's own knowledge of Dutch was fairly basic, one cannot know how informative Peter's discussions with his English interlocutors really were, but he clearly had the right people to help him.

My second category, hands-on experience of ship-handling, is perhaps a little less significant technically but was important for customer relations: it gave Peter a great deal of pleasure, as well as some sharp practical lessons in the need for specialist training in navigation and ship-handling. Peter was allowed to sail a yacht in the Thames and succeeded in ramming and seriously damaging the Royal yacht *Henrietta* and a bomb vessel, and cutting a cable, all expensive errors which were duly noted and costed in tight-lipped dockyard reports to the Admiralty.[28] It was perhaps fortunate that events in Moscow required Peter's hasty return overland and prevented him from carrying out his original intention of sailing the ship round the North Cape to Archangel.

My third topic, ships, is discussed more broadly by Richard Warner in his chapter in this volume, and I shall concentrate on the

Royal Transport, the ship which was the bait to lure Peter to England and secure the trade treaty. She is often described as a yacht, which is misleading to modern and non-specialist ears. In fact, the *Royal Transport* was a sixth-rate warship of experimental design, 90 feet long and 23 feet in the beam, guns variously reported as eighteen (in the Admiralty schedule), to thirty eight, and an unusually large complement of one hundred men. She was the first schooner-rigged ship in the English navy, with strongly raked masts and a very large sail area. She also had an unusual hull configuration, with bilge sections sweeping below the level of the keel,[29] possibly inspired by types of Dutch vessel, or perhaps influenced by Sir William Petty's experiments with twin-hulled ships some years before. At any rate this was presumably intended to increase lateral resistance and reduce leeway when the ship was sailing close-hauled or with the wind on the beam. She was reputed to be the fastest ship in the navy, if not in Europe, and could certainly sail closer to the wind than any of the conventional square-rigged warships of the period. Admiral Lord Carmarthen, her 'sole designer' as he stated in his letter to Peter,[30] had designed and built a number of ships, much to the disapproval of Admiralty officials. A memorial on the matter from the Admiralty Office to the Lord Justices (25 May) – an early but already well-polished specimen of the Whitehall memo – protested at the

> evil consequences that may attend giving power to particular persons to build ships ... such experiments ought not to be made on any of His Majesty's ships of war ... building His Majesty's ships according to the fancy and humour of particular persons will break through those wholesome Rules and Methods which have been found absolutely necessary for the well performance of His Majesty's Service[31]

A contemporary assessment of Carmarthen, admittedly by a protégé, was that he was the only man in Europe who really understood ship design, and that he was a great commander and had a fine collection of ship models.[32] The need for a fast and well armed vessel was, of course, very great at a time when the king and his representatives had to travel between England and Holland while at war with the French. The *Royal Transport*, as her name implies, was designed by Carmarthen, apparently at the king's request, for this purpose and seems to have met the requirements very well in point of speed. The logs record several journeys between Holland and the Thames of less than one day; in Luttrell[33] there is a reference to outrunning two French privateers (which may be presumed to have been fast craft and larger than the *Royal Transport*). Luttrell also describes the ship as being the 'best sailer' in the English fleet,[34] and there is a reference to her being used as a scout vessel.[35] Captain John Perry, in his *The State of Russia under the Present Czar*, describes the *Royal Transport* as 'much the fastest and best yacht then in England, built frigate-fashion [i.e. flush-decked] carrying twenty-four guns and contrived by my Lord Marquis of Carmarthen on purpose for the King's own use for crossing the sea during the war'.[36] Voltaire in his *Histoire de l'Empire de Russie sous Pierre le Grand*[37] also describes the *Royal Transport*: 'Enfin Guillaume lui fit présent du vaisseau sur lequel il avait coutume de passer en Hollande, nommé le *Royal Transport*, aussi bien construit que magnifique.' Carmarthen himself stated, in a letter to Peter dated 9 November 1697, of which only a Russian copy survives, that his intention in building 'this small vessel of my own invention' was 'not only its utility and convenience but also that she should be faster and stronger than other ships exceeding her size'.[38] Peter had undoubtedly got a gem of a present and knew what he had to do: the tobacco monopoly, albeit at a fairly high price, was granted to Carmarthen as the representative of a merchant consortium, with a substantial sum payable to him personally.

The *Royal Transport* was not the only ship acquired for Peter's new navy. In the following years ships, both naval and merchant, were regularly bought from Britain (for more detail see Richard Warner's chapter in this volume), several through the agency of Samuel Gartside, the shady entrepreneur who supplied the Russians with the *Bolingbroke* and *Victoria*, and who also entered into a shipbuilding partnership with a Russian merchant, Fedor Bazhenin, in Archangel – in fact by 1711 he claimed to have built nine ships in this way.[39]

This leads on to my fourth category: shipbuilders and shipbuilding. As we have already seen, Carmarthen is known to have discussed ship design and shipbuilding technology with Peter, and to have supplied him with a quantity of ship models.[40] These were of some importance to a would-be shipbuilder, and their availability may be explained by the requirement by the Admiralty Committee to the Naval Council in 1649 that detailed models of projected ships be prepared by their builders.[41] Two fine examples, including the model of the *Royal Transport*, reputedly made by Carmarthen himself, were in the Tercentenary Exhibition. The use of ship models for experiments in hull design had been proposed only ten years previously in the first edition of Newton's *Principia* (1687).[42]

Admirals Carmarthen and Mitchell are credited with finding the considerable list of shipbuilders and dockyard craftsmen who went to Russia following Peter's visit. The estimate of the numbers varies widely: Sir John Barrow in his *Life of Peter the Great*[43] gives a figure of nearly five hundred persons including three naval captains, twenty-five merchant captains, thirty pilots, thirty surgeons, two hundred gunners (a particularly improbable figure, even if it includes craftsmen for cannon foundries), four mast-makers, four boat-builders, two master sailmakers and twenty workmen, two compass-makers, two carvers, two anchor-smiths, two locksmiths, two coppersmiths, two tinmen. Some of these were no doubt politically disaffected: the deposed James II had been quite popular in the navy, and there were plenty of Jacobite sympathisers with reason to seek employment abroad. Others were in disgrace: men such as William Ripley, the first captain of the *Royal Transport* – who had been dismissed from the service for brutality and stealing ship's stores, and was now reinstated – or John Perry, absurdly imprisoned for debt for losing his fireship to the French, who went on to become a famous naval engineer. Perry is often described as having been hired by Peter to build a navy. In fact he did build one or two ships, but for the most part he was employed in building canals and docks; he was successful in these undertakings but always hampered by Peter's chronic shortage of cash. Eventually, after failing to get the promised reward of 50 000 ducats for finding a way of preventing Peter's ships from rotting (by removing planks in dry dock for ventilation, a method actually adopted by Peter)[44] he fled Russia disguised as a servant and claiming that he had only once been paid any of his salary during his fourteen years' service.[45] The English master shipbuilders who were the main builders of ships in Russia were Brown, Cozens, Joseph Nye (or Noy) and John Deane. Indeed, for a while British shipbuilders played the major role in Russia, displacing the Dutch (the last Dutch ship was reportedly built in 1703), and in the second-hand market Peter was prepared to pay up to

20 per cent more for ready-built British ships than for any other, including his next preference, ships built in Zealand. The scale of one order made through Prince Boris Ivanovich Kurakin, the Russian ambassador to Britain and Holland, in 1711, was considerable: five or more ships of forty-eight to sixty guns.[46] As late as 1716 the Russian ambassador in Britain was still buying second-hand British ships from British entrepreneurs.[47]

Some idea of the extent of British shipbuilding activity in Russia is given in a letter of 16 July 1719 from the British envoy in Russia, James Jefferyes, to James Craggs, secretary of state for the Southern Department, expressing alarm at the extent to which Peter's navy was growing and referring to the Act of Parliament recently passed 'to prevent the inconveniences arising from seducing artificers in the manufactures of Great Britain into foreign parts'. He says:

> I shall use my best endeavours to execute their Lordships' orders by inducing such of them as are in this service to return home; but I humbly entreat their excellencies to consider the difficulty I am like to meet with from the ship-builders. These are people who have taken their all with them into this country, who have no lands or tenements and consequently nothing to loose in Great Britain; they are come to this country with their families to seek their fortunes and have in some respects found the same, for their sallaries are considerable, two of them having 2000 rubles each p. annum, and the other three 800 each, besides presents upon occasion and other advantages. The respect paid to them is more than they could pretend to in any other country though they were persons of quality, for they are the most carressed by the Czar and consequently by all the great men of the kingdom: they partake of his diversions, and on festival-days sit at his own table when persons of the best quality are bound to stand and wait; – in short the Czar omits nothing that can endear himself to them or that may engage them to continue in his service during life.

He goes on to describe how the Russian fleet has grown:

> The Czar's fleet consisted 6 years ago of such ships as were either bought in foreign countries or built at Archangel by Hollanders which amounted to 17 or 18 in number; but these being for several reasons disapproved, ship-yards were made at St Petersburgh and they began to build His Czarish Majesty's ships-of-war at that place. In these yards none but English builders have the direction ..., by the care and diligence of who the Czar's fleet is now augmented to upwards of 30 sail, whereof 27 or 28 are ships of the line ... I say these are looked upon to be ships as good and as well built as any Europe can afford; besides these there are now 10 more of the line upon the stocks, whereof 7 (according to the Czar's own saying) will be ready to be launched by next spring.

Jefferyes then points out that cheap local materials for shipbuilding, and cheap labour, enable the tsar to fit out a man-of-war at a third of the cost of fitting out a similar vessel in England and that when the Ladoga canal is finished he will be 'able to build and fit out constantly one year with another 6 men-of-war at least'. He goes on to say that:

> There are 5 of these builders at St Petersburgh and one, I think, at Kazan, all good subjects and well affected to His Majesty's government; if therefore the half of what they have from the Czar be offered them in Great Britain, I am certain they will make no scruple of leaving this country, whereas, if they remain, they may by bringing the Moscovites into a good method, and by teaching their people the way of building do more damage to Great Britain than what a yearly expence of 20 times as much as the Czar allows them will amount to.[48]

I should like to turn now to my fifth topic: scientific instruments. In fact the first example of technological transfer in this field was probably not from England to Russia but the other way round: in 1618 John Tradescant brought a Russian *schety*, a kind of abacus still used, from Archangel to England.[49] Although it was faster than the counting board which was still in use in England at the time, it seems not to have excited any curiosity. Interest at court level in scientific instruments was not new in Russia. In 1614 a Russian merchant sold to Tsar Mikhail Fedorovich a telescope, facetted trick spectacles giving multiple images, a lunar phase calculator and a sundial (this is also the first recorded sundial in Russia).[50] Thereafter the tsars would regularly ask merchants to obtain telescopes (evidently for military purposes) and other instruments from abroad. The fact that tsars, and in particular Alexis Mikhailovich, were fascinated by scientific instruments and clocks was not lost on merchants, ambassadors and foreign monarchs. Not a few instruments in Russian collections were gifts to the tsar or his ambassadors. A pair of silver globes made in Magdeburg in the first half of the seventeenth century was presented to Alexis Mikhailovich by Charles X of Sweden[51] and a German silver celestial globe was presented to the same tsar by the Polish king.[52] A seventeenth-century 'polemoscopium', a telescopic periscope with five draw-tubes for observing the enemy from cover, which may also have been a gift, is in the Hermitage.[53]

In the reign of Peter scientific gifts became almost commonplace. Peter had already shown an interest in navigation and scientific instruments as a boy and is known to have been instructed in the use of the astrolabe by the same Dutchman, Franz Timmerman, who had explained the *botik* to him and communicated to the Royal Society in 1691 an observation of the 1688 eclipse of the moon in Moscow.[54] Although Timmerman clearly had some astronomical expertise, the textual context mentions measuring at a distance and we may assume that the astrolabe here was not a planispheric or mariner's astrolabe but a circumferentor, a land-surveying instrument usually called *astroliabia* in Russian.[55] Peter ordered one such instrument to his own design from Edmund Culpeper (dated 1721).[56] The Muscovy merchants, always anxious to obtain, keep or regain trading privileges, decided around 1714 to present Peter with a splendid scientific instrument. This was a very fine orrery (and one of the first) by John Rowley.[57] There were other presentation pieces by Rowley: two mechanical dials, one of them having both hour and minute hands (commissioned by George I in 1715 as a present for Peter) and also possibly a mural quadrant.[58] The 1741 catalogue of the Imperial Academy collections lists four more instruments by Rowley, including an 'astrolabium geodeticum cum telescopiis', as well as instruments by Joseph Moxon, Edmund Culpeper, Richard Whitehead, Isaac Carver, John Marshall, Matthew Loft and Jonathan Sisson. Peter in his turn liked to give scientific gifts and, for example, gave George I a compass which he may well have made with his own hands on a lathe.[59]

Peter did not rely on gifts alone for his scientific instruments; he needed them in quantity. While in England in 1698 he, or his scientific advisor the army officer James or Jacob Bruce (Iakov Brius), son of a Scot in Russian service, hired considerable numbers of craftsmen and bought instruments.[60] The first Russian doctor, Peter Postnikov, was also an agent for acquiring both instruments and instrument-makers: one of his acquisitions was a pneumatic pump for a diving mechanism. This cost 200 thalers.[61] A.K. Nartov and the tsar's librarian (in 1721), J.D. Schumacher, were also commissioned by Peter to buy instruments.[62]

The bill which the English merchant Henry Stiles, Peter's agent, presented to Peter on his return to Moscow included, beside the mysterious payment to the old man who had walked from Cambridge, the items in Table 9.1. Stiles continued to supply Peter with instruments: in 1706 Peter wrote to him with an order for three or four telescopes, one to be 12 feet in length, and two general-purpose lathes.[63]

Bruce, whom I mentioned as Peter's scientific advisor, was an interesting man of wide interests and with a claim to being Russia's first astronomer and certainly the organiser of its first observatory. He spent most of 1698 in England studying and buying instruments, and there is extant a telescope speculum made by him. He also appears to have spent a great deal on books: the catalogue of his library shows that 220 books, almost one third of the catalogue of known titles in his library, were English, mostly dating from just before 1698 and predominantly on mathematics, navigation and fireworks; the later books, sadly, were more commonly devoted to religion and the cure of gout.[64] Bruce was not the only man in Peter's close circle who possessed instruments. The most important of them, Alexander Menshikov – who accompanied Peter on his Grand Embassy abroad and was with him in England – almost certainly owned instruments and certainly acquired a number of English watches by leading makers of the time such as Daniel Quare and Thomas Tompion.[65] Andrei Matveev, Peter's ambassador in London for a while, who

Table 9.1 Part of the bill which the English merchant, Henry Stiles, presented to Peter on his return to Moscow

For mathematical instruments	6/10/–
To [Cul]peper for instruments	19/12/6 [66]
For a quadrant	1/5/–
For two magnets [? lodestones]	4/10/–
For three small globes	2/5/–
For four sandglasses	–/2/–
To Wynne for mathematical instruments	19/19/– [67]
For a gold watch	50/–/–
For the [geo]graph[ical] clock [from John Carte]	60/–/– [68]
To Coston [? John Colson] for two round table clocks and six pocket watches	160/–/– [69]
For medical instruments	250/–/–
For mercury and a glass tube	–/15/–

was arrested as a bankrupt in a famous diplomatic incident, had among his creditors Richard Colson, watchmaker, owed £2, and John Rowley, instrument-maker, owed £26/17/6.[70]

One product of Peter's visit was the Moscow Mathematics and Navigation School;[71] this is mentioned in more detail below, and here I shall only mention that the school faced a serious supply problem. When at the school, the students were supposed to have an arithmetic book, log tables, slates and slate pencils, rulers, backstaffs, sectors, quadrants, nocturnals, a book of charts and a set of drawing instruments; and the navigation course (which survives in manuscript) included instruction in the Davis quadrant and log and line.[72] This was just about the complete navigation equipment of a sea-going ship and the procurement of these books and instruments in the quantities required was a serious problem. At its height the school had over 1000 students, and proposals were put forward giving the school exclusive rights to buy instruments in Moscow, in effect to requisition them.[73] This problem was to be partially solved later when the instrument workshops under the direction of A.K. Nartov began to produce instruments.[74] Nartov himself had been a student at the Moscow Navigation School (from the age of twelve), became a skilled turner in the workshop attached to the school and later spent some time studying lathe-turning in England and acquiring lathes and moulds for their construction; he rose to be, for a while, the head of the St Petersburg Academy.

The connection of English instrument-makers with Russia continued to be strong. We know of several who set up shop in Russia: John Bradlee in Peter's reign was hired both to make instruments and to teach Russian craftsmen and worked in Moscow in the Artillery office from 1710 to 1716, and then in St Petersburg until 1743 for the Department of Artillery and Fortification;[75] and he was succeeded later in the century by Tangate, Benjamin Scott and Francis Morgan.[76] The exodus of skilled craftsmen from Britain to Russia prompted Parliament in 1718 to pass the Act already quoted to discourage skilled craftsmen from going abroad. The Act specifically mentions skilled workers in metals and clock and watch makers as well as shipbuilders.

So far we have seen how Peter on his trip to England was advised on how to set up a navy, how he observed shipbuilding and ship-handling, how he engaged seamen, shipbuilders, craftsmen, how he bought ships and ship models, how he bought scientific and navigational instruments. All that he needed now was to train Russians to sail their own ships.

My last category is navigation. Peter while in England visited Greenwich Observatory and took lessons with the mathematician and teacher of navigation John Colson.[77] But these by themselves could do no more than ensure that the tsar had some conception of what was required; it was not enough to start a navy. However, one of Lord Carmarthen's recommendations to Peter in setting up a navy was that he should hire as teachers of navigation some young men who had been trained at the Royal Mathematical School at Christ's Hospital, a school for poor boys which had been set up mainly to provide navigators for the British navy by Carmarthen's father as Treasurer of the Navy in 1675.[78] Carmarthen himself was one of its governors. Two youths from this school did indeed go to Russia: Stephen Gwynn, aged fifteen, and Richard Grice, aged seventeen. The Royal licence to 'Stephan Gwynn and Richard Grice, two mathematical boys of Christ's hospital to enter the Czar of Muscovy's service' was issued on 12 May 1698.[79] Gwynn eventually rose to the rank of professor in the St Petersburg Naval Academy; he died in Russia in 1720. Grice was murdered in the street in 1709 as he left the Navigation School. The Decembrist N.A. Bestuzhev, the first historian of the Russian navy, states that Carmarthen taught Peter navigation and advised him on the purchase of ship models, tools and instruments, as well as advising him on the hiring of Perry, Deane, Nye and Farquharson.[80]

This was Henry Farquharson and he was perhaps Peter's biggest catch. He was a mathematics teacher from Marischal College Aberdeen, and he was contracted to be the head of the projected new Mathematical and Navigation School in Moscow. This, the first non-clerical school in Russia, was of tremendous importance in that for the next forty years the English teachers, first at the Navigation School and then at its more advanced offshoot the Naval Academy in the new capital of St Petersburg, taught every Russian navigation officer and almost all the surveyors, cartographers, astronomers and not a few artillerymen of the first half of the eighteenth century.[81] Very many of Peter's new initiatives – military, naval, cartographical and astronomical – would have been impossible without them. Farquharson's contract promised a salary of 100 roubles per annum, and he was to receive free lodging, a food allowance and a bonus of £50 sterling for every successful student.[82] On arriving in Archangel in August 1699, Farquharson and his two young assistants found that Peter, no doubt more concerned with war against Sweden, had forgotten about his school and had failed to provide for them, so that they were left to the charity of English merchants Woolfe and Crevet. Eventually they had to petition Peter, in January 1701, not only for their promised pay, board and lodging, but also for a school to teach in, students to teach and books and equipment.[83] They asked for a large house, high enough to make astronomical observations, enough rooms to house them, a teacher of Slavonic literature and a scribe, a room to store books, globes, telescopes and mathematical instruments, a room to teach in, another to receive guests in, and accommodation for pupils if that was intended. This petition had its effect. An *ukaz* of 14 January 1701 orders Farquharson to start teaching mathematics and Grice and Gwynn navigation in an old linen mill.[84] After complaints that this was not a sufficiently elevated site they were moved to the Sukhareva Bashnia on the Zemlianoi val (a large building in Moscow Baroque style with a tower and striking clock, built in 1692–95).[85] This had an unimpeded view of the horizon and here Colonel James Bruce, who has already been mentioned, was entrusted with setting up the Navigation School, and he also established an observatory (the first in Russia), which was used by the staff and students of the school.[86]

Farquharson had a wide variety of duties. He not only taught, but in the absence of any usable textbook in Russian[87] he copied out textbooks for his students, and two copies are extant of a complete course in navigation which are clearly taken from English sources and which can only have been the work of Farquharson. This course was written in clear and fairly straightforward Russian, which Farquharson is reported to have learned to speak perfectly,[88] one reason perhaps why the English dominance in the teaching of navigation has left almost no trace in the Russian terminology of the subject. Further colour is given to his reported excellence in Russian by the fact that he translated and edited many scientific works and is credited with supervising thirty-eight translations by the Naval Academy's translators.[89] He is also credited with surveying the Petersburg to Moscow road with some of his students, and with the major enterprise of charting the Caspian sea, although in fact he probably had no more than a supervisory and planning role, and was evidently a valued scientific consultant in many of the scientific publishing projects of the time.

In 1715 the school had grown to 600 students and Peter ordered the more advanced navigation section to be moved to St Petersburg where it became the Naval Academy, the centre of scientific activity in Russia until it was eventually eclipsed by the St Petersburg Academy of Sciences.[90] Farquharson and Gwynn became the first professors of the Naval Academy; Farquharson continued to be entrusted with translating and editing mathematical and scientific books and training cartographers and his salary was increased to nearly 1000 roubles, twice the normal rate for foreign specialists. He was promoted to the rank of Brigadier in 1737 on the initiative of the Admiralty College, and the Empress Anna, writing to the College, remarked that every Russian sailor for nearly forty years had learnt his navigation from Farquharson.[91] This was certainly true, and his influence was not confined to the navy: graduates of the Navigation School and Naval Academy provided most of the teachers of mathematics for provincial schools and surveyors for Peter's geographical and cartographical projects.[92] Between 1714 and 1716 students of the school were ordered into all the provinces to teach mathematics to sons (and a few daughters) of the gentry and in monasteries and bishops' palaces. Farquharson died in 1739. It is perhaps a measure of his achievement and the reputation of British navigation that the Naval Academy immediately tried to find a replacement for Farquharson in England through the Russian envoy in London. Four candidates were found after a search of several years but the Academy was unable to meet their requirements for salary and conditions.[93]

*****

I have outlined six categories of maritime technology and expertise which Peter sampled in England. But we know how often Peter's projects faltered when he lost interest in them, or could not finance them, or they were overtaken by events, or were simply not feasible. So how real and how lasting was the English contribution? As far as hardware is concerned Peter certainly acquired ships, but not only from England; he certainly built ships and for nearly two decades British shipbuilders in Russia were predominant and the best paid, at least in St Petersburg and Archangel. Enough, perhaps, to leave a mark. Peter was shown in detail in England how an increasingly mathematical navy built its ships and trained its men, he acquired good navigation teachers and – after a shaky start – their school established a distinguished tradition of navigation and cartography. He acquired instruments from some of the best English instrument makers of the time, who were in fact among the best in Europe, and continued to import English instruments (although after his trip to Paris in 1717 and in the strained relations with Britain during the later part of his reign, he began to buy from French makers). His attempt to set up an instrument-making trade to supply the army and navy by bringing in English craftsmen was less successful: few instruments made in Russia survive from this period, Bradlee was not an outstanding maker, and the one or two extant pieces apparently made by his pupils were very poor. The many English craftsmen imported for other trades varied very much in quality and some had to be sent home as insufficiently skilled: out of five carpenters in one party sent to Russia three had to be sent home.[94] The naval officers – some of them disgraced or Jacobites – seem to have been for the most part no better and no worse than the various Dutchmen, Danes and Italians and other nationalities. And it is hard to gauge the long-term effect of the considerable number of Russians sent abroad to study, work as apprentices or serve in

English ships in Peter's reign and thereafter (an aspect of technology transfer which I have not discussed here). On balance I think it is true to say that Britain, and in particular British merchant entrepreneurs, did give Peter an extraordinary boost to build his navy during the period of his visit to England and immediately afterwards when the commercial and political incentives were strong. Those incentives changed fairly quickly and – although Britain needed to maintain supplies of essential shipbuilding raw materials *from* Russia (timber, masts, hemp, pitch) – there was never again an export of technology to Russia on such a scale. Moreover, the change of economic and political climate in Britain coincided with a relative decline in the importance of the navy in Russia after the death of Peter, which reduced demand and, ultimately, of course, the sale of expertise destroyed its own market by creating an ability in Russia to manage without foreign help. Already within Peter's lifetime the Russians could win naval battles against Sweden, not a negligible naval power. By the end of the eighteenth century the Russian navy could send squadrons of ships on round-the-world voyages of scientific exploration comparable with the best efforts of any of the major maritime powers.

NOTES

1 N.N. Molchanov, *Diplomatiia Petra pervogo*, Moscow, 1984, p. 65; E.V. Anisimov, *The Reforms of Peter the Great: Progress through Coercion*, Armonk and London, 1993 (abridged translation by J.T. Alexander of *Vremia petrovskikh reform*, Leningrad, 1989), pp. 48–9; L. Hughes, *Russia in the Age of Peter the Great*, London, 1998, p. 23.
2 For a detailed account of these projects see E.J. Phillips, *The Founding of Russia's Navy: Peter the Great and the Azov Fleet, 1688–1714*, Westport and London, 1995, pp. 13–28.
3 For example, the contemporary accounts of Narcissus Luttrell, *A Brief Historical Relation of State Affairs from September 1678 to April 1714*, 6 vols, Oxford, 1857; Gilbert Burnet, *Bishop Burnet's History of His Own Time*, Oxford, 1823; John Evelyn, *The Diary of John Evelyn*, ed. E.S. de Beer, 6 vols, Oxford, 1955, and later histories such as the still valuable Sir John Barrow's *The Life of Peter the Great*, London, 1832 (first published anonymously, but with later editions under Barrow's name); E. Schuyler,

Peter the Great, Emperor of Russia, 2 vols, London, 1884. More modern English studies dealing with Peter, England and the navy, include I. Grey, *Peter the Great*, London, 1960 (chapters 13–14); M.S. Anderson, 'Great Britain and the Growth of the Russian Navy in the Eighteenth Century', *The Mariner's Mirror*, 42, 1956, pp. 132–46, and Hughes, *Russia in the Age of Peter the Great*, pp. 80–9. The standard Russian works are N. Ustrialov, *Istoriia tsarstvovaniia Petra Velikago*, St Petersburg, 1858–59; M. Bogoslovskii, *Petr I*, II, Moscow, 1941; A.I. Andreev, 'Petr Velikii v Anglii v 1698 g.' in *Petr Velikii. Sbornik statei*, Moscow–Leningrad, 1947, pp. 63–103.
4 For a convenient recent overview see Hughes, *Russia in the Age of Peter the Great*, pp. 80–9.
5 *Britain and Russia in the Age of Peter the Great: Historical Documents*, ed. S. Dixon *et al.*, London, 1998.
6 On Carmarthen, and the *Royal Transport*, see W.F. Ryan, 'Peter the Great's English Yacht: Admiral Lord Carmarthen and the Russian Tobacco Monopoly', *Mariner's Mirror*, 69, 1983, pp. 65–87.
7 J. Cracraft, *For God and Peter the Great: The Works of Thomas Consett, 1723–1729*, Boulder, CO, 1982. For discussion and history of Peter's early naval experience, see Phillips, *The Founding of Russia's Navy*.
8 *Calendar of State Papers, Domestic, William III*, London, 1913–37: *1697*, pp. 295–7.
9 See Historical Manuscripts Commission, *The Manuscripts of the House of Lords, 1697–1699*, III, new ser., London, 1905, pp. 217–22.
10 Luttrell, *Brief Historical Relation*, IV, p. 158.
11 See note 57 below.
12 For details of the English tobacco trade with Russia see O.J. Frederikson, 'Virginia Tobacco in Russia under Peter the Great', *Slavonic and East European Review*, 21, 56, 1943, pp. 40–57, and the chief monograph on the subject, M. Price, 'The Tobacco Adventure to Russia: Enterprise, Politics and Diplomacy in the Quest for a Northern Market for English Colonial Tobacco', *Transactions of the American Philosophical Society*, 51, 1961. In fact Generals Gordon and Bruce, key figures in Peter's military establishment, had had limited rights to import tobacco since 1695 (*ibid.*, p. 20).
13 J. Flamsteed, *Historia Coelestis Britannica*, London, 1725, p. 341: 'J. Wolfias et Stileus mercatores Angliae'. 'J. Wolfias' was Sir John Wolfe, a city merchant who had met Peter in Moscow and who spoke Russian. The Stiles brothers played a consider role in Peter's English affairs.

14 The Dutch were the unlucky losers both on Peter's visit and on the later visit of Alexander I: see J.M. Hartley, 'England "Enjoys the Spectacle of a Northern Barbarian": The Reception of Peter I and Alexander I', in *A Window on Russia* (Papers from the V International Conference of the Study Group on Eighteenth-Century Russia, Gargnano, 1994), ed. M. di Salvo and L. Hughes, Rome, 1996, pp. 11–18 (17).
15 See *Britain and Russia*, doc. 2.
16 Historical Manuscripts Commission, *A Report on the Manuscripts of the Duke of Portland*, 3, 1907, p. 590 (hereafter HMC, *Portland MSS*).
17 *Ibid.*, p. 590.
18 London, PRO, Adm. 1/4086, f. 12.
19 General Adam Weide was one of Peter's inner circle. He had been an officer of the Preobrazhenskii regiment and was sent abroad by Peter to study foreign military methods and had been a prisoner-of-war in Sweden. He was much involved in the administrative reforms of Peter's reign, in particular the introduction of the collegial system based on the Swedish model and the recruitment of foreign specialists, including experienced lawyers. He drew up the first draft of Peter's Code of Military Law (*Voinskii artikul*), parts of which were also included in Peter's law code for the navy (*Morskoi ustav*). In 1717 he was appointed Vice-President of the College of War under Prince Alexander Menshikov.
20 Letter of 28 November 1697 from F.Ia. Lefort to Admiral Lord Carmarthen, in reply to a letter of November 23. See *Britain and Russia*, doc. 12.
21 S. Elagin, *Istoriia russkogo flota: Period Azovskii.* Prilozhenie, chapter 1, St Petersburg, 1864, pp. 478–9.
22 See Consett, pp. 214–5 in Cracraft, *For God and Peter the Great* (note 7 above).
23 Bogoslovskii, *Petr I*, II, pp. 268–73.
24 Carmarthen's constant presence is noted in many sources. Deane's is mentioned twice by A.K. Nartov in his reminiscences of Peter: see *Petr Velikii. Vospominaniia. Dnevnikovye zapisi. Anekdoty*, St Petersburg, 1993, pp. 247–326 (253, 257). Nartov was, however, writing some time after the event (1727), visited England only in 1718–20, and may well have confused Sir Anthony with his son John Deane, who entered Peter's service (see below, *passim*), or the other John Deane who published a history of the Russian fleet in 1724 (see D.B.S., 'The Authorship of *The Russian Fleet under Peter the Great*', *The Mariner's Mirror*, 20, 1934, pp. 373–6; also A. Cross, *Anglo-Russian Relations in the Eighteenth Century*, Norwich, 1977, p. 21).

25 *Britain and Russia*, doc. 11. The same point was made in a printed broadside from the Virginia merchants to the Board of Trade and Plantations: *ibid.*, doc. 14.
26 See *Britain and Russia*, docs 227, 228.
27 Ryan 'Peter the Great's English Yacht' (Appendix I).
28 London, PRO Adm. 100/3292, Dockyard letters, ff. 54v, 57, 59, 62v. This incident is described in some detail in Bernard Pool, 'Peter the Great in the Thames', *The Mariner's Mirror*, 59, 1973, pp. 9–12.
29 Carmarthen wrote to Peter: 'This ship also differs from other ships built before it in the shape of its hull and in other ways', Ustrialov, *Istoriia tsarstvovaniia Petra Velikago*, III, p. 466; English translation published in *Britain and Russia*, doc. 10.
30 *Britain and Russia*, doc. 10.
31 London, PRO, Adm. 7/3 34, p. 65.
32 Bogoslovskii, *Petr I*, II, p. 309.
33 Luttrell, IV, p. 290.
34 See also HMC, *Portland MSS*, III, p. 590.
35 *Calendar of State Papers, Domestic, William III*, London, 1913–37: *1697*, pp. 184–5.
36 J. Perry, *The State of Russia under the Present Czar*, London, 1716, p. 167.
37 1759, 1, p. 162.
38 RGADA, f. 35, Snosheniia s Angliei, op. 1, no. 265, ll. 6–9; published in Ustrialov, *Istoriia tsarstvovaniia Petra Velikago*, III, 466; English translation published in *Britain and Russia*, doc. 10.
39 See *Britain and Russia*, docs 126, 169.
40 Veselago states that Carmarthen had a large collection of ships models (Veselago, *Ocherk*, p. 111); Bestuzhev states that Peter bought, among other things, ships models on Carmarthen's advice (N.A. Bestuzhev, *Opyt istorii rossiiskogo flota (1825)*, ed. I.A. Livshits and G.E. Pavlova, Leningrad, 1961, p. 78). Although several sources mention ship models, and English ship models – including the model of the *Royal Transport* displayed at the 1998 tercentenary exhibition at the National Maritime Museum in Greenwich – certainly exist in the Naval Museum in St Petersburg, it is not known how many Peter actually acquired, although various sources mention up to four trunkloads. The bill presented by Henry Stiles for items paid for on Peter's account includes 'for 2 boxes for the ship and models, £1': *Britain and Russia*, doc. 19.
41 G. Naish, 'Ship Models' in *The Decorative Arts of the Mariner*, ed. Gervis Frere-Cook, London, 1966.

42 For discussion see I.B. Cohen, 'Isaac Newton, The Calculus of Variations, and the Design of Ships', *Boston Studies in the Philosophy of Science*, 15, 1974, pp. 169–87.
43 J. Barrow, *The Life of Peter the Great*, 3rd edn, London, 1839, pp. 106–7.
44 See [John Deane,] *History of the Russian Fleet during the Reign of Peter the Great by a Contemporary Englishman (1724)*, ed. C.H.G. Bridge, Navy Records Society XV, London, 1899, p. 73.
45 For Perry's specific points about his employment in Russia see Perry, *The State of Russia under the Present Czar*, pp. 20–21, 37–8, 53–5. Perry is the subject of a biographical essay in Samuel Smiles, *The Lives of the Engineers*, I, London, 1861, p. 73.
46 Instruction of Peter to Prince Kurakin, 18 October 1711: see *Britain and Russia*, doc. 125.
47 See *Britain and Russian*, doc. 175.
48 See *Britain and Russia*, docs 227, 228.
49 See W.F. Ryan, 'John Tradescant's Russian Abacus', *Oxford Slavonic Papers*, new ser., V (1972), pp. 83–8 and 'Bead Calculator' in *Tradescant's Rarities*, ed. A. MacGregor, Oxford, 1983.
50 See S.L. Sobol', 'Opticheskie instrumenty i svedeniia o nikh v dopetrovskoi Rusi', *Trudy Instituta istorii estestvoznaniia AN SSSR*, III (1949), p. 138.
51 See L.E. Maistrov, *Nauchnye pribory*, Moscow, 1968, p. 55, plates 94, 95.
52 *Ibid.*, p. 55, plate 93.
53 *Ibid.*, pp. 68–9, plate 153.
54 E.G.R. Taylor, *Mathematical Practitioners of Tudor and Stuart England*, Cambridge, 1967, p. 407; the circumstances of this observation and further details of Timmermann are given in Iu.Kh. Kopelevich, 'Frants Timerman i astronomicheskoe opredelenie dolgoty Moskvy', *Priroda*, 1973, 4, pp. 90–3.
55 W.F. Ryan, 'Some Observations on the History of the Astrolabe and of Two Russian Words: *astrolabija* and *matka*' in *Studies in Slavic Linguistics and Poetics in Honor of Boris O. Unbegaun*, New York and London, 1968, pp. 155–64.
56 Hermitage (Peter Coll.): see *Pamiatniki russkoi kul'tury pervoi chetverti XVIII veka v sobranii Gosudarstvennogo ordena Lenina Ermitazha*, Leningrad–Moscow, 1966, plate 52.
57 See V.L. Chenakal, 'The Astronomical Instruments of John Rowley in Eighteenth-Century Russia', *Journal for the History of Astronomy*, III, 2, 1972, pp. 119–35 (127–31); Chenakal's identification of this orrery with

the Pulkovo instrument destroyed in the second World War has been challenged: see J.H. Appleby, 'The Russia Company and John Rowley's Orrery', *Bulletin of the Scientific Instrument Society*, 36, 1993, p. 15 and *idem*, 'A New Perspective on John Rowley, Virtuosos Master of Mechanicks and Hydraulic Engineer', *Annals of Science*, 53, 1996, pp. 1–27 (4); this paper is also valuable for a general view of Rowley, on whom see also Taylor, *Mathematical Practitioners of Tudor and Stuart England*, pp. 294–5 and Gloria Clifton, *Directory of British Scientific Instrument Makers 1550–1851*, London, 1995, s.v.

58 See Chenakal, 'The Astronomical Instruments of John Rowley'; V.Iu. Matveev, 'Solnechnye chasy Dzhona Rauli', *Pamiatniki nauki i tekhniki 1987–1988*, Moscow, 1989, pp. 35–45: this also publishes the text and contemporary translation of Rowley's instructions 'The Description and Use of a New Sundial'. See also Appleby, 'A New Perspective', pp. 6–7.

59 Chenakal, 'The Astronomical Instruments of John Rowley', p. 124. Peter was fond of ornamental turning and is known to have sent specimens of his work to other rulers as presents.

60 See V.L. Chenakal, 'Iakov Vilimovich Brius, russkii astronom nachala XVIII veka', *Astronomicheskii zhurnal*, 28, 1, 1951, pp. 1–14 (8). For the fullest account of Bruce, see V. Boss, *Newton and Russia*, Cambridge, MA, 1972, especially pp. 15–18 'Newton and Bruce'; pp. 29–32 'Bruce and "Ivan Kolsun"'; chapter 3 'Russia's First Newtonian'; chapter 6 'Bruce as Translator and Instrument Maker'.

61 For a further request for diving equipment in 1715 see *Britain and Russia*, doc. 167.

62 See Boss, *Newton and Russia*, p. 89.

63 See *Britain and Russia*, doc. 67.

64 See E.A. Savel'eva, *Biblioteka Ia.V. Briusa*, Leningrad, 1989.

65 L. Iakovleva, 'Chasy, prinadlezhavshie A.D. Menshikovu', *Soobshcheniia Gosudarstvennogo Ermitazha*, 50, 1985, pp. 11–14.

66 Edmund Culpeper, 1660–1738, one of the best known mathematical and optical instrument makers of the time. His shop also sold mathematical books. See Taylor, *Mathematical Practitioners of Tudor and Stuart England*, p. 277 and Clifton, *Directory of British Scientific Instrument Makers*, s.v.

67 Probably Henry Wynne of the Clockmakers Company, free 1662, died 1709, four recorded addresses in Chancery Lane. He was a respected maker of all kinds of scientific instruments and his shop also sold mathematical books. See Taylor, *Mathematical Practitioners of Tudor and Stuart England*, pp. 242–3 and Clifton, *Directory of British Scientific Instrument Makers*, s.v.

68 John Carte was a clockmaker, originally from Coventry, free of the Clockmakers Company in 1695, who was working in London at the time of Peter's visit and advertised a 'Great Geographical Clock' which had a thirty-year almanac on its face – evidently the clock mentioned here. See Taylor, *Mathematical Practitioners of Tudor and Stuart England*, p. 292 and Clifton, *Directory of British Scientific Instrument Makers*, s.v.

69 Probably John Colson, fl. 1671–1709, mathematician, teacher of navigation and mathematics (he had had sea-going experience), and publisher of mathematical books. He was one of the examiners at Christ's Hospital School on behalf of Trinity House. He appears to have instructed both Peter and Bruce. See Taylor, *Mathematical Practitioners of Tudor and Stuart England*, p. 264 and Boss, *Newton and Russia*, pp. 29–32 'Bruce and "Ivan Kolsun"'.

70 See *Britain and Russia*, doc. 84.

71 See N. Hans, 'The Moscow School of Mathematics and Navigation (1701)', *The Slavonic Review*, 29, 73, 1951, pp. 532–6. Unfortunately Hans does not give the sources of most of his information (it seems to have been Veselago) and some of his assertions are inaccurate. See also F. Veselago, *Ocherk istorii Morskogo kadetskogo korpusa*, St Petersburg, 1852; P. Pekarskii, *Nauka i literatura v Rossii pri Petre Velikom*, 2 vols, St Petersburg, 1862; A. Viktorov, *Opisanie zapisnykh knig i bumag starinnykh dvortsovykh prikazov (1616–1725)*, vyp. 2, 'Zapisi o Navigatskoi shkole', Moscow, 1883; *Kolybel' flota. Navigatskaia shkola: Morskoi korpus. K 250-ti letiiu so dnia osnovaniia Shkoly matematicheskikh i navigatskikh nauk, 1701–1951*, Paris, 1951, pp. 12–37, 52–3; M. Okenfuss, 'Education in Russia in the First Half of the Eighteenth Century', PhD dissertation, Harvard University, 1970.

72 For a detailed account see W.F. Ryan, 'Navigation and the Modernization of Petrine Russia: Teachers, Textbooks, Terminology', in *Russia in the Age of the Enlightenment: Essays for Isabel de Madariaga*, ed. R. Bartlett and J.M. Hartley, London, 1990, pp. 75–105.

73 S. Elagin, *Materialy dlia istorii russkogo flota*, St Petersburg, 1866, p. 293: letter of A.A. Kurbatov to Golovin, 16 July 1702.

74 On Nartov see most recently M.E. Gize, *Nartov v Peterburge*, Leningrad, 1988.

75 V.L. Chenakal, 'John Bradlee and his Sundials', *Journal for the History of Astronomy*, 1973, 4, pp. 159–67, illustrated.

76 See V.L. Chenakal, *Watchmakers and Clockmakers in Russia from 1400 to 1850*, London, 1972, s.v.

77 See note 66 above.

78 This school was one of the results of the many proposals and enterprises in the later sixteenth and seventeenth centuries designed to meet the ever-increasing need for mathematically trained navigators. See D.W. Waters, *The Art of Navigation in Elizabethan and Early Stuart Times*, London, 1958, *passim* (index, s.v. 'mathematics').
79 On Gwynn see *Russkii biograficheskii slovar'*, vol. *gaag-gerbel*, Moscow, 1914, pp. 293–4.
80 N.A. Bestuzhev, *Opyt istorii russkogo flota*, ed. I.A. Livshits and G.E. Pavlova, Leningrad, 1961 (written in 1825), p. 78. Hans has suggested that Mitchell recruited Farquharson, solely on the ground that both men were from Aberdeen. This is not in fact so, and most of the evidence points to Carmarthen as the prime mover in supplying Peter's manpower needs.
81 For the most recent account see Ryan, 'Navigation and the Modernization of Petrine Russia'.
82 Veselago, *Ocherk*, p. 5.
83 See *Britain and Russia*, doc. 35.
84 S. Elagin, *Materialy dlia istorii russkogo flota*, St Petersburg, 1868, III, p. 289.
85 *Ibid.*, pp. 289–90.
86 Chenakal, 'Iakov Vilimovich Brius', pp. 1–14.
87 It is known that Magnitskii's *Arifmetika*, the first serious mathematical work to be published by a Russian, was not used, despite the fact that Magnitskii was in charge of the lower courses at the Navigation School and was well regarded. On Magnitskii and his book see most recently a substantial article by A.V. Lavrent'ev, *Liudi i veshchi*, Moscow, 1997, pp. 69–108; this suffers from a failure to consult non-Russian work in the field, except for three largely irrelevent references to Wittram, Max Okenfuss and myself.
88 Pekarskii, *Nauka i literatura*, p. 272.
89 Veselago, *Ocherk*, p. 101.
90 For some further assessment see chapter 7 'Newton and the Naval Academy' in Boss, *Newton and Russia*.
91 *Russkii biograficheskii slovar'*, XXI, Moscow and St Petersburg, 1901, pp. 22–3, s.v. *Farvarson*.
92 See M.I. Belov, 'Rol' Petra I v rasprostranenii geograficheskikh znanii v Rossii' in *Voprosy geografii petrovskogo vremeni*, Leningrad, 1975, p. 20 (Belov speaks of 'a pleiad of great names, among them Soimonov, Kirilov, Chirikov, Pronchishchev, Cheliuskin, and Malygin', to which he might have added the astronomer N.G. Kurganov); V.L. Chenakal, 'Prakticheskaia astronomiia v Rossii dopetrovskogo i petrovskogo vremeni', *ibid.*, pp. 56–7.

93 A.G. Cross, *'By the Banks of the Thames': Russians in Eighteenth-Century Britain*, Newtonville, MA, 1980, p. 96. It is, however, possible that a Mr Newberry continued the tradition from about 1755 to 1762: an advertisement in the *Daily Advertiser* for 23 November 1762, reads: 'Mr Newberry, late Professor of Mathematics and Navigation, Corps of Noble Cadets at St Petersburgh ... received the generous Approbation of the Gentlemen of the British Factory.' I am indebted to Alan Morton of the Science Museum, London for this information.
94 *Britain and Russia*, doc. 58.

Part V

Diplomatic and Military History

10 Peter the Great and the Conquest of Azov: 1695–96

Graeme Herd

Peter's conquest of Azov caused a stir across Europe, with the news reported in all major capitals. Andrei Vinius, in a letter to Nicholas Witsen, the Burgomaster of Amsterdam, passed the news of Russia's victory over the Turks on to William III. The siege was reported in the *London Gazette*, which noted the impact of the conquest on the Ottoman Empire's ability to reinforce front-line troops stationed in Central Europe:

> The Loss of this Place is like to be very ill consequence both to the Turks & Tatars. It giving the Moscovites passage into the country of the latter, who will be thereby hindered from sending any assistance to the Turkish Army in Hungary.[1]

Although the two Azov campaigns have been overshadowed by the defining event of Petrine rule, the Great Northern War (1700–21), the conquest of Azov in the mid-1690s was in many ways a precursor to that war.

Indeed, when Franz Lefort contacted the British Representative in Stockholm, Robinson, with news that the campaigns against the Tartars in the south were underway, Robinson reported to the Duke of Shrewsbury that 'As others, so this Court will be well pleased the Czar employ his troops on that side, being otherwise apprehensive it may take him in the head to make an attempt at Liefland, where not a few of the Gentry are discontents, & inclined to change Masters.'[2] This relief that Russian forces had not been directed against Swedish territories on the Baltic coast underscores the training role that these campaigns played in Petrine imperial ambition; practice in the command and control of artillery, infantry and cavalry – not least marines and a flotilla – were perfect preparation for the rigours of warfare with one of the major European powers of the seventeenth century, the Swedish Empire.

In themselves, the Azov campaigns were remarkable. They represented Peter's first foreign-policy success. They signified the first use of the Russian navy in active maritime operations and provided a watershed between the various play (*poteshnye*) warfare exercises which characterised Peter's activities in the early 1690s and the real military struggles which both defined the nature of Petrine rule and shaped Peter's personality.[3] As well as having a central role in Peter's military development, the capture of Azov raised Russia's diplomatic profile across Europe, by providing the ostensible reason for the Grand Embassy (March 1697 – August 1698). The Grand Embassy was to recruit trained professional soldiers, naval and artillery experts to fight against the Ottoman Empire and so fulfil Russia's treaty obligations to the Holy League. This Embassy brought the image of Peter onto the international stage and pushed Russia firmly into European consciousness, signalling its desire to be treated as one of the major European powers.

The Azov campaigns were also instrumental in helping to mobilise internal military and political opposition to Peter's rule. The Grand Embassy, prompted by the success of the Azov campaigns, exacerbated the perceptions of the conservative and orthodox elements within Russian society that Petrine modernisation would prove inimical to 'traditional' state evolution. When *strel'tsy* regiments mutinied first in April and then more seriously in June 1698, the campaigns provided ammunition for *strel'tsy* complaints over the discriminatory treatment they had allegedly endured at the hands of foreign officers. Thus the Azov campaigns help explain why the Grand Embassy was cut short and Peter forced to return hurriedly to Moscow. The campaigns provided a key pillar of complaint against Petrine rule, bringing into focus the ill-defined but heartfelt distrust felt by traditional military elites for Petrine perceptions of progress.

This chapter utilises two key unpublished contemporary sources. Ambassador Charles Whitworth, the first permanent British Resident to Russia, began his diplomatic duties in Russia at the beginning of the eighteenth century (February 1705–12), and he was thus not a contemporary witness to the events he described. He does, though, rely upon three contemporary sources that were available to him, which he synthesised into one account in 1708. One of these sources he names as the 'Diaries of General Patrick Gordon of Auchleuchries (1635–99)', but the other two are unattributed. Gordon wrote a 35 000-page diary in six volumes, currently housed in the Russian State Military Historical Archive (RGVIA) in Moscow. Part of volumes 5 and 6 covers the Azov campaigns in great detail. Whitworth annotated Gordon's diaries both with pen marks in his own hand beside those passages to be utilised and with short passage summaries in the margin. Thus, for example, on 21 June 1696, Whitworth enters in the margin 'Lutina surrenders'.[4]

Whitworth's account is a fifty-page manuscript. It is in the British Library (BL), but it is misleadingly catalogued as written by Patrick Gordon, an error which may be due to a cursory reading of the superscription which states: 'writ by General Gordon who commanded a considerable part of the army.'[5] However, as the document is dated 1708 (Gordon had died in November 1699) and refers to Gordon in the third person (a feature not consistent with the first-person narrative of Gordon's own diaries), it is clear that Gordon was just one of the contemporary sources Whitworth drew upon to create his account.[6] As Whitworth writes in the first paragraph of the manuscript:

> Having got some relations or rather Diaryes of the sieges of Assov in this and last year by diverse intelligent persons who were present and eyewitnesses of all that passed and finding some things or passages therein worthy of observation I resolved and indeed for diversement in the intervals of my business to redraw them into one discourse tho not so exact and perfect as I wish or may be expected.[7]

WHY PETER WENT TO WAR IN 1695

The town of Azov, on the sea of Azov at the mouth of the river Don, was originally a Greek colony and then a factory town of the Genoese Empire, and both Gordon and Whitworth noted in their accounts the presence of the arms of Genoa decorating the inner wall. The Turks captured Azov from the Genoese empire in 1475 and held it until the 1690s. For a brief period, however, the Don Cossacks had captured and held the weakly defended town (1637–42) from the Turks. The Cossacks fortified the town 'with bulwarks according to the modern way of fortifying, made it seems by some foreign and experienced person'.[8] They were forced to relinquish control in 1642, having held off a 20 000 strong Turkish assault the year before with 'private' Russian assistance, as Tsar Mikhail Fedorovich had not been prepared publicly to commit forces to hold it and so break a peace treaty with the Ottoman Empire.

Azov stood on high ground and was surrounded by a stone wall punctuated by strong bastions. Within this wall lay two others, dividing the town into three concentric segments, 'so that it makes three Townes, one called the Greater, the other the Lesser and the third the Castle.' As the Account relates:

> In the towns are some houses built of stones, the Mosques and a Greek Church (though very few Christians live in it; especially when the Towne is apprehensive of any seiges). The rest of the houses are most of wood, or rather Poles and stakes, plotted about with willow or other yerlding shrubs dabbed within and without with clay, as most of the cottages over Ukrania are ... It is distant from the river about 20 or 30 fathome, in this walls are two gates one to the greater town, the other to the lesser or gordock which is as much as a Cittadell or Castle.

That Peter went to war in the 1690s is not in itself surprising. The Russian historian Kliuchevskii has noted that in the whole of the seventeenth century Moscow was only at peace for thirteen years, constantly battling with Sweden and Poland in the west, the Turks and their Tartar vassals in the south and intermittently with the Chinese in the east. The experience of warfare was central to the Petrine period, too; however, can that experience be placed within a coherent interpretative framework? In retrospect, some historians have attempted to uncover strategic imperatives and overarching foreign-policy objectives which give a shape and a meaning to Petrine imperial expansion. Four foreign-policy objectives appear, in hindsight, to have dominated Peter's reign:

- gaining access to the Black sea;
- a 'window to the west' through Baltic conquest;
- expansion into the Caspian sea and Siberia; and
- the promotion of Russian diplomatic status in western Europe.

However, there is little consensus amongst historians as to whether Peter pursued an overarching strategy, following a well-thought-out blue print of imperial expansion, or rather whether he operated on an ad hoc and incremental basis, as an opportunist responding to events and a master of contingency action. If we analyse the Azov campaigns and the causal explanations to which contemporaries attributed the conquest, then the evidence suggests, at least in the mid 1690s, that a mixture of strategic, tactical and personal motivations shaped Peter's decision-making.

The primary reason for going to war, as we have noted, was to fulfil treaty obligations. Since 1686 Russia, in alliance with Poland and Austria, had technically been at war with Turkey. Russia did not sign an armistice following the disastrous Crimean campaigns of 1687–89, which precipitated the fall of the regent Sophia and strengthened Peter's status as co-tsar until the death of his brother Ivan V in 1696. The Crimean campaigns may have been military failures, but diplomatically they ensured Russia's continued role in the alliance and hence secured her formal role in European international relations. However, by the mid-1690s Russia's military contribution to the viability of the alliance through her Crimean contribution was a dim memory amongst her European partners. Both 'the Roman Emperour and the King of Poland had by the Envoys and missives being continually soliciting and pressing the Czar to sop something for the common Good conformable with the treaty made with the Poles.'[9] Poland placed pressure on Russia to strike southwards against the Turks or risk the resumption of a separate Polish–Turkish peace, and so the collapse of the alliance and consequent isolation of Russia.

External international pressure coincided with Muscovite internal self-interest, namely a desire to reassert Muscovite authority on the steppe. Although the Turks were on the retreat on the Danube, this was partially compensated by an increasing presence in the Caucasus and the Black sea region. The Black sea coast fell within the Ottoman Empire's traditional sphere of influence, and imperial Ottoman power projection was underpinned by the control of a linked network of key fortresses and garrisons, located especially at the mouth of the major rivers. Because Ottoman maritime control was absolute, both resupplies and reinforcements were unimpeded.

These military assets acted as a springboard for repeated Crimean Tartar incursions into Russian territory. In 1692, for example, 12 000 Tartar cavalry had struck north as far as Nemitzov, unsettling the Don and Zaporozhian Cossacks, who were Muscovite allies. A strong Russian response had the added benefit of restoring the authority of Hetman Ivan Mazepa amongst the pro-Moscow Cossacks of Ukraine. It would:

> keep the Cossacks in action and from minding any mutinies or innovations amongst themselves, especially to attempt the taking of the forts on the River Boristhenes to which the Cossacks living at Setsky persuaded and pressed passionately: thereby to have freedom of fishing and a clear passage to the Euxean Sea as they have had before the Rebellion of Chlmielnitsky.[10]

Peter's curiosity and a proven personal desire to master the new and technologically progressive military techniques provided another layer of motivation. Throughout the early 1690s Peter had been experimenting in naval affairs, rapidly casting aside rowing boats on the Iauza for yachts on lake Pereiaslavl' in 1692 for full-scale naval manoeuvres on the White sea in 1693, commanding Dutch ships anchored at Archangel for the winter. The capture of a Turkish coastal garrison raised the possibility of creating Russia's first warm-water port, so justifying the construction of a flotilla or fleet which could be permanently based in the sea of Azov and then the Black sea. The construction of a port on the sea of Azov had an added advantage: it was an easier task than the capture of one of the Baltic ports – such as Reval (Tallinn) – held by Sweden, as the Battle of Narva in 1700 was to prove.

There was also a religious motivation that underpinned and legitimised the campaign. Dositheus, the Orthodox Patriarch of Jerusalem, had written to Peter in 1691, taunting him with the words: 'The Crimean Tatars are but a handful, and yet they boast that they receive tribute from you. The Tatars are Turkish subjects, so it follows you are Turkish subjects.'[11] However, it is most probably more personal considerations that persuaded Peter, namely a desire for glory. Franz Lefort had advised Peter that Azov represented a 'win–win' proposition: victory would enhance his status and profile in Europe, but defeat would not bring the Tartars to the gates of Moscow. In evaluating Peter's motivation for war, Whitworth appears ambivalent and cautious as to the overriding imperative. He notes that the 'Cabinet Council' which met to discuss both the merits and disadvantages of the proposed invasion, ultimately decided against war 'as not agreeable with their interests or humours'. However, despite this recommendation, Peter opted for war:

> Whether the Czar Peter Alexeovitz thinking the taking of Azov an easy task or matter, resolved to have the Honour of it himself [or] more maturely deliberated the matter to himself found it agreeable with the Interest of his Empire I cannot nor dare not tell.[12]

THE FIRST CAMPAIGN, 1695

The 1695 campaign was based not on the strategy of a direct military attack across the steppe with wagon supplies as logistics support, but rather a two-pronged thrust southwards on either side of the Crimean peninsula. These drives to the east and west of the Crimean peninsula were designed to capture the Turkish forts at the mouths of the Dnieper and Don. The western army was to be led by the boyar Boris Petrovich Sheremetev and its task was to attack along the Dnieper to the Turkish fort at its mouth. It was expected that such an attack would serve a multiple purpose. It would sever the links between the Crimean Tartar cavalry and the Turkish army in the Balkans and so aid Russia's allies on the Danube. It would also cut Crimean land communications westwards with their Nogai Tartar allies; this Russian threat to the Tartar hunting and grazing grounds would draw off and divert other Tartar cavalry units from operating on the Azov front.

This subsidiary Dnieper battle zone was in support of the main eastern advance on the Don side of the peninsula, against a range of possible targets, including the Turkish forts of Kazi Kerman, Aslan Ordek and Azov. Azov was chosen as the primary objective because it was easiest to resupply by boat from the Russian controlled upper Don and Voronezh, with Tsaritsyn utilised as a staging post. This task was left to the eastern army, in which three generals and Peter were to form an uneasy command structure.

A 31 000-strong army, including traditional *strel'tsy* regiments and Peter's new guard regiments, formed the bulk of this force. Command of this army was split between the Generals Franz Lefort, Avtamon Golovin and Patrick Gordon, whilst the tsar relegated himself to the rank of 'bombardier Peter Alekseev'. The Account describes how through 'no small danger and hazard' he 'was indefatigable in the preparing and throwing of Bombs having attained good perfection of skill therein.'[13] Peter, despite his low artillery rank, could still exert control over his generals through 'advice' and correspondence. On 22 June 1695, for example, Gordon received four letters from Peter 'about advice in all businesses, two whereof were writ particularly with his majesties owne hand'.[14]

Ominously for the conduct of this campaign, the failures of the Crimean campaigns had not been eradicated from strategic planning. The lack of a supreme commander or unified command system led to poor communication between differing Russian units, even within the same army. This was compounded by the fact 'that the Generals were not in amity nor cordially affected towards each other, so that the reliefs for succours from the other armys could not be expected.'[15] Contingency exacerbated supply difficulties when an arms depot at Achterk (consisting of 12 000 muskets and carabines) was 'by great mischance all burnt which was the reason that the soldiers of the town could not be got armed'.[16]

More generally, Russian units suffered from poor intelligence, reconnaissance ability and tactical manoeuvring. Peter, in a letter to Vinius on 19 May 1695, discussed the handling of barges transporting troops down the Moscow, Oka and Volga rivers to Tsaritsyn. He laconically noted: 'The winds delayed us badly, but most of all Our delays have been due to stupid pilots & workmen, who call themselves masters, and who are as far from being masters as heaven is from earth.'[17]

But the failure of the Russians to capture Azov during the first campaign can be perceived as much a Russian defeat as a Turkish victory. The Turks managed to resupply Azov unchallenged on 18 June 1695 with 18 supply ships, so breaking the siege on the seaward side. The Russians, with no naval forces of their own, were thus unable to isolate the fortress. Moreover, the Turks made fine use of contingency. Jacob Jansen, a Dutch seaman originally from Archangel, had been converted to Russian Orthodoxy and served in the artillery at Azov under Gordon's command. His defection to Azov's defenders allowed the Turks to exploit fundamental weaknesses in Russian military dispositions, prompting the undertaking of a series of successful raids against poorly defended Russian positions, particularly artillery redoubts.[18] Turkish Tartar allies were also effective in both harassing Russian foragers (they even managed to surround and wipe out an entire regiment during the Russian retreat) and maintaining communications with Azov through the Russian siege lines.

THE SECOND CAMPAIGN, 1696

After leaving 3000 troops in two watchtowers which the Russian army had built, in September 1695 the bulk of Russia's military forces began to retreat northwards. The return to Moscow took several weeks through heavy autumn rains. However, the majority of Russian forces were quartered at Voronezh during the winter months of 1695 and into early 1696. Here Peter regrouped his armies and considered afresh the campaign planned for the following summer.

Voronezh was a military and proto-industrial centre, situated 250 miles north of Azov on a tributary ten miles upstream of the Don. Peter, determined to rectify the failures of 1695, focused on the two key limitations of that campaign. First, the lack of a Russian naval presence in the sea of Azov with which both to launch amphibious operations against the fort in support of infantry attacks and to hamper Turkish resupply and reinforcements would have to be rectified. Second, he was determined to strengthen Russia's balefully inadequate resupply network. Siege engineers were ordered from Austria and Prussia and Venetian and Dutch galley construction experts travelled south from Archangel to supervise the construction of a powerful shallow draught flotilla. In just five months 30000 labourers had felled 7000 trees and created two warships, twenty-three armed galleys, four fire ships and hundreds of riverboats.[19] Water-driven mills speeded the process, but Whitworth attributes this remarkable achievement to Peter's constant pressure and determination:

> The building of the galleys being a thing impossible to be brought to perfection yet by the extraordinary care and indefatigable industry of his Czarish Majesty 30 galleys greater and lesser were in a short tyme in good forwardness, as to the hulls according to a modell brought from Holland the Dutch fleet wintering att Archangel it was very opportunately, a carpenter from each ship being fetched up and put to work.

The second campaign began on 3 May 1696 when Russian forces marched south supported by the fruits of winter: improved logistics networks and a formidable flotilla. Peter also learned from the strategic errors of the previous year; the army was not divided along two independent fronts. All Russian infantry and artillery forces were concentrated in one consolidated column consisting of 46000 Muscovites, 20000 Cossacks (5000 Don and 15000 Ukrainian) and 3000 Kalmyk allies. The siege began in early June 1696 and Russian artillery very quickly came to dominate the battle. A rolling rampart of earth allowed the artillery to fire from an elevated position directly onto selected targets within the town. The first Russian marine amphibious operations had the desired effect: Turkish resupply ships were deterred from reaching Azov and the town was battered from artillery fired from the seaward side. By 19 June 1696 the town fell, and Peter immediately informed Moscow by letter 'written in Our conquered town of Azov'.

Both Gordon and Whitworth note the care Peter took upon surrender to observe the formalities of victory during negotiations with the Turkish side. It is clear that the rules of warfare, particularly the etiquette of negotiating and accepting surrender terms following a siege, were scrupulously followed by Peter. His only demand was that the 'traitor Jacob' be handed over to the Russian side before the Turks were able to march out of the town in good order in a formal ceremony, carrying small arms. In Azov Peter ensured that two former mosques were consecrated as Orthodox churches, so symbolising Peter's intention for Russia to incorporate the region into its cultural sphere of influence.

The success of this campaign can be attributed to a number of interrelated factors, not least Peter's ability to learn from mistakes and rectify past errors. A single large command was unified under the Boyar General A.S. Shein, so improving the chain of command within the Russian forces. Peter had promoted himself to the rank of naval captain, commanding one of the twenty-three armed galleys. The Russian navy broke the Turkish chains across the mouth of the Don. Once they had penetrated the sea of Azov they proved to be effective in keeping Turkish resupply ships from breaking through to Azov with much needed supplies. The use of 4000 marine troops taken from the Preobrazhenskii and Semenovskii Guards' regiments allowed the Russians greater tactical mobility. The second campaign was marked by the successful application of new tactics and this was reflected in the adoption of technical expressions to describe the new military techniques and tactics.

*****

Azov had fallen to a victorious Russian army. What were the implications and consequences of Peter's first foreign-policy victory for Russia and the West? Above all, the capture of Azov projected Russian power on her southern flank. It projected Russian military power and political authority across the southern steppe and into the sea of Azov. A systematic shipbuilding project was initiated, with monasteries ordered to build one ship per 8000 peasant households, and noble landowners one ship per 10 000 peasant households. By 1699 Russia had fourteen ships of the line in service on the sea of Azov, the largest with sixty-two guns, and this naval presence was underlined when the first permanent Russian ambassador, Emel'ian Ukraintsev, entered Constantinople aboard the forty-six-gun *Krepost'* (fortress) in 1700. The Ottoman invitation to Russia to create a permanent ambassador in Constantinople finally signified a Europe-wide acceptance of Russia's new status as a Great Power.

The Russian infantry presence was also dramatically increased around Azov and the new port of Taganrog. Patrick Gordon initially supervised these construction works, in the face of strong *strel'tsy* grumbling, through late 1696 and into 1697. Three thousand *strel'tsy* from Kazan and the same number from Moscow were ordered to garrison Azov, so breaking the tradition that *strel'tsy* troops campaigned in the summer but returned to their urban garrisons during the winter. Twenty thousand men were also conscripted from Ukraine and ordered to begin construction of the Volga–Don canal under the command of the German engineer Colonel Breckel and then Captain John Perry.

The diplomatic impact of the conquest was mixed. While it provided the ostensible reason for Peter's Grand Embassy, the Embassy itself failed to ensure the continuation of a pan-European alliance against the Turks. Austria withdrew her support at the treaty of Karlowitz, and as a consequence the Russians failed to take the straits of Kerch and gain access to the Black sea. Russia entered negotiations with the Ottoman Empire between November 1699 and June 1700. The Russian negotiators pushed for military and religious privileges. Russia demanded naval access to the Black sea through the acquisition of the straits of Kerch, the renunciation of tribute payments to the Crimean Tartars and a guarantee that Tartar raids would cease. Ambassador Ukraintsev pushed for the return of the Holy Sepulchre in Jerusalem to Orthodox possession. This was denied but Russia was to gain the right of pilgrimage to the Holy Land. In 1700 Turkey acceded the secession of Azov during a thirty-year truce, and a permanent Russian diplomatic mission to Constantinople, placing Russia on an equal footing with other European nations.

The *strel'tsy* troops who had fought at Azov and served in the port construction projects around Taganrog revolted in 1698. Amongst their many petitions listing outstanding grievances was the perception that Lefort had used them as cannon fodder during the campaign itself. They objected to having to serve on campaign during the winter months, foregoing the traditional return to their permanent bases in cities, particularly in Moscow and Kazan.[20] They also claimed that Peter favoured the 'foreign' guards' regiments above the traditional *strel'tsy* units. (Gordon, it may be noted, commented upon the lack of professionalism in the *strel'tsy* regiments during the Azov campaign: 'the laziness, unwillingness or unskillfulness of the *strel'tsy*'s retarded their work very much'.[21])

Azov also had an important role in shaping Peter's self-image and our image of Peter in the 1690s. Peter dated his duty and service to the state from the Azov campaigns, signifying his belief that the campaigns represented the start of his reform process and his own personal service career. Indeed, Petrine plans for the reconstruction of the badly damaged fort of Azov reveals a desire to create a second fort across the river, to be named 'Petropolis', prefiguring perhaps the imperial capital of St Petersburg or echoing the imperial Byzantine (Constantinople) or Hellenic (Alexandropolis) past. The medal he had struck to commemorate the victory was of an imperial Roman design. On the obverse side in the Latin alphabet we read 'Petrus Alexii' the 'Russor Mag. [Magister] Caesar', encircling a profile of Peter complete with Roman breastplate and laurel wreaths. The reverse side reveals a winged Athena Nike-type figure, naked to the waist, bestride fallen Turkish colours, arms and a half-crescent moon, holding aloft a crucifix. Although the coin ostensibly celebrated the victory of Christianity over Islam, it was remarkable for both the lack of traditional Orthodox iconography and symbolism and the intertwining of Greek and Roman motifs.

This tendency towards cultural borrowing was even more in evidence during the subsequent victory parade, which took place on the evening of 30 September 1696. It began at Kolomenskoe, a residential palace south of Moscow, passing through a triumphal arch (to the sound of a thirty-six-piece-cannon salute) over a stone bridge crossing the Moscow river, and 'having marched through the castle of Kremlina all were dismissed to their respective homes.' The triumphal arches were decorated with Roman and Greek mythological allegorical figures – Neptune, Hercules, Mars – allusions to heroic Petrine physical and military prowess. The spectacle of the parade was as dramatic as the fusion of triumphal classical pagan and Christian motifs in the heart of Orthodoxy's 'Third Rome'. It was thus emblematic of Russia's passionate, not to say discriminate, embrace of European traditions.

Whitworth notes that 'the marines with their admirals captains and other officers in good order being about 4000 men' had pride of place at the start of the parade. These novel naval military elements were followed by General Shein at the head of sixteen captured Turkish colours and assorted prisoners. General Golovin followed, leading the Preobrazhenskii regiment with the hapless Jacob, the defector in 1695. Jacob was bound to a scaffold on wheels, a half moon and star hung over him, and a Turkish inscription was tied to his neck. Next came Gordon's Butyrskii regiment: 'being clad in white Turkish Coates with Turbans on their heads and the officers with feathers and plumes in their hats, which show drew the spectators eye and gave great content to them all.'[22]

The impact of the victory parade upon conservative Muscovite society must have been startling. The campaigns had destabilised the already insecure identity of the *strel'tsy* regiments and the victory secured Peter advanced recognition in Europe, perfect pre-publicity for the Grand Embassy. Within the traditional boyar elite, the Azov victory helped secure the positions of a new stratum which emerged, flourished and was promoted through their loyalty to Peter and their ability to embrace Petrine reform. Reading the Whitworth account, we can note that the Peter Matveevich Apraksin ('Boyar Peter Mastfeovitz Apraxin') commanded two redoubts with three artillery batteries in Golovin's army during the first campaign[23] and Prince Iakov Fedorovich Dolgorukii ('Kniaz Jacob Fiodorovitz Dolgorukoy') commanded a strong detachment of 4000 with artillery and both were promoted as a result of their Azov successes. Both these individuals were to enjoy leading elite positions within the Petrine state.

Azov encapsulated the central themes of Peter's reign and the whole Petrine order: reorganisation for war, the reinvention of the

Russian imperial system and the rise of Russia as a Great European power. These themes found full flowering in the Great Northern War when victory in 1721 confirmed the title 'Great' upon Peter and signified the consolidation of Peter's imperial image as the head of a young and vigorous European empire. The siege of Azov is central to our comprehension of this tradition as it marks the first real attempt by Peter to construct an imperial identity. The capture of Azov, this formative educational experience in Peter's life, explains the subsequent shape and power of that identity. The experience of Azov was the secure foundation stone upon which both the Empire rested and the Petrine myth was to flourish.

NOTES

1 *The London Gazette*, 7–10 September 1696. Issue no. 3217, Hamburg, 11 September. This was the first news about Russia reported in *The London Gazette* since 1689.
2 Robinson to the Duke of Shrewsbury, 6 April 1695, Public Record Office, State Papers 95/14 (Sweden), fol. 276.
3 E.V. Anisimov, *The Reforms of Peter the Great: Progress Through Coercion*, New York, 1993; N.I. Pavlenko, 'Peter I', in *Rossiia v period reform Petra I*, Moscow, 1973, pp. 72–3.
4 Gordon, Diary, 21 July 1696, Russian State Military Historical Archive (RGVIA), f. 846, op. 15, VI, p. 60ob.
5 Charles Whitworth: 'Account of the Seiges of Asof in 1695 & 1696: writ by General Gordon who commanded a considerable part of the army', British Library, Additional Manuscript, 96 970, fols. 425–52. Hereafter Whitworth, 'Account' plus fol. no. See also Graeme P. Herd and Alexander Nekrasov, 'Britanskii istochnik XVIII v. ob Azovskikh pokhodakh Petra I', *Istoricheskii arkhiv*, 1997, 3, pp. 195–205; Charles Whitworth, *Account of Russia as it was in the Year 1710*, London, 1758.
6 This interpretation is still open to question. In fol. 431 Whitworth writes of the 1689 events: 'and every day skirmishing till our pty [party] at last was routed and beat.' The use of the word 'our' suggests that the author was a contemporary to the events of 1689 and had participated in them. This, however, is the only reference in the first person throughout and may have been an oversight on Whitworth's part.
7 Whitworth, 'Account', fol. 425.

8 *Ibid.*, fol. 428r. This episode is celebrated in *The Tale of the Don Cossack*.
9 Whitworth, 'Account', fol. 431r.
10 *Ibid.*, fol. 431r. 'Setsky' refers to the Zaporozhian Sich (camp) on the Dnieper (Boristhenes) river.
11 Cited in S.M. Soloviev, *History of Russia, Peter the Great: A Reign Begins*, XXVI, L. Hughes, ed., Gulf Breeze, FL, 1994, p. 118.
12 Whitworth, 'Account', fol. 432.
13 *Ibid.*, fol. 442r.
14 *Ibid.*, fol. 434r.
15 *Ibid.*, fol. 438r.
16 *Ibid.*, fol. 432.
17 *Pis'ma i bumagi Petra I*, I, St Petersburg, 1887, p. 30.
18 Alexander Gordon, *A History of Peter the Great in Russia*, 3 vols, Aberdeen, 1755, III, p. 100; *A Memoir of the Life of Peter the Great*, London, 1832, p. 37; Gordon, Diary, 15 July 1695, RGVIA, f. 846, op. 15, V, p. 497ob.
19 For references to forest management around Voronezh, see Aleksei Karimov's paper in this volume.
20 V.I. Buganov, *Vosstanie moskovskikh strel'tsov. Sbornik dokumentov*, Moscow, 1980, pp. 40–1.
21 Gordon, Diary, 1–6 June 1695, V, pp. 46–47ob.
22 Whitworth, 'Account', fol. 452r. The detail of this passage surpasses that of Gordon's diaries. For comparison, see Gordon, Diary, 30 September 1696, VI, p. 78ob.
23 Whitworth, 'Account', fol. 437r.

11 Peter the Great and the Baltic

David Kirby

Peter the Great was not the first Russian ruler to pursue an active and determined Baltic policy, but he was the most successful. Ivan III managed to obtain a foothold on the coast in his wars against the Livonian Order at the end of the fifteenth century, and Ivan IV briefly held the port of Narva between 1558 and 1581; but in the uncertainty and chaos after the death of Ivan IV, the Russian presence on the Baltic came to an end.[1] For most of the seventeenth century, Muscovy played little active part in Baltic affairs. Trading links established by the English and Dutch during the preceding half century became weaker and less certain, with a concomitant decline in knowledge of or interest in things Russian; this was described by Matthew Anderson as 'a period of stagnation, and even of decline'.[2]

In these circumstances, Peter's sudden and spectacular incursion into European affairs was bound to excite attention. His success in pushing Russia's frontiers westwards ensured that his fame would leave a lasting legacy. Within less than a quarter of a century Russia had emerged as the dominant great power in north-eastern Europe, pushing a territorially diminished Sweden into the northern shadows and establishing an ascendancy over Poland–Lithuania which was to prove fateful for that Commonwealth. Less than one hundred years after Peter's death, Russia's western frontier flanked Silesia and East Prussia; from the Åland islands, Russian troops guarded the short sea crossing to Stockholm. Russia's westward expansion brought into an Orthodox state peoples of different religious, cultural and social traditions, and, whilst this proved mutually beneficial in many ways, the experience was not without its tensions and problems.

In western and central European historiography, the Baltic is generally portrayed as an area of penetration and colonisation, of crusading knights and militant churchman pushing the frontiers of Latin Christendom to the shores of lake Peipus, and of merchants of the German empire gradually establishing a commercial ascendancy over the region, before being supplanted in their turn by the Dutch and English in the seventeenth and eighteenth centuries. This is an overall picture not without its blemishes and disagreements, but it is one that does impose itself in concrete form, such as the undeniably 'Hanseatic' look of the medieval cities of Livonia, or the incontrovertible fact that the castle of Viipuri (the present Russian city of Viborg) was built under the orders of the Swedish commander Torgils Knutsson at the end of the thirteenth century.

The Russian view of the Baltic rests rather more on traditional claims. These claims are not simply twentieth-century inventions, as the wealth of monuments and plaques and the assertions of historians and other image-makers might lead us to believe. Long before the statue of Peter the Great was erected in 1910 in Viipuri to commemorate the conquest of that city two hundred years earlier, the Russian claim to ancient dominion over the region was being made by Peter's chief apologist, P.P. Shafirov.[3] The subsequent fate of that statue – replaced by the Finnish lion during the interwar period, briefly restored by the Russians in 1940, cast down by the occupying Finnish forces in 1941 and restored once more to its plinth by the Soviet authorities in the 1950s – is illustrative of the way in which claims, backed by force and might, have been asserted in the eastern Baltic.[4]

On the whole, however, historians outside Russia have paid scant attention to such claims, preferring instead to direct their attentions towards commerce or power politics in their search for what motivated the contenders in the struggle for dominance in the Baltic.[5] Trading considerations certainly featured prominently in the policies and thinking of the maritime nations during the late seventeenth and early eighteenth centuries, not least with regard to Russia. Charles Whitworth was sent to Russia in the first place to represent the business interests of the Russian merchants; and even the French envoys to Russia were primarily concerned with matters of trade and commerce.[6] Yet it would be unwise to form a picture of Peter's motives and policies in the light of the concerns of foreign powers seeking their own ends. For westerners, Peter was always something of a puzzle: a man who clearly embraced many of the outward signs and values of 'western' society, but whose actions were still conditioned by rather different practices, traditions and attitudes. Dutch and English merchants were foxed by his involvement and direction of trade, for example, and his dynastic policy clearly caused problems for diplomats and statesmen. The sudden incursion of a hitherto distant and very alien country into the affairs of the Holy Roman Empire, and Peter's involvement in central and northern European politics was unexpected, and it threw the European concert momentarily out of balance. Indeed, this occurred at a time when the concert was in the process of forming, or re-forming, after a long and exhausting series of wars. Retrenchment and the consolidation of positions was a common concern of government in Paris, London and Vienna after the signing of the peace of Utrecht in 1713. Spain remained a problem, and Russia threatened to become one. The difference was that Spain had been the main bone of contention in the last of Louis XIV's wars, whilst Russia had been and continued to be caught up in another, separate conflict. The final collapse of Swedish power in Europe between 1710 and 1715 threatened not only to disturb the 'balance of the North' (a favourite expression of English diplomats), but also to undermine the stability of the Empire, and hence the system of stability striven for in Europe since 1648.

In truth, the balance of the North had already been irrevocably upset before the final conquest of Livonia and Finland. Russian forces managed to secure a firm grip on Ingria and eastern Estonia, and Peter was able to found and successfully defend his new capital on the Baltic. He was well aware of the value of trade as a bargaining counter. As early as May 1705, he declared through his chancellor his willingness to assure Charles Whitworth:

> that in case the Commerce on the East Sea can be transported from the Kingdom of Sweden to the Haven of His Czarish Majesty, all sort of Monopolies shall be entirely broken:

whereof the Envoy himself should immediately see the effect if he would but give such an assurance under his hand ...[7]

He could not have been unaware of the Royal Navy's need for naval stores, pitch and tar during a critical moment of the war against France, or that trade was what mattered for the maritime powers. The Swedes did their cause little good by blockading the ports of the eastern Baltic, and by unleashing privateers; and however many warnings were made against Russia becoming too mighty – and there were many as the propagandists got to work – the fact that Russia came into possession of a good stretch of the eastern Baltic and was a potentially major supplier of vital commodities and of luxury goods from the Orient was probably decisive. Much as the merchants might grumble about the capricious nature of the tsar's commercial policies, they were obliged to trade through Russian-held ports; and this in turn conditioned and influenced the policies of their governments.

The restoration of the status quo ante bellum after 1705 was, to most perceptive observers, unlikely: Peter would never give up 'his belov'd Petersburgh', and Sweden was unlikely to regain it by military force. Peter's conquest of Livonia in 1710 added several new dimensions to the problem. In the first instance it brought under Russian control a major and well-known international port, Riga, which for the first time raised the prospect of a real shifting of power in the Baltic (the use of St Petersburg as a port at this time should really be seen in the context of the Archangel trade, rather than the Baltic trade). It also brought back onto the agenda the claims of Augustus of Saxony (Augustus the Strong), the deposed king of Poland, to the possession of Livonia, as agreed in 1699. These were claims that Peter publicly promised to honour (though he was clever enough to make the handing-over of Livonia conditional upon the consent of the Polish Sejm), but which increasingly looked more fragile. Peter was adept at playing on the tensions between Saxony and Poland. After being defeated by the Turks in the Pruth campaign in 1711, Peter returned to his old line of promising nothing until the peace was concluded, and he took measures indicating a wish to incorporate Livonia, such as the naming of Menshikov as governor-general. Several observers were inclined to see Peter seeking compensation from Sweden for the loss of Azov and, from 1712 onwards, there are more and more hints that Peter intended to keep Livonia for himself.[8]

A third aspect of the conquest of Livonia, and one which is often overlooked, is that, at the same time as Peter's troops were reducing the province, envoys from the duke of Courland were in St Petersburg, negotiating a marriage alliance. Amongst other things they sought to secure perpetual neutrality and freedom of trade for Courland, with the enfeoffment of or hereditary regency over Livonia. Although unsuccessful in their desires, they did achieve a marriage – that of Peter's niece, Anna Ivanovna, to eighteen-year-old duke Friedrich Wilhelm – which was solemnised with much drinking in December 1710. The duke's death early in the new year offered Peter a fine opportunity to interfere and direct the affairs of the duchy, which was ruled badly and ineffectively by the childless Duke Ferdinand from his residence in Danzig.

Six years later Peter married off another of his nieces, Ekaterina, to the duke of Mecklenburg, making an agreement obliging him to aid the duke against his internal and external enemies with the assistance of 9–10 infantry regiments, and the promise of diplomatic support at the Imperial court in the quarrel between the duke and the nobility of the duchy. Russian merchantmen were to be allowed free access to Mecklenburg harbours, which were to act as warehouses for Russian goods. The tsar promised to support the duke's claims to Wismar and Warnemünde at the peace, and Russia was to have the use of a military base and magazine 'if HM the tsar should have need to send his troops or warships to the Roman Empire against his enemies or to assist his allies'. There had been earlier rumours of Peter seeking a seat in the Reichstag by restoring Livonia to the Reich, and these resurfaced at the time of the Mecklenburg marriage.[9] There is, however, little evidence to support this and, indeed, one can only conclude that Peter's dynastic policy, if such it can be called, was something of a failure. To be sure, the eventual marriage in 1725 of his daughter Anna to the duke of Holstein-Gottorp was a clever move, and it had consequences after Peter's death. Peter had also realised the nuisance value of the Gottorp claims in regard to Denmark and Sweden and was able to achieve some of his most noteworthy diplomatic successes by threatening to play that card. He was not, however, able to use so effectively his stake in Courland through the widowed Anna Ivanovna, unnecessarily arousing the suspicions of his Prussian ally. His Mecklenburg policy was even more unsuccessful, committing him to a highly unreliable ally, worsening Russian relations with the court in Vienna and making of George I an enemy. The last in particular was a serious error, for it also had an impact on Russia's relations with other countries. The Russians tried to drive a wedge between George the German prince and his British subjects, but were notably unsuccessful in this endeavour.

It is possible, indeed likely, that Peter was looking for a base in Mecklenburg from which to attack Sweden, rather than for a bridgehead by which to enter Germany, and a Russian presence there may at least have prevented Denmark from making a separate peace with Sweden, as Prince Dolgorukii observed at the beginning of 1717.[10] But Mecklenburg was expendable. Peter expressed his willingness to evacuate his troops in his negotiations for a French alliance and to guarantee the peace settlement of 1713. His main objective here, as in so many other instances, was the conclusion of peace with Sweden.

Peter's policy during the second decade of the eighteenth century cannot really be understood without reference to his adversary. It was the refusal of Charles XII to treat that forced the tsar to engage in a diplomatic game in which he had little experience and few wholly reliable advisers. Furthermore, in spite of his resounding victory over Charles XII at Poltava in 1709, Peter lacked either the confidence or the resources to complete the final military victory over Sweden. Although his galley fleet had proved its worth in the conquest of Finland in 1713–14, he recognised the need of Danish naval forces to complete the plan to invade Sweden. He hoped to secure British support as well, dangling the prospect of a treaty of commerce. The year and a half Peter spent in western Europe in 1716–17 produced little of any real value to the tsar. The plans for an invasion of southern Sweden came to nothing. George I was bringing increasing pressure to bear on the tsar to quit Mecklenburg, and the king of Prussia was kept on side only by further guarantees of his claim to Stettin. The French promise of mediation in the war against Sweden was of little value; indeed, Kurakin specifically denied France any such role in his discussions with the Swedish plenipotentiary Baron Görtz.[11] In the end, the only concrete result was the opening of talks with Sweden on the island of Lövö. The flight of Tsarevich Alexis to Vienna and Peter's own ill-health also cast uncertainty on the future. There were rumours of courtiers waiting only for the tsar's death to return to Moscow, abandoning St Petersburg and all his conquests.

The Åland island negotiations which opened in the spring of 1718 were conducted by two graduates of the university of Jena: the highly inventive Baron Georg Heinrich von Görtz for the Swedish side and Heinrich Johann Friedrich Ostermann for the Russian side. Neither man enjoyed the full confidence of his colleagues and both were skilful intriguers. As the talks meandered through the summer, both sides were playing the field elsewhere: the Swedes were trying to win over George I and the Russians were momentarily caught up in the ambitious plans of the Spanish minister Alberoni. Nevertheless, the fact that Peter did not break off talks on the Åland islands even after the failure to reach agreement on the plan worked out by Görtz and Ostermann during the summer is a fair indication of how serious he was about concluding the war with Sweden. The plan would have committed the tsar to supplying forces to aid Charles XII's war effort against Hanover and Saxony, should agreement be reached over the terms of the peace. To agree to such commitments at a time of consolidation of the western powers in the Quadruple Alliance was risky; but the prospect of a new northern alliance, possibly backed by Spain and giving support to the Jacobites, persuaded the government in London to reopen its lines of communication with St Petersburg. At the same time, however, George I was careful to make sure of the friendship of the emperor Charles VI and Augustus of Saxony, and his hopes of a separate settlement with Charles XII had by no means evaporated.[12]

This complicated quadrille was ultimately broken up by a stray bullet, which ended the life of the king of Sweden at the end of November 1718. The year 1719 went badly for Peter. He was unable to prevent Prussia signing an alliance with Britain and Hanover; George I was now working actively to bring about peace between Sweden and her enemies in the west, and an eighteen-year alliance with Sweden was concluded to repel any Russian invasion and to secure a favourable peace settlement in the Baltic. The *Plan projetté pour la paix générale du Nord*, drawn up by the three principal negotiators of the Imperial–Saxon–Hanoverian alliance in

January 1719, and which was widely circulated, envisaged Livonia, Finland and all other Russian conquests with the exception of Petersburg, Kronstadt and Narva returning to Sweden in compensation for the loss of territories in Germany. Should Peter not agree and the war continue, the pre-1700 frontiers in the North would be restored, with Smolensk and Kiev being conquered for the Poles and incorporated as a barrier against the insults and vexations of the Russians.[13]

The verdict of the British envoy James Jefferyes that Peter suspected the purpose of the alliance was 'to reduce the Czar within due bounds and to force him within his old limits again', may well have been not far off the mark; but the tsar himself had a better hand than Jefferyes seems to have imagined.[14] Indeed, there is good reason to argue that it was during the last five years of his reign that Russia really emerged as a mature and powerful player in the game of international politics. Peter was undoubtedly aided by growing dissension and internal problems amongst the western European powers, though he was also able to secure a few diplomatic successes of his own. In spite of the efforts of George I's English and Hanoverian ministers, neither the Turks nor Prussians joined the anti-Russian coalition. He used the Holstein-Gottorp card skilfully, having learnt at an early stage how duplicitous the duke's advisers could be. In the case of Denmark, he backed the duke's claims for the restitution of his lands in Schleswig as a means of securing duty-free passage of his ships through the Sound. By seeming to back Duke Karl Friedrich's claims to the Swedish throne (which on the death of the childless Charles XII had passed to one of his two sisters, married to Friedrich of Hesse; the other sister was Karl Friedrich's mother), Peter helped persuade the Swedes to conclude peace. Though clause 7 of the Nystad treaty bound Peter not to interfere in Sweden's internal affairs, and was thus a rebuff to the duke's ambitions, the existence of a Holstein party in Sweden enabled the tsar to fish in troubled waters. In 1723 the Secret Committee of the Riksdag agreed to accord the title of 'royal highness' to the duke and to recognise Peter's imperial title. As Mikhail Bestuzhev reported:

Things are going well for the duke of Gottorp. It would have been possible at this Riksdag to secure for him the succession to the throne of Sweden, but it would have cost a lot of money, for although the duke has many supporters, they will do nothing for free.[15]

The treaty concluded in Stockholm at the beginning of 1724 has been seen by Hans Bagger as the foundation stone of Russia's alliance system, an effective counter to British-Hanoverian influence in Denmark and northern Germany, and a provider of security for Russia within the Baltic. The secret clauses bound both countries to the preservation of the Polish constitution and to use their good offices for a satisfactory resolution of Karl Friedrich's claims to restitution of his lands. Herein lay ample opportunity for further interference and involvement in the affairs of Russia's western neighbours in the Baltic, which in the case of Poland was to end in that country's disappearance within seventy years.[16]

Bagger may be attaching too much importance to the question of restitution as a touchstone for the new Russian empire within the European states system, although he is right to draw attention to the issue of prestige. If there is one thing that runs through Peter's life as ruler of Russia, it is a strong desire to be respected. The discourteous treatment accorded to the tsar in Riga during the outward part of his Grand Embassy in 1697 grew in proportion into what became at times an obsession. In the words of his chief apologist, Petr Pavlovich Shafirov, Peter wished only to be treated as a Christian and civilised (*poli*) gentlemen, who had driven much of the barbarism out of the Russian nation, but the Swedes continued to treat him as if he were a barbarian.[17] Peter's long tussle with the Swedes for territorial hegemony in the Baltic was as much concerned with status and standing in the eyes of the world as it was about land. He was perhaps fortunate in that his reign coincided with major shifts and realignments elsewhere in Europe; Sweden, Poland and the Ottoman empire were waning powers, and France was no longer in a position to influence the affairs of the north as it had been earlier in the reign of Louis XIV. George I was potentially a powerful rival, but he had his own problems as ruler of two territories with very different political and other interests. Peter was not always best served by his favourites and advisers – the activities of Prince Menshikov in Livonia and later in Mecklenburg spring to mind here – and there does seem to have been a tension, or at least a dividing-line, between his Russian and non-Russian senior officials. The man himself led a peripatetic life, much like his arch-rival Charles XII. It was never easy for foreign diplomats to keep tabs of his movements or his intentions, and his naughty habits added to their cautiousness. Like Charles XII, he was unconventional, which caused further confusion for the highly formalised courts of Europe. The darker aspects of his life – his early childhood, the defection of his son and heir, the foot-dragging of his subjects and his own mental state – clearly had a bearing on his conduct of affairs and may go some way to explaining his desire to establish a firm Russian presence in the Baltic. But in the end, the Baltic was just one part of Peter's activities, given a high profile by the foundation of a new capital by its shores. St Petersburg established the direct link between Russia and the West, and this helped draw Russia into the mainstream of European life, much as Peter's new subjects in the Baltic lands helped disseminate European ideas and practices throughout his empire.[18] The balance of the North – a matter of great moment to George I's ministers – was upset. Russia acquired Sweden's eastern Baltic territories and was able to exercise a degree of remote control over Sweden's affairs through bribery, patronage and, above all, by wielding the Holstein-Gottorp card. At times, Sweden in the 'Age of Liberty' seemed destined to follow down the same path as the Polish-Lithuanian Commonwealth.[19] That it did not says much about the different social and constitutional composition of the two states, but that Russia played a far more consistent and decisive role in the fate of Poland–Lithuania during the eighteenth century may also indicate where the empire's priorities now lay. Charles XII was difficult to defeat militarily, but easy enough to outwit diplomatically. Augustus of Saxony (Augustus the Strong) was a tougher proposition, as the researches of Jan Gierowski have shown, and it is in his handling of the Saxon king and the Polish question that Peter showed his true skills. He initiated a process of mediation and pressure which under his successors would end with the final expunging of the Commonwealth from the map of Europe.[20] Less dramatic than the war against Sweden, and lacking the definitive character of the peace of

Nystad, Peter's Polish policy was arguably of far greater importance for the future.

NOTES

1 On the nature of Russia's 'exclusion' from the Baltic, see I. Shaskol'skii, 'Byla li Rossiia posle Livonskoi voinyi otrezana ot Baltiiskogo moria?', *Istoricheskii Zapiski*, 35, 1950, pp. 294–303.
2 The Soviet historian Boris Fedorovich Porshnev argued, however, for a significant Muscovite input into Swedish policies during the Thirty Years' War; see B.F. Porshnev, *Muscovy and Sweden in the Thirty Years' War 1630–1635*, ed. Paul Dukes, Cambridge, 1995. The Estonian historian Helmut Piirimäe has also shown that Swedish-Russian relations were rather lively after the treaty of Kardis (1661), which ended a brief war between the two powers; see H. Piirimäe, *Kaubanduse küsimused Vene-Rootsi suhetes 1661–1700 a.*, Tartu, 1961. See also M.S. Anderson, *Britain's Discovery of Russia 1553–1815*, London, 1958, p. 48.
3 P.P. Shafirov, *A Discourse Concerning the Just Causes of the War between Sweden and Russia: 1700–1721*, introduced by W. Butler, Dobbs Ferry, NY, 1973, pp. 2, 242. On previous Russian claims, see Erik Tiberg, 'Moskau, Livland und die Hanse, 1487–1547', *Hansische Geschichtsblätter*, 93, 1975, pp. 13–70, and 'Die Politik Moskaus gegen alt-Livland, 1550–1558', *Zeitschrift für Ostforschung*, 1976, pp. 577–617.
4 The fate of Peter the Great's statue in Viipuri, and the claims of Russian historians and others, is charted in O. Jussila, *Venäläinen Suomi*, Porvoo, 1983, pp. 33–54.
5 The commercial motive features strongly in the writings of A. Attman; for example in *The Struggle for Baltic Markets: Powers in Conflict 1558–1618*, Göteborg, 1979. Much importance is also attached to commercial motives in Peter's north German policy in W. Mediger, *Mecklenburg, Rußland und England–Hannover 1706–1721*, Hildesheim, 1967. See also K. Zernack, 'Von Stolbovo nach Nystad: Rußland und die Ostsee in der Politik des 17. und 18. Jahrhunderts', *Jahrbücher für Geschichte Osteuropas*, NF 20, 1972, pp. 77–100, reprinted in K. Zernack, *Nordosteuropa. Skizzen und Beiträge zu einer Geschichte der Ostseeländer*, Lüneburg, 1993, pp. 105–31.
6 See the letter from one of those merchants, Francis Stratford, to the consul in Moscow, Charles Goodfellow, 28 March 1704: '[T]his is to acquaint you that at the Sollicitation of the Tobacco Comp^a here Her Majesty hath been pleased to order an Envoy Extraord^y to be sent to the Czar for redressing of

our grievances.' Whitworth Letter Book, 1702–05, British Library, Additional Manuscript (hereafter BL, Add. MS) 37353.
7   Whitworth to Lord Harley, 20/9 May 1705, BL, Add. MS 37353.
8   Whitworth to St John, 2/13 October 1711, *Sbornik Imperatorskago Russkago Istoricheskago Obshchestva,* St Petersburg, 1888 , LXI, pp. 21–2. Ludvig Weisbrod, secretary to the British embassy in Moscow, reported a conversation with a Russian, who told him that they found Riga a 'place much more convenient for Trade than Archangel; and that for the future most part of the product of their Country should be sent that way, which is a Sign that they have *no mind* to *renounce* Liefland if other conjunctions do not oblige them to it'. Weisbrod to Nicholas Rowe, 6/17 September 1711, BL, Add. MS 37360.
9   On the treaty and the rumours, see R. Wittram, *Peter I: Czar und Kaiser*, Göttingen, 1964, II, pp. 225–30, 274–9 and H. Bagger, *Ruslands alliancepolitik efter freden i Nystad,* Copenhagen, 1974, p. 62 for the quotation.
10 Wittram, *Peter I*, p. 296.
11 Wittram, *ibid.*, p. 323ff. On these negotiations, see C. Nordmann, *La crise du nord au début du XVIIIe siècle*, Paris, 1962.
12 The Åland island negotiations were given detailed treatment by K. Hartman, *Åländska kongressen och dess förhistoria*, Åbo, 6 vols, 1921–31. The standard Russian work is S. Feigina, *Alandskii kongress*, Moscow, 1959. See also R. Hatton, *Charles XII*, London, 1968, pp. 446–61.
13 Wittram, *Peter I*, p. 410.
14 Cited in Wittram, *ibid.*, p. 409.
15 Cited in Bagger, *Ruslands alliancepolitik*, p. 128.
16 Bagger, *ibid.,* p. 132
17 Wittram, *Peter I*, p. 286. In his apologia for the tsar's actions, Shafirov launched a counterattack, detailing instances of Swedish barbarity. See *Discourse Concerning ...*, p. 297ff.
18 On the impact of the Baltic Germans in Russian public life, see E. Thaden, *Russia's Western Borderlands, 1710–1870*, Princeton, NJ, 1984, pp. 9–14; see also the major work by E. Amburger, *Geschichte der Behördenorganisation Rußlands von Peter dem Grossen bis 1917*, Leiden, 1966.
19 A point noted by Gustav III on the eve of his coup d'état in 1772: L. Konopcynski, 'Polen och Sverige I det adertonde århundradet. En historisk parallel', *Historisk Tidskrift*, 45, 1925, p. 101.
20 See the contribution by Gierowski in J. Kalisch, J. Gierowski, eds, *Um die Polnische Krone: Sachsen und Polen während des Nordischen Krieges 1700–1721*, Berlin, 1962, pp. 254–90. Zernack, 'Von Stolbovo', pp. 121–5.

12 Why St Petersburg?

Robert E. Jones

The creation of St Petersburg is surely one of the most impressive and enduring components of Peter the Great's legacy and legend. With a singular combination of authority, vision and will Peter transformed the inhospitable wasteland at the delta of the Neva river into a thriving, civilised metropolis. Uninhabited in 1703, the new settlement held 40 000 people by 1725. By 1790 it would surpass Moscow as Russia's largest city; and by 1811 it would rank as the fifth largest city in Europe, with a population of 336 000.[1]

Conquering that uninhabited wasteland cost Russia twenty-one years of warfare. Turning it into Russia's capital with forts, an admiralty, palaces, canals, warehouses, thoroughfares and residences entailed such enormous expenditures of money and manpower that the distinguished economic historian Arcadius Kahan considered St Petersburg 'the most massive Russian investment of the [eighteenth] century'.[2] Peter may never have questioned the cost of that investment, but we may ask what he hoped to gain from it. What did he have in mind? Why did Peter focus so much attention, so much effort, so much money on the delta of the Neva?

The site itself was hardly inviting. Except for the small Swedish fort and settlement at Nyenskans a few kilometres upstream, the delta of the Neva had remained uninhabited for centuries before Peter took possession of it in May 1703. And for good reasons. It lay on the border between Russia and Sweden, on the very edge of those empires. Its climate is cold, damp and notoriously unhealthy. The Neva normally freezes in November and does not thaw until April. When it does, a westerly wind can raise the water level by as much as three meters, which is enough to flood most of the delta. Even less appealing is its dependence on distant sources for almost all necessities, including food. As the statesman Grigorii Teplov observed in 1772, the persistent scarcity and high price of food in St Petersburg were, in his words:

> The consequences of creating this capital city in such a region of the empire, which either from the characteristics of the soil or of the climate, is itself unproductive and in which nothing that is nourishing grows satisfactorily, but all is, of necessity, brought from far away with great difficulty.[3]

So, what was it that attracted Peter to such a place? One possibility is that his appreciation of the site and his ambitions for it evolved gradually over time. Peter's first action was to capture the length of the Neva river and so divide Swedish forces in Karelia from those in Estland. Then he built a fort at the mouth of the river to prevent the Swedes from sailing upstream and reversing his conquest. Possession of a river flowing from lake Ladoga to the Baltic enabled Peter to construct a fleet that he then used to drive the Swedes from the Gulf of Finland and the eastern Baltic. Once that had been accomplished that same route could be used to ship Russian goods to Western Europe. In the course of the long war with Sweden Peter found it expedient to reside near the front to direct operations and gradually brought the rest of the government to his headquarters; the result of this was that St Petersburg became the capital of Russia.

That is more or less the sequence in which Peter carried out his aims, but that does not mean that he formulated those aims in that sequence. To assume that events led Peter to commit unpremeditated acts of enormous importance for the future of Russia is to push the law of unintended consequences to its illogical conclusion. Not only does it ignore Peter's lifelong interest in commerce and trade routes, but it also begs the question of why Peter launched his war against Sweden. Did he do so only to recover Ingria as a part of his patrimony that Sweden had taken from his forefathers in 1617? If so, then why was Ingria, ostensibly empty and worthless, worth a war?

Another possibility is that Peter went to war against Sweden expressly for the purpose of gaining a port on the Baltic from which

Russian goods could enter the world market. Timber, tar, hemp, hides, lard, iron, grain and other goods that Russia produced in abundance commanded far higher prices abroad than they did at home. Selling them at prices Europeans would pay could enrich Russia, its subjects and its ruler.[4] Ivan the Terrible had understood that simple fact when he founded the ports of Kholmogory and Archangel in the far north and waged war for twenty-five years in his ultimately futile effort to acquire the Baltic ports in Livonia. So had A.L. Ordin-Nashchokin, a leading statesman of the 1660s, who had urged the government to acquire ports on the Baltic. The Swedish government also understood the potential value of Russian exports. While deliberately excluding Russia from the Baltic, the Swedish government tried repeatedly to attract Russian exports to Narva and Nyenskans; however, the Russian government, unwilling to put its foreign trade under the control of a foreign power, had responded to Swedish pressure with discriminatory tariffs and other measures aimed at directing Russian commerce to the Russian port at Archangel.[5]

Archangel, located near the spot where the Northern Dvina river empties into the White sea, was the only seaport under Russian control at the time Peter came to power. Although it served to demonstrate the profitability of foreign trade, Archangel was too remote from both the producers and the consumers of the goods Russia wanted to sell. A voyage from western Europe to Archangel and back around the dangerous North Cape of Norway took three times as long and cost proportionally more money than one to ports on the Baltic or the Gulf of Finland.[6] When Peter visited Archangel for the first time in 1693–94, he was fascinated by the sea and the prospects it offered to Russia, but his subsequent actions suggest that he also gained an understanding of Archangel's inadequacies. Much of the rest of his life would be spent trying to acquire and develop seaports that would bring Russian producers closer to European consumers.

Peter's first effort to acquire such a port led him to Azov, an Ottoman fortress near the mouth of the Don river in the far distant south. Ultimately his effort to make Azov a new and better Archangel failed, but it is worth examining because it reveals Peter's objectives and methods and does much to explain his subsequent actions at St Petersburg.

Russia was already at war with the Ottomans when Peter seized the reins of government from Sophia in 1689. Instead of attacking the Ottomans' Crimean vassal, as the previous regime had done, Peter led his forces against the port of Azov and captured it in 1696 with the help of ships constructed at a shipyard (*admiralteiskii dvor*) in Voronezh upstream on the Don. Once he had conquered Azov, Peter took immediate steps to make it the pivot of a trade route that would connect the products of the Russian interior with the commerce of the Mediterranean basin. He hired foreign engineers, including the Englishman John Perry, to construct two canals to link the Don with the Oka and the Volga rivers and make it possible to transport goods to Azov by water from Moscow, the central Russian heartland and the Ural mountains. At Azov itself Peter ordered the construction of new fortifications along contemporary European lines and took a close personal interest in their design. Across the river from the fort a civilian settlement was to be constructed in accordance with a rational, orderly plan and given the significant name 'Petropolis'. That Peter intended it to be a city of considerable size and importance can be inferred from his instruction to the Orthodox Church to appoint a senior bishop or metropolitan for this new settlement.[7] Peter established an annual trade fair at Azov, and in 1701 he ordered Ukrainian merchants to bring their wares to Azov and not to sell them at other fairs or in other towns.[8]

Looking outwards to the sea, Peter ordered soundings and surveys of the Don, the sea of Azov and the Black sea. The findings were quickly incorporated into regional maps and nautical charts of the sea route from the lower Don to Constantinople. These persuaded Peter to locate his military and commercial port not at Azov – some forty kilometres above the mouth of the heavily-silted Don – but at Taganrog, on salt water – some fifty-five kilometres from Azov.

Azov could claim a number of advantages that Archangel and the future St Petersburg might envy:

- Its harbour and the waterways leading to it were free of ice for seven months a year;

- Russian goods could be transported downstream to Azov by way of the Don and canals connecting it to the Volga and the Oka; and
- Grain for consumption as well as for export could reach it by way of the Don, which flows for hundreds of kilometres through a fertile steppe region capable of producing grain in abundance.

Azov's greatest disadvantage was one that Peter never fully appreciated despite his maps and charts: for large merchant vessels the sea route from Taganrog to Constantinople was difficult, dangerous and sometimes completely impassable.[9] Azov's other disadvantage – and one that Peter understood with perfect clarity – was Ottoman control of the straits between the Black sea and the Aegean. To remove that obstacle Peter sought a new alliance against the Ottomans that would open Russia's way to the Mediterranean and the markets of Europe.[10] Had he succeeded in forging such an alliance, St Petersburg might never have been created at all. A long war against the Ottomans or a decisive victory would have concentrated Peter's energies and attention on the south rather than the north, and one can easily imagine Peter moving Russia's capital to the scene of action, with consequences no less significant though very different from those that followed its transfer from Moscow to St Petersburg.

On his Grand Embassy to Europe in 1697–98, Peter learned that his scheme to dismember the Ottoman Empire had no appeal to European statesmen preoccupied with the question of succession to the throne of Spain and the Spanish Empire.[11] He also learned that the rulers of Saxony and Denmark wanted him to join them in attacking Sweden and seizing its possessions in the Baltic. Those discoveries altered Peter's field of operations, but they did not alter his goal of obtaining a port from which Russian goods could enter the European market. Consequently, when Peter met the other members of the anti-Swedish coalition at Preobrazhenskoe in November 1699 to work out the terms of their alliance, he insisted that the price for Russia's participation in a war against Sweden would be access to the Baltic, and he succeeded in having that point included in one of the first articles of the alliance agreement.[12]

Peter did not create St Petersburg in order to defeat Sweden; he fought Sweden in order to create St Petersburg, and he would go on fighting for as long as necessary in order to keep it. In January 1707 Peter was prepared to make significant concessions to Charles XII in the hopes of forestalling a Swedish invasion of Russia. He instructed his diplomats to begin by offering to return the fortress of Dorpat but, if Charles demanded more, Peter was ready to return all of his other conquests in the war except the city of St Petersburg. And '[a]bout giving it back', he wrote, 'there is to be no thought'.[13] In 1709, within hours of his decisive victory over Charles at Poltava, Peter wrote to Admiral Apraksin informing him of the victory and declaring, 'Now, with God's help, the final stone in the foundation of St Petersburg has been laid.'[14] Peter understood his war aims quite clearly, and access to the Baltic at the mouth of the Neva was the first and most important of them.

When Peter first gained that access with the capture of Nyenskans in May 1703, he largely repeated what he had already done at Azov. He constructed a European-style fort to safeguard the site and bar the waterway to his enemies. On the opposite shore he projected a planned settlement, to be called 'Sankt Peterburg' rather than 'Petropolis' in keeping with its different location and orientation. A shipyard upstream at Olonets replicated the one at Voronezh, and the saltwater port at Kronstadt the one at Taganrog. Work began on a canal to link the new city and harbour with the Volga and the Russian heartland. However, with Archangel open but the Swedes blockading St Petersburg, Peter waited until 1713 before he began to repeat his efforts to divert commerce to the new city. He then introduced a series of measures compelling merchants to bring goods for export to St Petersburg rather than Archangel, under penalty of confiscation.[15] It is worth noting that Peter's construction projects in and around Azov continued, though at a slower pace than before, until the so-called 'disaster on the Pruth' in 1711 forced Peter to abandon the Black sea coast.

Military victories in 1710, confirmed by the peace of Nystad in 1721, brought Russia several additional ports on the Baltic, but none capable of replacing St Petersburg as the focus of Peter's ambitions. Three of them – Narva, Reval (Tallinn) and Riga – had valuable assets, but none could match St Petersburg's potential for increasing the export of Russian goods. Narva had enjoyed a brief period of success as Russia's Baltic port in the time of Ivan IV, but by Peter's time its harbour had become too shallow to accommodate large merchant ships. The waterways leading to Narva were interrupted by the deep waters of lake Peipus that threatened to capsize shallow river craft and by a waterfall just a few kilometres inland from the port; more importantly, however, they did not provide access to Narva from areas beyond the western periphery of Russia.[16] Reval possessed a fine harbour, but with no water transport from the interior it served mainly as a port for agricultural commodities hauled overland from estates nearby in Estland.[17] Riga, on the other hand, received commodities by way of the Western Dvina river from an extensive agricultural hinterland that included the western edge of Russia and a part of the northern Ukraine. Even though they were separated from Riga by the lands of the Polish-Lithuanian Commonwealth, which imposed tolls and tariffs on Russian goods, those regions could profitably send their surplus commodities to Riga for export.[18] For other regions, however, Riga was too distant and too remote in comparison to St Petersburg. Peter was pleased to annex Riga and collect tolls and duties on its exports, but its already flourishing maritime trade offered little prospect for expansion, especially for the export of goods produced in Russia as opposed to the Polish-Lithuanian Commonwealth or Lifland.

The great advantage that St Petersburg held over the other Baltic ports that Peter acquired from Sweden was its accessibility by water from the Russian heartland. That advantage was decisive because water transport offered the most profitable and in many cases the only profitable means of moving heavy, bulky goods over long distances. The Neva river flows to St Petersburg in a broad, deep channel from lake Ladoga, a large catch basin for the waters of north-western Russia. To the south and east of the lake only a relatively low and narrow divide stands between several of the rivers that feed lake Ladoga and several tributaries of the Volga. If two of those rivers could be joined by a canal across the divide, then goods could be brought to St Petersburg by water from as far away as Astrakhan, the northern Ukraine and the Ural mountains, or, at even greater remove, from central Asia, Iran and the Caucasus (see Plate 9). Such a canal would, in effect, make St Petersburg the seaport of the Volga and provide that landlocked river system with the outlet that nature had denied it. The potential value of a seaport that could be connected by water to the Volga far surpassed the value of one that could not, and thus St Petersburg, like Azov before it, offered Peter an advantage unobtainable elsewhere.

In 1701, after Peter had gone to war against Sweden but before his armies had occupied the delta of the Neva, Peter sent John Perry and a Russian by the name of Korchmin to investigate possible sites for a canal across the divide between the watershed of the Volga and the rivers leading to lake Ladoga. When Perry and Korchmin quickly identified three already existing portages where a canal or series of canals could open a continuous waterway from the Volga to the Gulf of Finland, Peter impatiently chose the route that could be opened in the least amount of time with the least construction. In January 1703, four months before his armies reached the Gulf of Finland, Peter put Vasilii and Matvei Gagarin in charge of constructing a canal between the rivers Tsna and Tvertsa at Vyshnii Volochek, a coaching station (*iam*) on the road between Moscow and Novgorod.

It is possible that at that moment Peter wanted a canal cut across the divide in order to supply his military operations against the Swedes, rather than a future city on a site he did not possess and had not seen, but it is by no means certain or even likely. If that was his motive, Peter either foresaw a war of many years duration, or he seriously underestimated the amount of time it would take to bring that canal into operation. In 1709 a simple, direct canal 2.8 kilometres long with a lock at each end allowed the first river craft to transport cargo from the Volga to St Petersburg without portage, but a faulty design limited its usefulness and eventually required a complete reconstruction that lasted until 1722. Only then did the Vyshnii Volochek canal begin to solve the problem of transporting goods from the Volga to St Petersburg. The amount of cargo passing through its locks rose from an average of 2166 metric tonnes per year for the period 1712–19 to an average of 156 600 metric tonnes for the period 1722–31. In 1731 the opening of the Ladoga canal in 1731 around the dangerous waters of that lake permitted a further expansion to an average of 216 000 tonnes by the 1750s.[19]

Although a number of hazards and bottlenecks remained after 1731, the so-called Vyshnii Volochek System of waterways supplied the new city on the Neva with the commodities on which its commerce and even its very existence depended. In a memorandum on commerce and transportation prepared for the Empress Catherine II in 1763, General N.E. Murav'ev pointed out that 'the well-being not only of St Petersburg but also of the surrounding regions, which supply the capital with goods and themselves depend on products brought from the southern provinces, depends on the good condition of the waterways'.[20] In 1810, as work on two additional waterways linking the Neva with the Volga approached completion, the Director of Water Communications reminded Tsar Alexander I of the indispensable role the Vyshnii Volochek System had played up to that point: 'By this one route', he observed, 'the capital has been supplied up to now with products from the interior of Russia for its own needs as well as for export overseas.'[21] Not only had Peter understood the vital importance of such a canal for St Petersburg, but he had also foreseen it before his army had wrested control of the Neva from the Swedes.

The reopening of the Vyshnii Volochek canal in 1722 increased the delivery of Russian goods to St Petersburg one year after the Peace of Nystad had cleared the way for their passage through the Baltic. Reinforced with Peter's *dirigiste* commercial policies, those two developments made St Petersburg a successful replacement for Archangel. Between 1719 and 1725 the value of exports from St Petersburg–Kronstadt rose from 268 600 roubles to 2 035 200 roubles while the value of Archangel's exports suffered a corresponding decline from 2 344 200 roubles to 120 000 roubles.[22] As shown in Table 12.1, the number of ships using the port of St Petersburg–Kronstadt also rose dramatically in that same period and

Table 12.1 Number of Ships Using the Port of St Petersburg–Kronstadt, 1718–97

Year	1718	1720	1722	1724	1760	1766	1773	1784	1790	1797
arr.	52	75	114	270	338	394	676	890	932	1267
dpt.	n.a.	n.a.	n.a.	n.a.	325	363	669	n.a.	n.a.	1224

Source: *Ocherki istorii Leningrada*, I, Moscow and Leningrad, 1955, pp. 86, 288.

continued to rise throughout the eighteenth century.

By the 1780s and 1790s, exports from St Petersburg accounted for 60 per cent of the total value of all exports from the Russian Empire.[23] In that same period tariff collections in St Petersburg provided 12 per cent of the government's annual revenue.[24] Exports through St Petersburg also provided income for Russia's nobles, peasants and merchants, and yielded additional revenue for the government in the form of taxes of various kinds on the latter two categories. Boris Mironov has also argued that the linking of the Russian economy with that of Europe produced a price revolution in Russia between 1707 and 1810 that raised Russian prices to European levels, increasing them by 400–570 per cent.[25]

Peter's decision to establish a seaport on the delta of the Neva demonstrated a brilliant understanding of economic geography, but if that was his only goal then his decision to establish Russia's capital on that same site defied many considerations of economics and geography. Unlike Washington, New Delhi, Canberra, Brazilia, Islamabad and other newly created capitals that followed it, St Petersburg was intended to serve as a centre of commerce as well as government, and to do both in a remote and desolate region far from its sources of supply. Geography can explain why Peter created a seaport on the delta of the Neva. It does not, however, explain why he made that seaport his capital.

Although the creation of a seaport and naval base and the transfer of the central organs of government occurred more or less simultaneously, they were separable developments, as the Supreme Privy Council understood in the late 1720s. Faced with the expense and difficulty of ruling Russia from a remote corner of the empire, the council considered moving the capital back to Moscow and might have done so if its power had survived the succession crisis of 1730. Such a move would have left St Petersburg to serve as an outlet for Russian exports, like Archangel, and as a naval base.

From an economic as well as an administrative point of view, the idea of returning the capital to Moscow had much to recommend it. Transporting goods to St Petersburg at considerable expense made sense when those goods could be sold to foreign merchants at a profit, but not when those goods were used to shelter, clothe and feed multitudes of people there rather than in Moscow, where virtually everything was cheaper. In 1786 a committee of dignitaries appointed to investigate the shortage and high price of flour in St Petersburg replied to Catherine II that:

> this capital, according to its geographical location, lying almost on the edge of the empire and unable to bring grain from the districts surrounding it, is deprived of the advantages by which all populous cities attract to themselves rural inhabitants with their domestic produce, but must supply itself with grain brought here by water at the cost of a whole year.[26]

What the committee said about grain could be said of virtually all other necessities consumed in St Petersburg.[27]

The need to transport goods for domestic consumption, especially building materials and foodstuffs, strained the carrying capacity of the waterways from the Volga to St Petersburg. In a decree dated 26 June 1720, Peter's government assigned the highest priority for goods in transit through the waterways to timber and foodstuffs destined for use in the city even though they interfered with the delivery of goods destined for export.[28] Other decrees of the Petrine era forbidding or seriously restricting the export of timber and grain from St Petersburg adversely affected St Petersburg's exports and the income therefrom for nearly a century.[29] Finally, in 1797–98, concern over deliveries of timber and cereals convinced Paul's government to take on the expense of opening two additional waterways, the Tikhvin and Mariiansk canals across the divide between the Volga and lake Ladoga.[30]

Peter's willingness to limit St Petersburg's exports for the sake of its development as a capital and metropolis does not contradict the hypothesis that he intended St Petersburg to be Russia's primary seaport, the outlet of the Volga and the entry point for Russian goods on to the European market. Instead, it indicates that he intended it to be something more than just a seaport, more than just a replacement for Archangel. On that essential economic base Peter also intended to create a large, magnificent city from which he and his successors would rule the Russian empire.

In the absence of any explanation from Peter himself, it is not clear precisely when he decided to turn the new settlement on the delta of the Neva into a major European city and the capital of Russia, but it is quite possible that he made that decision as soon as he had occupied the site, if not sooner. Although he did not officially move Russia's capital to the new city until 1713, as early as 4 September 1704 Peter referred to St Petersburg as the capital (*stolitsa*).[31] Equally indicative of his intentions to create an imposing city on a grand scale are his close personal involvement with the planning and construction of the city and the financial and human resources he was prepared to commit to the project from the time he conquered it until he died.[32]

Unlike Washington, Brazilia and the other the newly created capital cities that followed it, St Petersburg was conceived at a very early date, if not from the start, as an imperial metropolis, a world-city that would be both a locus of political power and a centre of international trade. As a city created to serve both purposes, St Petersburg has no real successor in modern history and no predecessor in Russian or European history since the late Roman Empire. The only real precedents and quite possibly the inspirations for St Petersburg were Constantinople and, more distantly, Alexandria, two cities founded by eponymous emperors who also wanted to shift the political, cultural and economic centres of their realms.[33]

Peter's opponent, Charles XII of Sweden, revered Alexander the Great and strove to emulate his military successes. Was Peter's ambition to move Russia's capital from its historic location, now mired in intrigue and antiquated customs, to a bustling centre of international commerce similarly inspired by the example of Constantine the Great? There is no direct evidence, but the parallels seem more than accidental, especially in the light of Peter's many conscious and pointed references to the examples of ancient Rome and Constantinople. In St Petersburg, as in Constantinople, a senate and a synod governed the state and the church under an emperor who could designate his own successor. There, on 21 October 1721, the Senate celebrated the signing of the Treaty of Nystad by conferring on Peter three titles – *otets otechestva* (father of the fatherland), *imperator vserossiiskii* (emperor of all Russia) and *Petr Velikii* (Peter the Great) – replicating the Latin titles – *pater patriae*, *imperator* and *maximus* – that the Roman Senate had bestowed on a number of emperors, including Constantine the Great. Accepting those titles, Peter made yet another historical reference when he warned the Senate that despite recent victories 'we should not slacken in the military area, lest we suffer the same fate as the Greek monarchy.'[34]

Why did Peter create St Petersburg? Most certainly he created it to enrich his realm by exporting Russian products to Europe, but that is not the whole story. On that indispensable commercial base – from the beginning or at least soon thereafter – Peter intended to create an imperial metropolis the likes of which had not been seen in Christian Europe since the fall of Constantinople.

NOTES

1 Robert E. Jones, 'Getting the Goods to St Petersburg: Water Transport from the Interior 1703–1811', *Slavic Review*, 43, 1984, p. 414. There is some question as to when St Petersburg surpassed Moscow in population. *European Historical Statistics*, London and Basingstoke, 1980, pp. 86–8, lists the largest cities in Europe in 1800 as follows: London (1 117 000), Paris (547 000), Naples (427 000), Moscow (250 000), Vienna (247 000), and St Petersburg (220 000). At the end of the eighteenth century Heinrich Storch, *The Picture of St Petersburg*, London, 1801, p. 86, put the population of St Petersburg at 230 000 behind only Constantinople, London, Paris, Naples and Vienna.
2 Arcadius Kahan, *The Plow, the Hammer, and the Knout*, Chicago, IL and London, 1985, p. 247.
3 *Doklady Grigoriia Teplova o vozvyshaiushcheisia dorogovizne s estnykh pripasov v Peterburge*. Russkii Gosudarstvennyi Arkhiv Drevnikh Aktov (hereafter RGADA), f. 16, d. 496, l. 39ob.
4 B.N. Mironov, *Khlebnye tseny v Rossii za dva stoletiia (XVIII–XIX vv.)*, Leningrad, 1985, pp. 45, 52.
5 Michael Roberts, *The Swedish Imperial Experience 1560–1718*, Cambridge, 1979, pp. 110–12. Artur Attman, 'Swedish Aspirations in the Russian Market during the Seventeenth Century', *Acta Regiae Societatis Scientiarum et Litterarum Gothoburgonsis Humaniora*, 1985, 24, pp. 28–41.
6 This was the finding of a study of Russian trade undertaken by the Swedish government in the mid-seventeenth century. Sweden hoped to

persuade or force Russia to conduct its trade with western Europe through Nyenskans or Narva but failed to do either. Attman, 'Swedish Aspirations', p. 16. On Archangel's limitations as a commercial port see also J. Jepson Oddy, *European Commerce*, Philadelphia, PA, 2 vols, 1807, I, pp. 91–5.

7 James Cracraft, *The Petrine Revolution in Architecture*, Chicago, IL and London, 1988, pp. 114–21.

8 *Polnoe sobranie zakonov Rossiiskii Imperii*, 1st series, 45 vols, (hereafter *PSZ*), St Petersburg, 1830, IV, no. 1826

9 On the shortcomings of Azov and Taganrog for maritime trade, see Oddy, *European Commerce*, I, pp. 171–4.

10 Evidence that Peter's goal in the south was to expand Russia's foreign trade can be found in the initial demands Russia put forward in negotiations for a peace treaty with the Ottomans: acceptance of Peter's conquest of Azov and several fortresses on the lower Dnieper, and the right of free passage for Russian vessels on the Black sea. He dropped the latter demand in his haste to conclude a peace with the Turks before joining the war against Sweden. Edward J. Phillips, *The Founding of Russia's Navy: Peter the Great and the Azov Fleet, 1688–1714*, Westport, CT and London, 1995, p. 102.

11 Peter's emissary, E.I. Ukraintsev, offered another explanation of Peter's failure to secure a new alliance against Turkey. He informed the tsar that the maritime powers supported Turkey because they opposed Peter's efforts to enter directly into maritime trade. The text of Ukraintsev's communication was published in S.M. Solov'ev, *Istoriia Rossii s drevneishikh vremen*, Moscow, 15 vols, 1962, VII, p. 617.

12 I.I. Rostunov *et al.*, *Istoriia severnoi voiny*, Moscow, 1987, p. 20.

13 *Pis'ma i bumagi imperatora Petra Velikago*, 13 vols, St Petersburg–Leningrad, 1887–1992, V, p. 61.

14 Quoted in Cracraft, *The Petrine Revolution*, p. 179.

15 In 1701 Peter had ordered that export goods from Novgorod, Pskov and other towns near the Swedish frontier be sent to Archangel. *PSZ*, IV, no. 2387. In 1713–14 he decreed that hemp and Russian leather (*iuft*) be exported exclusively from St Petersburg. In 1714 he ordered merchants to send half their export goods to St Petersburg and half to Archangel. In 1717 he changed the proportion to one-third to Archangel and two-thirds to St Petersburg. *PSZ*, V, nos 2732, 2737, 2784, 2760, 2793 and VI, no. 3195.

16 Oddy, *European Commerce*, I, p. 145. On Narva's history as a precursor of St Petersburg see Walter Kirchner, *Commercial Relations*

between *Russia and Europe, 1400 to 1800: Collected Essays*, Bloomington, IN, 1966, pp. 59–76.
17 Oddy, *European Commerce*, I, p. 146.
18 N.N. Repin, 'Izmenenie ob"ema eksporta Arkhangel'skogo i Peterburgskogo portov vo pervoi polovine XVIII v.' in A.A. Preobrazhenskii, ed., *Promyshlennosti i torgovlia v Rossii XVI–XVIII vv.*, Moscow, 1983, p. 186. In 1721 Peter ordered Ukrainian merchants sending goods to Riga to use a new route that avoided as much territory of Poland as possible. *PSZ*, VI, no. 3860. That problem was eliminated by the first partition of Poland.
19 The figures for 1712–19 and the 1750s are from S.V. Bernshtein-Kogan, *Vyshnevolotskii vodnyi put'*, Moscow, 1946, pp. 21–6. The figure for the period 1722–31 has been calculated by combining the average number of boats per year passing through the locks, as given in V.A. Gorelov, *Rechnye kanali v Rossii*, Leningrad and Moscow, 1935, p. 167, n. 205 with the capacity of 90–100 tonnes per boat given in Bernshtein-Kogan, *Vyshnevolotskii vodnyi put'*, p. 28. Using the minimum capacity of ninety tonnes, I arrived at a conservative figure of 156 000 tonnes per year.
20 Quoted in S.M. Troitskii, 'Zapiski senatora N.E. Murav'eva o razvitii kommertsii i putei soobshcheniia v Rossii (60e gody XVIII v.)' in A.L. Narochnitskii, ed., *Istoricheskaia geografiia Rossii XII – nachalo XX v. Sbornik statei k 70-letiiu professora Liubomira Grigor'evicha Beskrovnogo*, Moscow, 1975, p. 238. In June 1765 the Vyshnii Volochek System, the Ladoga canal and the Neva river were placed under Murav'ev's authority 'for their better maintenance'. E.G. Istomina, *Vodnye puti Rossii vo vtoroi polovine XVIII – nachale XIX veka*. Moscow, 1982, p. 5.
21 Quoted in E.G. Istomina, 'Vyshnevolotskii vodnyi put' vo vtoroi polovine XVIII v.' in Narochnitskii, ed., *Istoricheskaia geografiia Rossii*, p. 206.
22 Repin, 'Izmenenie', p. 177.
23 F.G. Virst, *Razsuzhdeniia o nekotorykh predmetkakh zakonodatel'stva i upravleniia finansami i kommertsieiu Rossiiskoi imperii*, Supplement, Table 19, St Petersburg, 1807. The twenty-eight tables appended to Virst's book are bound separately in an unpaginated supplement.
24 In two letters to General P.D. Erapkin, Governor-General of Moscow, written in the spring of 1787 while she was visiting the Black sea coast, Catherine II claimed that St Petersburg, which had once been slandered as severely as her new acquisitions in the south, now produced one-eighth of the state's annual revenue. Iakov Rost, ed., *Vysochaishiia soobstvennoruchnyia pis'ma i poveleniia blazhennoi i vechnoi slavy dostoinoi pamiati gosudaryniimperatritsy Ekateriny Velikiia k pokoinomu Generalu*

Petru Dmitrievich Erapkinu i vsepodanneishiia ego doneseniia v trekh otdeleniiakh, Moscow, 1808, pp. 247, 258.

25 Mironov, *Khlebnye tseny*, p. 45.

26 Sankt Peterburgskii Filial Instituta Rossiiskoi Istorii, f. 35, (Vorontsovykh), op. 1, d. 410 (Dela komissii o khlebe uchrezhdennoi v 1786), l. 36ob.

27 In Peter's time John Perry pointed out that 'all manner of Provisions are usually three to four times as dear, and Forage for their Horses at least six or eight times as dear as it is at Moscow; which happens from the great expense of it at St Petersburg, and the small quantity which the Country thereabouts produces, being more than two thirds woods and bogs'. Perry, *The State of Russia under the Present Czar*, London, 1716, pp. 261–2.

28 RGADA, f. 397 (komissiia o kommertsii), opis 1, d. 226 (Dela o borovitskikh porogakh i o vyshnee voloshchikh sliuzakh, 1761), l. 3ob. Preserved among the papers of the Commission on Commerce, this decree was not included in the *PSZ*.

29 Peter banned the export of grain from St Petersburg whenever the price of rye in Moscow rose to one rouble per chetvert. *PSZ*, IV, nos 1872, 2672. After 1762 the government permitted the unrestricted export of wheat from St Petersburg, but rye and rye flour could only be exported by special permission. In the early 1780s the regular export of rye and rye flour was also permitted, but it was banned again after the famine of 1786. In the early nineteenth century among the twenty-two most significant goods exported from St Petersburg, wheat ranked thirteenth (by volume not by value) and rye was not listed at all. Virst, *Razsuzhdeniia*, Table 25. Virst complained, pp. 258–60, that the prohibition on exporting wood and timber was depriving Russia of valuable export earnings and added 'and the situation is the same with grain'. A.L. Shapiro, 'O roli Peterburga i vserossiiskogo rynka v XVIII – pervoi polovine XIX v.' in V.I. Shunkov, ed., *Goroda feodal'noi Rossii. Sbornik statei pamiati N.V. Ustiugova*, Moscow, 1966, p. 391, estimated that from 1738 to 1839 grain constituted twenty-seven to thirty per cent of the value of all goods arriving in St Petersburg from the interior of Russia.

30 This concern is evident in the correspondence between the Director of Water Communications, Jakob Sievers, and other government officials including the tsar. Rossiiskii Gosudarstvennyi Istoricheskii Arkhiv, f. 156, opis 1, d. 1 (Departament vodianykh kommunikatsii), ll. 90–105.

31 In a letter to A.D. Menshikov, dated 4 September 1704, Peter wrote that 'In three or four days we will be in the capital, St Petersburg (*v stolitsu, Piterburkh*)', *PiB*, III, no. 725.

32 S.P. Luppov, *Istoriia stroitel'stva Peterburga v pervoi chetverti XVIII veka*, Moscow and Leningrad, 1957, especially pp. 23–4. Also Cracraft, *The Petrine Revolution*, pp. 174–81.

33 Although St Petersburg was officially named for Peter's patron saint rather than for the emperor himself, it was commonly referred to by Peter and others as Peterburg, Piterburkh and even Piter. Cracraft, *The Petrine Revolution*, p. 174 points out that documents dated July 1703 and later also refer to the city as Petropolis and Petropol'.

34 *PSZ*, VI, no. 3840.

13 Seven Years with Peter the Great: the Dutchman Jacob de Bie's Observations

Thomas Eekman

In May 1711 the Netherlands States General decided to send an 'extra envoy' to Poland and Livonia in order to find a peaceful solution to the conflict between Poland and Russia, on the one hand, and Sweden on the other.[1] The embassy's secretary was Jacob de Bie, on whom there is practically no background information, beyond the fact that he was born in 1681 in Nantes, France.[2] The mission was not successful: the Northern war lasted for ten more years; but de Bie was travelling in eastern and central Europe for some time, becoming well acquainted with the scene, the political problems of the area and the mutual relations and conflicts between the governments involved in the war. In July 1711 the States General appointed him their permanent representative ('resident') in the Russian capital, following the death of Hendrik van der Hulst, who had held that post from 1699 until his death in 1710. De Bie arrived with his wife and their belongings in St Petersburg and presented his credentials. He took up his duties in the same year in which Prince Boris Ivanovich Kurakin was appointed the Russian representative in The Hague.[3]

Hardly had de Bie settled in his new function and environment than the tsar decided to visit his allies around the Baltic and lead the war operations. The Dutch resident followed him (and so did the British envoy Charles Whitworth), first to Iaroslavl' (September 1711), then to Danzig, Elbing, Königsberg, Riga, and

Reval (Tallinn) (January 1712). Like a newspaper correspondent, he followed Peter wherever he went (except to Torgau, where Peter and his wife Catherine attended the wedding of Peter's son, crown prince Alexis, to Princess Charlotte of Wolfenbüttel). Unfortunately, de Bie's missives to the States General are rather short, dry and formal and do not present a colourful picture of the places Peter visited, his actions or his deliberations; there are, however, a few exceptions. For example, from Königsberg he writes (23 November 1711):

> His Highness the Duke of Holstein-Beck, accompanied by four state counsellors, received His Majesty the Tsar in the name of His Majesty the King of Prussia, with the citizenry under arms, while the gun on the quay was roaring, then led His Majesty up to the castle, where apartments had been furnished for him. However, His Majesty the Tsar, after having a bite, did not want to stay there and went to Mr Major Negelen, where he stayed until his departure, which was yesterday, again contrary to expectation. But Mr Duke was unable to persuade His Majesty to stay any longer.

This little scene illustrates Peter's self-willed behaviour, as well as de Bie's laconic style.

Back in St Petersburg, on 2 February 1712, de Bie reported to his superiors on 'the miserable state into which commerce and navigation in the Baltic have lapsed'. As a result of the constant wars in the region, and also because of growing international competition – as well as the constantly higher export taxes which Russia, implicated in a long and costly war, was exacting from the foreign merchants – the once flourishing Baltic trade was now languishing. In Riga de Bie ascertained that the entire timber trade (important to Holland which bought and needed pinewood for ship masts) had gone over into the hands of agents of the notorious Prince Aleksandr Danilovich Menshikov, Peter's friend and protégé, known for his unscrupulous ways of enriching himself.[4] The commandant of Riga, Polonskii, turned out to be Menshikov's favourite and collaborator. The Dutch captains and crew were exposed to all kinds of harassment, with the result that 'there is virtually no skipper who doesn't swear never to sail to the Baltic again'. De Bie claims that most abuses never were brought to the tsar's attention; when he talked to him and mentioned some of them, the tsar refused to believe him. Menshikov also discredited the stories.

The supreme commander in the city of Reval was, according to de Bie, 'a malicious and vicious man, and You High Mighty Gentlemen would certainly be fed up if I would bring up all his wiles and describe them to you'. He encloses a letter written by a Dutch skipper to the States General, complaining of the maltreatment he had undergone in Reval. The commander, de Bie discovered, was the son of Peter's 'court jester', who played the part of a pseudo-patriarch[5]; his son could be certain of the Tsar's protection. Again, this commander shared his spoils with Prince Menshikov.

De Bie urges the States to take a firm stand in these matters; he himself tried to do the same. But then he adds:

> However, the situation at the court is different from other courts: the access to His Majesty the Tsar's residence is blocked, nobody is admitted to it or to the Prince [Menshikov] anymore, unless by special order ... The sentinels repel everybody who wants to see him, so one has no other recourse than to the Grand Chancellor, who will hear a person out, but only makes some notes, so nothing can be effected unless with the utmost trouble and patience, as long as the great authority of Prince Menshikov will last. (2 February 1712)

This seems to contradict the fact that on many occasions the Dutch representative would 'sit at His Majesty's left side' at a banquet or have other occasions to talk freely to him. Did Peter become less accessible in his later years and did he shield himself behind 'the prince'? He could be very critical of him, if we believe de Bie's words; two weeks later he writes:

> I have been informed by a reliable source that His Majesty the Tsar has addressed him [Prince Menshikov] with the following words: 'I have to tell you that your behaviour is most disgusting to me. You are trying to shield rascals, pre-

senting them to us as honest men, and honest men as rascals, but I warn you for the last time: change your ways if you don't want to fall into the worst misfortune. You are now supposed to go to Pomerania; perhaps you think you can play havoc there like you did in Poland, but you will be dead wrong!' (16 February 1712)

On 23 May of the same year de Bie reports that Peter has summoned all the members of the Senate to move from Moscow to Petersburg, where the new capital was now formally established. The Senate was going to discuss a number of grave complaints lodged by British and Dutch residents. De Bie must have been aware of the fact that the Senate was not a strong or influential body; the senators have often been described as lazy and corrupt. In this letter he renders the following little scene, which again does not confirm his statement about Peter's inaccessibility:

> As soon as His Majesty caught sight of me he was so gracious as to come up to me, saying: 'We are surely much obliged to you [he meant the States General for mediating in the peace negotiations between Russia and Turkey] for the service and all the work your ambassador has done for us, and I congratulate you on the results.' Upon which I congratulated His Majesty on his happy arrival and successful expedition and replied that ... You High Mighty Gentlemen had acted as good and sincere friends of His Majesty. His Majesty then embraced me and, noticing that I wanted to talk to the State Counsellor, referred me to him.[6]

In the same letter he reports that 'His Majesty regaled the tsaritsa in her summer residence, where Your High Mighty Gentlemen's resident also had the honour of being invited and [the pleasure of being] present.' He also mentions that the Dutchman Scheltinga – 'in recognition of his good services' – was appointed the 'Captain Commander' of the tsar's navy. Two weeks later (letter of 7 June) he writes about his conversation with the tsar at the wedding of Field Marshal Sheremetev.[7] In fact, the Dutch resident, taking an active part in daily life at the court, had plenty of opportunities for contact with the monarch, who as a rule was well disposed and even cordial towards him.[8]

Most of de Bie's missives deal with problems, controversies and complaints in connection with trade. Innumerable (and practically unsearchable) are all the merchants, shopkeepers, artisans, dockers, etc, the *Rusluie* (Russia-goers) who in the course of the seventeenth and eighteenth centuries came from the Netherlands and established themselves in a number of Russian towns, usually in the special foreigners' quarter. As these people could count on very little protection by law, they would turn with their problems to the representative of their country in the capital. These are some examples of issues arising: There was the supplication of the Dutch shopkeepers in Moscow who, by a decree of the tsar, were suddenly notified they had to close their shops, although they had been assured they could freely set up their business. There was the question of the taxes which Dutch exporters had to pay, whereas the British, by a special treaty, were exempted. There was the demand of the Russian authorities that the Dutch ships approaching or leaving Archangel should give a salute to Russian war vessels (letter of 7 June) (an agreement was reached on that issue). There was the protest by eight Dutch cargo ship captains in Reval, who came to load grain, but were told there was an order from the tsar prohibiting the loading of grain in that city, for no apparent reason (31 August 1713). Several other captains or ship owners lodged complaints because of damage or unfair treatment they had experienced in some Russian sea port. The authorities in Archangel suddenly levied an extra tax of 9 per cent on grain and wine, which was going to ruin the exporters (as de Bie pointed out in a letter to the tsar). In 1715 a plan to introduce a grain monopoly in the hands of the government provokes his comment: 'This would totally destroy our trade with these lands [that is, with Russia].' A complete state grain monopoly was never enforced, perhaps partly thanks to de Bie's protests.

Such official duties, obligations and chores were alternated with more pleasant, or occasionally even adventurous, events. In late June 1712 he states:

On the 10th of June occurred His Majesty's birthday, when he turned 43 [a mistake: in 1712 Tsar Peter turned 40], which event was celebrated in his summer residence. On the 12th and 13th the wedding of Prince Dolgorukii and a Circassian princess took place. And on the 19th His Majesty invited all foreign diplomats to gather at a certain place to assist at the marriage of a certain Russian [the name is omitted, unfortunately]. All the notable gentlemen and ladies, and also His Majesty himself, the tsaritsa and all the princesses appeared in old-time Russian attire; such clothes had also been sent to the foreign representatives, and they had put them on, the undersigned among them, when they assembled. After the couple was joined in matrimony there was food, there were drinks and some old Russian, now obsolete ceremonies were performed. Then we all boarded a Finnish vessel that was well equipped for this occasion; the ladies went into the hold, the men stayed on deck. Thus we were rowed, in bad, rainy weather, to a house of His Majesty called Pieters Hoff [Peterhof], which is twenty versts from here, half way to Cronslot [later Kronstadt]. There we had dinner and spent the night. The next day we boarded – in our own clothing – some yachts and boyers; we had to tack in a strong wind to Cronslot, and most of the distinguished ladies and gentlemen were very sick. Finally we arrived, only late at night. The next day the whole company was invited for lunch by the Admiral General [F.M. Apraksin] on his ship, called the Viborg, with fifty pieces. We ate and had, under the roar of the guns, several drinks. Then we all boarded the vessels again, and during the night this distinguished company returned home.

His Majesty [de Bie continues] had the complaisance of pointing out to the foreign representatives the situation in this area, the depths and shoals of the harbour, and described to us the city he is planning to build on the island of Ritzov [?], where only merchants will live, in stone [brick] houses. The city will be adorned with canals and bridges, just like in Amsterdam.

About two weeks later:

> [T]he entire nobility, of both sexes, plus the foreign residents that were available, were invited to attend the launching of the ship 'Poltava', that will carry 54 metal, 24- and 72-pound guns. When we were all there, the ship was successfully launched, which very much delighted His Majesty, who himself is its captain. Later the whole company had to come aboard, where there was a banquet and very strong drinks were served until late at night.

A few days later de Bie accompanied the tsar to Riga, where he celebrated the third anniversary of the battle of Poltava in June 1709.

> His Majesty the Tsar had already given orders to prepare everything for a dinner party. Invited were not only his entire retinue and the officers of this garrison, but the nobility of the province and the magistrature of this city [Riga], even all the skippers, of whom there may be about forty, English and Dutch. His Majesty was again extremely merry; he showed a special preference for the Dutch captains, often getting up from the table and joining them to drink a glass in his quality of Rear Admiral (all this from a long letter of 10 July 1712).

These quotes give an idea of life in and around the imperial court in those early Petersburg days. De Bie was sometimes invited to the palace without an immediate cause, just to chat with the tsar and tsaritsa (as appears from a letter without a date, probably from November 1713).

The voyage to Riga mentioned above was just the beginning of a long journey the tsar undertook within a year after his previous trip; and once more de Bie accompanied him. Again there are dispatches from Danzig (July–August 1712), Berlin, Hamburg (January 1713), then again Berlin and Danzig, until he writes again from St Petersburg in August 1713. This time Peter acted during his journey as an army commander-in-chief, fighting the Swedes together with his Danish and German allies. Militarily not much was achieved, except that the Russian army dispelled the Swedes from Finland and totally destroyed Helsingfors (Helsinki). De Bie's missives read again like the reports of a war correspondent.

The year 1713 marked the end of the Spanish War of Succession by the Peace of Utrecht, which in fact was a debacle for the Netherlands, whose role as a great European maritime and economic power came to an end. Yet there were a few successes as well, and there was relief that the war with France was finally over. The States General suggested that their representative in Russia celebrate this joyful fact. To this de Bie responded that the 300 guilders put at his disposal would be far too little, as:

> there is a multitude of notable persons I will have to invite, such as senators, generals, admirals, boyars and other nobles at the court and officers of His Majesty the Tsar, as well as agents of foreign nations. It could very well be that His Majesty will appear with his high family to grace the event with their presence; and the whole crowd will be so considerable that the cost of the wine alone would far exceed the mentioned budget – and I did not begin to calculate the food and other necessities which in these regions, exhausted by plague and war, are very expensive and hard to obtain. (3 June 1713)

Therefore, he asks for a higher allowance, consulting with the States whether he should 'let the wine flow in front of my house for the people, and come up with illuminations and other signs of joy'. It is not likely that the celebration took place; in a letter from early August he begs to be exonerated from this task.

When de Bie returned from his peregrinations in Germany to St Petersburg, he received the startling news that Russian war ships had opened fire on five Dutch freighters in Helsingfors harbour, set them alight and sunk them, with great loss of life (we are never told how many victims there were) and of freight. De Bie reported this to his principals and soon a claim for damages was put in by the Netherlands government in the name of the surviving relatives and the shipowners. This affair will from now on come up in almost all of de Bie's letters. The tsar, the state chancellor (G.I. Golovkin), the vice-chancellor (P. Shafirov), the Senate and other high authorities were approached and became involved, but only some evasive answers and vague promises ensued. It was a war situation, it was said; the ships should not have been there in the first place; and they did not indicate clearly enough that they were Dutch, not Swedish ships (this was vehemently disclaimed by the few survivors). Of course, Russia was at war and suffered a severe financial crisis; nobody wanted to take the responsibility and agree to spend money on such an inconsequential matter, even a boring matter, which it became more and more as time went by. From de Bie's letter of 15 February 1715 it appears that the tsar had ordered his ambassador Kurakin to pay a sum to the victims, but not the full requested amount. Perhaps this unpleasant affair is just one small symptom of the general decline of the Netherlands as a maritime world power and of their prestige in the early eighteenth century.

A second, and more important, theme in his letters from 1713 onward is the 'treaty of commerce' (*commercie tractaat*) which the Dutch government wanted to conclude with Russia. The Dutch merchants and shipowners had complained for a long time that no such treaty or agreement between the two countries existed, and yet it would be most helpful and indispensable to carry on trade under the protection of such a contract that existed between many European countries. The Dutch wanted freedom of trade, of buying and selling, of settlement and setting up businesses, offering the Russians the same rights in the Netherlands. But the Russians did not come in large numbers to the Dutch Republic; and at home they were traditionally antagonistic towards foreigners, resenting it when the latter poked their noses into Russian customs or put Russian merchants out of business. Peter himself and his close collaborators (Golovkin, Shafirov, Menshikov) hesitated: they needed the income of high export taxes as state revenue, especially for the money-eating war machine. The treaty of commerce was repeatedly formally proposed by the States General and fervently advocated by their agent in St Petersburg; however, it was never accepted nor totally rejected. Several stipulations of the proposed treaty were acceptable to the Russians, but the idea of free trade for the Dutch merchants met with insurmountable objections. The Dutch considered such a treaty a *sine qua non* because, as de Bie put it in one of his letters, 'in the continuing absence of it [the treaty] nothing else but the total ruin of the already agonising trade on Russia and the Baltic has to be anticipated' (27 September 1713). A significant passage in his letter of 29 October 1714 reads:

> Mr Osterman[9] told me later in private: 'Shall I tell you the real truth, sir? We have nobody here who understands these matters. Yet I can assure you His Majesty is actually working on it.'

De Bie sometimes became desperate at the slow process of communication with his principals.

> In these lands [that usually meant Russia] there are such amazing and unruly goings-on with the mail that I cannot well describe it to you. The foreign agents always receive their letters two or three days after they have arrived and after the Chancellor has decoded and read the mail and reacted to it through his channels. I believe I have reasons to suspect that the postmaster in Riga has received the order to send all mail that looks like official mail via Moscow – which also was the case with Your High Mighty Gentlemen's secret resolution of 28 June. In short, they are trying here to make the foreign agents as useless as possible and to frustrate the tasks they have to perform in the interest of their principals by holding up their letters and orders. (25 October 1713)

Another matter that generated considerable correspondence and deliberations was Peter's decision to divert all commerce from the port of Archangel to that of St Petersburg. This made some sense, but in this case the Dutch seem to have been more conservative than the Russians; they were not really willing to give up Archangel and certain privileges they enjoyed there (although they often had conflicts with and suffered losses from Archangel's greedy governor). It is true that the ongoing war remained at least a temporary obstacle for the Baltic trade: Ships bound for Russia were sometimes held up and searched by the Swedish navy. But both de Bie and the tsar felt easier on that score when:

four Dutch commercial vessels had arrived in Petersburg after the captains were summoned to come over to the Swedish vice-admiral Lillie's ship, where they were asked what their destination was. When they answered: 'Sint Pietersborg', the vice-admiral had remarked: 'I see, going to our enemies!' To which the captains replied: 'We sail to where we hope to make a little money, it makes no difference to us whether our bosses send us to Sweden or Russia.' Finally, the vice-admiral said: 'Sail with God,' and he had let them go. He took two barrels of wine from them, and paid for them. (19 May 1714)

Some of de Bie's letters are quite substantial, numbering ten to eleven pages. The one of 2 June 1714 is fourteen pages long; it describes in (for de Bie) lively detail a conversation he had with the tsar and a report of the tsar's visit to his navy (partly newly arrived from Holland). His Majesty led the naval exercises and the preparations for a battle against Sweden. This would be the battle of Cape Gangut (Hangö) that ended in a brilliant Russian victory in August (July O.S.). However, the victory was overshadowed by the autumn storm which reportedly sank eleven of the tsar's ships with six hundred men. The dispatch of 5 November 1714, in which this is reported, dwells on the tsar's bad mood, partly to be attributed to this loss, partly to bad news from his armies in Germany and partly to the grave difficulties caused by the project of letting St Petersburg take over Archangel's role as the main Russian port. During such periods, when he was down in the mouth, Peter suffered, as it is described in this letter:

from deep chagrin and melancholy, [with] a serious colic and pains in all his limbs, [for] His Majesty's constitution, which has been very strong, is considerably weakened as a result of the great fatigues and worries of these recent years; but the main cause is his bad corpulence, which remains because of his drinking: he regales himself upon everything and at all times.[10]

Perhaps Peter's poor health and consequent bad temper contributed to the 'heavy inquisition' that started in November 1714.

> It was on the fourth of this month [recalls de Bie] in the evening after the celebration of Prince Menshikov's birthday, when His Majesty in strong terms threw him [Menshikov] in his face his bad conduct and that of his favourites, stating that they had shamelessly enriched themselves in a few years by their extortions and thefts, whereas His Majesty's coffers were exhausted and revenues had dried up; that he had often times warned him not to patronise such people anymore; he saw now that his admonitions had been in vain and was going to investigate the situation and give people what they deserved. The first examples of this could be seen on the morning of 6 November, when His Majesty had all employees of the state offices in the city, of the admiralty and the government of Ingermanland arrested, and also the senator Volkonskii, who already had been tortured and run the risk of losing his life. The prince's vice-governor Korsakov has also been arrested and will be tortured; he already had his arm broken when he was run in and may also be killed, as His Majesty regards him as the worst of all the prince's creatures. Mr Kikin of the Admiralty, who was always considered a favourite, and who for a number of years held the reins of the whole Admiralty, has also been arrested and was struck with apoplexy.

And de Bie goes on mentioning names of high dignitaries, among them the governors (or past governors) of Archangel, Narva and Reval.

> This inquisition is still spreading and will have numerous consequences, but was, as everybody agrees, highly necessary. Yet His Majesty supposedly passed the message on to Prince Menshikov that he should not anticipate any trouble. However, it is to be expected that he will suffer a lot

indirectly, because of the punishment inflicted on his creatures.

On 25 January 1715 he writes that 'the inquisition is still going on'; on the other hand, he mentions that the ex-vice-admiral Cornelius Cruys was pardoned and was coming back from Kazan, where he was exiled. In his letter dated 15 February 1715 he reports that 'the great inquisition' will 'affect wallets rather than lives: I have been assured by a reliable source that His Majesty has already received over six million rubles out of it', while the tsaritsa supposedly had been given over two pounds of jewels alone (in gratuities).

In the epistle of 25 June 1715 there are a few remarks that may shed some light on the relations between Peter's allies in the war against Sweden. The Prussian court counsellor (*Hofrat*) Achenbach had come to ask Peter for a contingent of 16 000 Russian military to help him fight the Swedes on Prussian soil; but he was met with a refusal, partly because the Polish envoy Lose:

> by special order of his court, protested against a march of this Russian corps through Courland, pretending this would give the Turks an opportunity to make trouble ... There is quite some amazement here at the lack of harmony among the Northern allies; it is really worth noticing that even between the Danish, Prussian and Polish agents here there is not a bit of cooperation, to the contrary, the Prussian and the Pole counteract the Dane wherever possible and frustrate his negotiations as much as they can. However, His Majesty the tsar has the strongest confidence in and affection for the King of Denmark.

De Bie now follows the preparations for a new attack on Sweden. Peter and Menshikov will be leaving for Riga and Reval 'shortly after the wedding of the soi-disant Patriarch,[11] which will finally start next Sunday and will last for three days' (letter of 25 January 1715). In his next letter (1 February) he describes this wedding; it was:

very burlesque. There were several hundreds of disguised wedding guests and a ditto Patriarch, dressed in papal outfit. His Majesty the Tsar himself, together with Prince Trubetskoi and lieutenant-general Buturlin, beat the drum; they were followed by the so-called Tsar of Moscow [Prince F.Iu. Romodanovskii], who was sitting on a high sledge representing King David, but instead of a harp he was holding a bagpipe made of a bear's skin under his arm.

In the next letter, of 15 February 1715, one senses a certain well concealed bitterness.

I know from very good sources that there is some discontent here that His Majesty the Tsar has a permanent ambassador in The Hague,[12] whereas You Mighty Gentlemen keep only a resident; the Russian ministers maintain that it is a sign of contempt, and that in these matters equality should be observed. This has been repeatedly brought to my attention and I thought it would be good to mention it to You High Mighty Gentlemen.

There was a hitch in the appointment of a French 'commissary', which elicits the remark: 'The tsar just hates France – notably since, years ago, the royal French ships put an affront on his flags and ships.'

The next month it was Carnival week, which 'His Majesty has the habit of spending, together with his courtiers, sailing, eating and drinking'. On the last day of Carnival, a Sunday evening:

the Dutch merchant Jan Lups [visiting from Moscow], sitting with Mr De Lange, son-in-law of Vice-Admiral Cruys, was informed that His Majesty with his company was coming to visit him. He took some chairs, benches, tables, etc from the vice-admiral and Mr De Lange and several bottles of good French plus two bottles of Hungarian wine, and went home. Before long His Majesty arrived, who, if I may say so, had been drinking rather much elsewhere. Mr Lups offered His Majesty two glasses, one with Hungarian and one with

French wine. The first was selected, tried and condemned as being mixed with mead or honey – upon which His Majesty decried Mr Lange in Russian as a miser, a Jew etc. The latter, wanting to show his innocence, mentioned that he had received the wine from Mr Cruys, who in his turn had been presented with the bottles by Mr Raguzinski but it was all in vain. His Majesty's wrath grew worse, to such an extent that he told Mr Lups he had the power to take all his possessions and punish him with the knout. Whereupon he left, and a police sergeant came in to ask Mr Lups for his sword. He said he had left it in Moscow; then he was arrested and three soldiers with a petty officer were stationed in his room; however, at about 11.30 p.m. they were removed. When I asked the merchant for the reason of this unpleasant affair, he said he knew of no other reason than the fact that he had noticed, after arriving in Petersburg, that in the Senate and other institutions [*prikazy*] of His Majesty, that owed him large sums of money, they were unwilling to settle accounts, so he complained that commerce in these lands was by the day made more difficult for foreigners and that, instead, they should agree upon a commercial treaty and put it all on a firm, regular footing. Then he declared he had the intention of repatriating with his possessions and family, which His Majesty and some of his Gentlemen Senators took very much amiss of him, and they flew into a passion, as His Majesty cannot stand it when foreigners in his country, blessed by God and by their own diligence, think of returning to their homeland. The meeting has surprised this merchant even more so because he thinks he has, on very many occasions, in Russia and abroad, done great services to His Majesty.

A week later, on 15 March, de Bie reports that Lups 'in the meantime has been brought back to the tsar's court and treated very well. However, he sticks to his decision to repatriate as soon as possible.' De Bie talked several times with Lups and Jan van Gent, another merchant, who said that a commercial treaty had no chance and that:

Dutch trade is deteriorating day by day: not one tenth of Dutch merchandise and manufactured goods is being consumed as compared to some time ago, and most of what is imported has been brought from Holland by Armenians, who (because of their great privileges in this country) can sell their wares at a much lower price.

In 1716 there is, in de Bie's dispatches, regularly some news about the naval activity under Admiral Apraksin against Sweden. He mentions the conflict with the Tartars of Kazan that had flared up again (24 February). And he reports on the downfall of Prince Dolgorukii (16 October), who a year ago had been the leader of the 'grand inquisition' against Prince Menshikov's creatures. Prince Menshikov himself was accepted again and in full control. De Bie reports in the same letter how he was invited by Menshikov to a banquet in celebration of the battle of Lesnaia (where the Swedish general Count Löwenhaupt had been defeated a few years earlier). Obviously he was 'brainwashed' by Menshikov, who tried to convince him of his innocence, his positive role and the fact that so much injustice was done to him. De Bie was urged (and did comply) to invite Menshikov and a number of his friends to a party in his home.

On 21 November 1717 de Bie wrote a petition to the tsar asking for the release of the Dutch freighter *Galei*, seized by the Russian navy when a Swedish officer had been found on it (he had been admitted not by the ship's owner, but by the captain). This is the last activity of de Bie in Russia that we know of.

In 1716 the tsar left once more on a journey abroad; he visited Holland for the second time, then France. After his return very unpleasant things happened to our resident. In June 1718 Prince Kurakin conferred with the States General and reported on 'the unwanted [literally: unnecessary] demeanor of Mr De Bie' and requested his dismissal. On 14 June he was interrogated in St Petersburg about inadmissible correspondence with the States concerning Tsarevich Alexis.[13] He had in some of his reports alluded to the conflict between Peter and the prince and to the latter's sad fate, without much commentary; however, agents of Peter had opened his mail, including his official diplomatic dispatches, and found some comments that could be construed as critical of Peter. Then a letter by de Bie was brought to light that was highly critical, a sort of pasquinade, directed against the tsar and some of his dignitaries. De Bie always maintained that this letter was a fraud. He had to undergo some very unpleasant interrogations, his house was ransacked and all his papers were confiscated. The States General protested, but to no avail. De Bie was forced to leave and returned to the Netherlands. The confidence the Dutch government had in him was shown by the fact that the next year (1719) he was sent on an important diplomatic mission to Stockholm. Several of his missives from there have been preserved; but that is another story.

De Bie's dispatches do not present, of course, a complete picture of Tsar Peter's reign during the period 1711–18. Many facets of that reign, even many aspects that have to do with Russia's relations with Holland and the West, are not reflected in his letters. He does not describe, for example, the Russian debacle at the Pruth river against the Turks in 1711, the subsequent loss of Azov and the treaty of Adrianople (1713); nor does he mention Peter's invasion of Mecklenburg in 1716 with the intention of attacking Sweden from there; nor the treaty he concluded with France and Prussia in 1717. He also fails to report on Russia's turn towards Asia – Siberia, the Middle East, Persia – in the period of his residency. He pays no attention to the establishment of the Senate in 1711 or of the collegiate boards in 1717. He did not note the opening of the Naval Academy in St Petersburg in 1715. We could go on. However, we should not expect from him a detailed chronicle of political, court, social and economic life in Russia. He was sent to the Russian capital to represent the government of the United Republic and to guard the interests of Dutch citizens in Russia, although he also had to watch and report, of course, what was going on, mainly in connection with foreign policy, in government circles, at the court and among the other accredited diplomats. It is more than likely that he and other residents, in addition to what is kept in official archives, sent other, secret messages that have not been preserved; and even some of de Bie's regular missives are missing. Yet there are interesting details in his letters, especially regarding Peter the Great; these are details that are not known from other sources and that have at least an illustrative value.

NOTES

This paper is based on material from the General State Archive (Algemeen Rijksarchief) in The Hague, Netherlands, Liassen Muscovie 7364, 7366, 7367 and 7397. Some of de Bie's letters are in the Anthonie Heinsius Archive in the Rijksarchief. All translations from the Dutch are the author's.

In his missives de Bie followed the New Style (Gregorian) calendar, according to which, for example, Peter's birthday, 30 May in the Old Style (Julian) calendar still in use in Russia, which was eleven days behind New Style, occurs on 10 June.

1 Compare J.S.A.M. van Koningsbrugge, 'The Dutch Republic, Sweden and Russia, 1697–1708, and the Secret Activities of Cornelis Cruys and Johannus van den Bergh', *Russia and the Low Countries in the Eighteenth Century (Rossiia i Niderlandy v XVIII veke)*, ed. E. Waegemans, Groningen, 1998, pp. 51–61.

2 See L. Bittner, L. Gross, eds, *Repertorium der diplomatischen Vertreter aller Länder seit dem Westfälischen Frieden*, I: 1648–1715, Berlin, 1935, s.v. Jacob de Bie.

3 Kurakin, who was married to the sister of Peter's first wife, was to replace Andrei Artamovovich Matveev, who had been Russian minister in The Hague for many years. Matveev was an interesting figure, the author of a whole series of books, including an autobiography (see M.A. Alpatov, *Russkaia istoricheskaia mysl' i Zapadnaia Evropa: XVII – pervaia chetvert' XVIII veka*, Moscow, 1976, 275 ff.).

4 According to Kurakin, Menshikov 'found great favour [with the tsar] and climbed so high that he actually reigned over the entire empire, received the title of field marshal and was made by the tsar an imperial count, and soon thereafter a prince ... Talking about his character, I can be brief: he was quite mediocre, uneducated, he could not even write, but had only learned to put his signature; for he was of very low birth, lower than the gentry' (B.I. Kurakin, 'Gistoriia o tsare Petre Alekseeviche, 1692–1694 gg', in B.V. Anan'ich *et al.*, eds, *Petr Velikii: Vospominaniia, dnevnikovye zapisi, anekdoty*, St Petersburg–Moscow, 1993, p. 83.

5 This must have been Nikita Moiseevich Zotov, who constantly played the part of Prince-Pope in the 'Council of Fools and Jesters' with whom Peter amused himself. See M.I. Semevskii, 'Petr Velikii kak iumorist' in his *Slovo i delo!, 1700–1725*, St Petersburg, 4th printing, 1884; reprinted, Moscow, 1991, pp. 279–334. Zotov died in 1717 and was succeeded by Peter Buturlin as new 'Prince-Pope'. His son, Konon Nikitich, rose to high rank in the Russian navy.

6 Etiquette required that a ruler was never referred to with a personal or possessive pronoun, but always with his title and name. Likewise, the States General could never be addressed with 'you', but only with 'You High Mighty Gentlemen' (*U Hoogmogende Heeren*).

7 Boris Petrovich Sheremetev, member of a leading boyar family, received the title of *graf* (count) in 1706 (he died in 1719); as a Field Marshal, he commanded the Russian armies during most of the Northern War; he also had been the Tsar's emissary to the Viennese court.

8 It is unclear in which language they spoke; as is known, the only foreign language Peter knew was Dutch, but he was not fluent in it. We do not know how well, if at all, de Bie spoke Russian.

9 Andrei (Hendrik) Osterman was the son of a Lutheran pastor from Westphalia. He had studied at Jena University and knew Latin, French and Dutch as well as German and Russian. He came to Amsterdam and enlisted on a ship bound for Russia; on the personnel list he figures as 'second mate' (*onderstuurman*), but not long after his arrival in Moscow he became Admiral Cruys' secretary. In Russian state service since 1711, he was involved in diplomatic activities and was appointed in 1718 to the Russian delegation at the Aland Congress (which was to lead to the Treaty of Nystad in 1721). See P. Dukes, *The Making of Russian Absolutism 1613–1801*, London, New York, Longman, 1982, p. 79 and J. Scheltema, *Rusland en de Nederlanden beschouwd in derzelver wederkeerige betrekkingen*, II, Amsterdam, 1817, p. 96.

10 Peter's apoplectic fits are described by Just Juel, the Danish envoy to the tsar in 1709–11, who left a diary of his Russian years. Juel was dumbfounded by the amounts of food and drink Peter and his entourage consumed every day. The diary confirms and adds to the image of the tsar which the Dutch residents present in their letters. See 'Zapiski Iusta Iulia' in Anan'ich *et al.*, *Petr Velikii*, pp. 85–125.

11 This was the mock patriarch Zotov. The whole 'wedding' was apparently a hoax.

12 Prince Boris Kurakin had just been promoted to the rank of Russian ambassador to the Netherlands government.

13 See N.N. Bantysh-Kamenskii, *Obzor vneshnikh snoshenii Rossii*, 4 vols, Moscow, I, 1894, s.v. 1714 and 1718.

Part VI

The Court and the Arts

14 Catherine I, Her Court and Courtiers

John Alexander

Catherine I, the second wife of Peter the Great and his successor as ruler of Russia from 1725–27, lives on in history as an intriguing figure of obscure background.[1] Neither the year of her birth (1679?, 1683?) nor her parentage nor ethnicity is certain.[2] Jewish origins have been bruited, and Alexander Menshikov's cunning sponsorship derived from intimate knowledge of Catherine and Peter.[3] Her ascent astonished all, then and now. Indeed, the rise to celebrity of 'the Livland Zolushka' (Cinderella) betokened extraordinary powers physical, psychological and parapsychological.[4] No wonder she was compared to the legendary viragos Semiramis of Babylon, Tamara of the Scythians and the several Amazon queens.[5]

Her Amazonian physique is affirmed by various portraits (see Plate 10) such as a recently reprinted sketch in a revealing robe.[6] That she was the first woman to be crowned empress and gain the throne of the Russian Empire, inaugurating seven decades of 'Russian matriarchate', sealed her fame and fortune. If her own reign (28 January 1725 – 6 May 1727) proved 'far too short to accomplish anything noteworthy', it did at least avoid Petrine excess.[7]

Her Russian name (Ekaterina) adorned palaces at Ekaterinhof on the edge of Petersburg, at Katharinenthal outside Reval (Tallinn) and at Tsarskoe Selo, as well as Ekaterinburg in the Urals. Her portrait was painted by Karl Moor in Amsterdam in 1717 and in enamel miniatures by Grigorii Musikiiskii, while her elder daughter, Tsesarevna Anna Petrovna (1708–28), sat for foreign and Russian portraitists.[8] The Order of St Catherine, with its motto 'For Love and Fatherland', celebrated her survival skills amid the Pruth disaster of 1711. 'Without Regard to the Imbecility and Tenderness of her Sex, ... in that critical Juncture she behaved herself not like a Woman but a Man', Peter later affirmed, 'wherefore our whole Army will witness, and can testify to our whole Empire.'[9] Catherine received the new award for elite women on her nameday, 24 November 1714.[10] Dedicated to ransoming prisoners of war, it was the single Russian knightly order reserved for women and was regularly conferred on prospective imperial spouses, notably her namesake, the future Catherine II, in 1744.[11] In 1723 Peter transferred his flag to the ship of the line *Sv. Ekaterina*.[12]

MISTRESS, TSARITSA, IMPERATRITSA

Contradictory qualities animate the images associated with Catherine over the centuries. Nikolai Pavlenko ranks her 'among women of the rarest destiny', speculating that her influence on Peter proceeded through three phases: as mistress from 1702 to 1711, as tsaritsa 1712–24 and as empress 1724–25. Her sway arose from a rare blend of human and feminine traits comprising tact, submissiveness and stubborn independence.[13] Certainly she admirably filled the role of imperial wife and mother with her frequent pregnancies and family concerns.[14]

Catherine exhibited 'Amazon' attributes of hardiness and endurance, ingenuity and initiative, muscular strength and 'heroic health' in travelling thousands of miles through Russia, the Baltic lands and Northern Europe.[15] She even gave birth at Wesel on 2 January 1717 to a baby boy, Pavel Petrovich, who lived barely three hours and whose tiny coffin was sent to Petersburg three weeks later.[16] That she was survived by only two daughters (from an estimated twelve live births) also befits the myth of the ancient Amazons, who supposedly annihilated their male offspring. Reflecting the Amazons' equestrian skill, Catherine rode astride like Muscovite elite women since the sixteenth century and at the head of the line en route to the Pruth campaign.[17] Later she mainly travelled by carriage, and by boat as far as Derbent during the

Persian campaign of 1722, a venture to the Amazon homeland that no Russian ruler or spouse had seen before.[18]

Blessed with an attractive exterior, good humour and great vitality, Catherine wore a colourful Amazon outfit amid Shrovetide masquerades in Moscow in 1722 and 1723 and St Petersburg in 1724. When crowned at Moscow on 7 May 1724 she was lauded as a peer of Semiramis, Tamara and Penthesileia of the Amazons (see Plate 11). Even so, the coronation outfit weighed so heavily that, already weakened by three days' prayer and fasting beforehand, she paused several times amid the ceremony to catch her breath.[19] Towards the end of the month she fell ill, only returning to Petersburg a month after Peter on 8 July, still weak and fatigued.[20] She did not accompany Peter on his last trips outside Petersburg but attended a comedy about her coronation on 10 October for which she tipped the players 150 ducats.[21] Soon after Peter's return on 27 October the Willem Mons embezzlement scandal broke, alienating the consorts over the last ten weeks of Peter's life. Catherine's chancery was investigated and revenues withheld so that she had to borrow 1000 ducats from her court ladies.[22] Mons was beheaded and his accomplices scourged and exiled on 16 November 1724 whereas the tsar-emperor expired on 28 January 1725. Their daughter Natalia Petrovna (1718–25) died of 'spotted fever' on 3 March 1725, supposedly infected by the 'miasma' from Peter's corpse lying in state. She was buried a day after her father on 11 March.[23]

Catherine was rumoured to have poisoned Peter, ostensibly in revenge for the execution of her lover, Mons.[24] Some suspected that she and Menshikov conspired against Peter's recovery and that Menshikov later poisoned her with tainted bonbons.[25] Recent reconsideration of this period rejects such tales, however, contending that the consorts were reconciled before his death, and that she truly mourned him.[26] And while accepting her infidelity as proven, Pavlenko and others acknowledge Peter's own double standard and attribute his death to drunkenness, debauchery and venereal disease.[27]

THE COURT

Catherine's career coincided with the emergence of the imperial court as a Europeanised (and feminised) institution. Like other European courts of the early modern era, the early imperial Russian court resists definition.[28] In one sense the court comprised the ruler, the ruling family as a whole and the ruler's immediate entourage. In the broader administrative sense the court encompassed many institutions of the highly centralised state. It employed a substantial support staff to house and feed the ruling family, and to minister to familial, religious and dynastic needs and interests. At its upper levels the court comprised three kinds of elite servitors: officers of the court, courtiers and court ladies.[29] When the family's ceremonial functions are added, the support structures and personnel expanded dramatically.

The earliest full roster of court personnel, from 1730, listed 625 persons with annual money salaries totalling 83 571 roubles.[30] Presumably the Petrine court – or courts as more Romanovs received at least minimal household establishments – was somewhat smaller.[31] Whatever the exact number of servitors, they were far fewer than the 2000 service personnel living at the Winter Palace in the mid-nineteenth century or the 1600 court personnel employed in 1914.[32] The new imperial court consumed some 450 000 roubles annually (figure for 1725), or 4.4 per cent of total state expenditures.[33] Expenses varied wildly from year to year in accordance with official travels and special celebrations such as Catherine's coronation. A roster of horses assigned to the consorts upon their return from abroad in December 1717 listed sixty-nine for Peter's entourage and ninety-eight for Catherine's.[34] The Stables Bureau had been one of the largest court-related administrations in Muscovite times, with over 700 personnel by 1673, and though Peter and Catherine were less 'horse crazy' than their predecessors, the court's frequent travels and ceremonies required large numbers of horses and stable personnel.[35]

The city of St Petersburg, primary seat of the court from about 1712, blossomed into a European-type *Residenz Stadt* with many newly reformed offices 'in residence' and a population approaching 40 000 by 1725.[36] But Moscow remained the empire's largest city and retained many central institutions and functions. The court invariably spent time in both capitals, Russia's 'two hearts', which also housed in city or in hinterland many imperial palaces and gardens.[37] To be sure, diplomats routinely spoke of the Court of St Petersburg as a shorthand for the imperial Russian government.

The court comprised a whole series of institutions and offices such as the Court Staff, the Court Stables Chancellery, the Chamber-Stallmaster Office, the Workshop and Arms Chamber, the Senior Huntmaster Chancellery, the Petersburg and Moscow Court-Inspector's Office, and the Estates Chancellery of His Imperial Majesty. Many of these had evolved under the Muscovite Chancellery of the Great Palace, from which the peripatetic Peter I extracted a Palace Campaign Chancellery in Petersburg in 1704. Two decades later *Ober-Gofmeister* Matvei Olsuf'ev (who is profiled below) petitioned for service rank and jurisdiction, and on 2 June 1724 he informed the Senate that by imperial decree all matters of the former Chancellery of the Great Palace were under his supervision. The Main Palace Chancellery in St Petersburg, with a branch in Moscow, formally assumed jurisdiction in 1726. This minimalist court administration employed only thirty-one servitors in 1723, up from twenty-two in 1718.[38] Seventy military men were listed in 1718 but none in 1723, perhaps reflecting the end of the Northern War. During the consorts' visit to the Olonets waters in February 1722 Catherine tipped 104 soldiers of the Chernigov Regiment a rouble each for doing sentry duty.[39]

The German or barely Russified names of the court offices originated in the flood of foreign terms drenching Petrine Russia, the foreign ranks carefully equated to Muscovite equivalents. Although their placement in the general hierarchy of service was established by the Table of Ranks in 1722, many ranks were never awarded nor specific duties explicated; several were barely used and soon died out.[40] The 1730 listing began with *ober-gofmeister, ober-kamerger, gofmarshal, kamergery* (chamberlains), *kamer-iunkery* (gentlemen of the bedchamber), *freiliny* (maids of honour) and also included *karlitsy* and *karly* (female and male dwarves), *arapy* (Arabs or Blackamoors) and several kitchen ranks – for example *zil'berdiner, kellermeister, kofi-shenk, konfekturir, tafel'dekery* – and *pazhi* (pages), *musikanty*, etc.[41]

How court personnel were chosen is uncertain. Apparently Catherine had much to say in the matter and often acted on the advice of friends and relatives of appointees. On 10 April 1723, for example, she instructed Matvei Olsuf'ev to hire Sidor Lazyrev, a serf cook who had petitioned to join the imperial household.[42] Emperor Peter, however, approved the petition of Baroness Maria Stroganova in 1724 to appoint her son *kamerger*, but this may have been a stray instance.[43] Many courtiers of both sexes were related or became related to others at court, and there was much continuity in court families over the generations.

High officials such as Alexis Vasil'evich Makarov (1675–1750), Peter's cabinet-secretary from 1704 and head of the tsar's personal secretariat, wielded weight in court affairs without holding court office. Of modest provincial background, Makarov first married the daughter of a minor Senate official and later, his own status having risen impressively, the wealthy widow Princess Anastasia Ivanovna Odoevskaia.[44] He accompanied the consorts on their frequent travels, thanking Anna Ivanovna (the future empress) from Reval in May 1721 for her hospitality and attention to his wife at Riga earlier that spring.[45] His court-related duties increased after the death of the dowager Tsaritsa Praskovia Fedorovna in October 1723 to include supervision of the estates of her daughter Ekaterina Duchess of Mecklenburg and her sisters.[46] His court connections, correspondence with a multitude of persons, and accommodating personality – 'this Makaroff is esteemed an ingenious man and was a great favourite of the late Czar and Czarinna', commented the English envoy Rondeau in September 1728 – conferred extraordinary authority and further ascent until a sudden fall under Empress Anna.[47]

The Romanov family had proliferated from the mid-seventeenth century, as Tsar Alexis Mikhailovich during his long reign (1645–76) sired thirteen children with Maria Miloslavskaia (1626?–69) and three with Natalia Naryshkina (1653–94). Ten of these offspring were females who lived longish lives; five survived into the 1700s and yet none married. Only three males even reached adulthood (Fedor died in 1682 at age twenty without issue, despite two marriages), and only Peter I left any male heir through the male line among an estimated fifteen children from two marriages – his grandson, Peter Alekseevich (1715–30). Moreover, his half-brother Ivan Alekseevich (1666–96) fathered five daughters, and Ivan's formidable widow Praskovia Fedorovna née Saltykova (1664–1723) presided over a substantial court and was buried with imperial pomp in St Petersburg's new Alexander Nevskii monastery.[48] Three of her five daughters reached adulthood: Ekaterina Ivanovna (1691–1733), Anna Ivanovna (1693–1740) and Praskovia Ivanovna (1694–1731). All three married, two into European princely houses. Anna Ivanovna, who lost her husband a mere few weeks after their wedding in St Petersburg on 31 October 1710, reigned as dowager duchess of Courland from 1710 until her surprise selection as empress in 1730. Ekaterina Ivanovna ('Svet-Katiushka' to her mother) resided briefly in Mecklenburg after her marriage in 1716 before returning in 1722 with her daughter, later known as Anna Leopol'dovna (1718–46). Praskovia Fedorovna, sickly from youth, secretly married Senator and General Ivan Il'ich Dmitriev-Mamonov (1681– 1730), whom she barely outlived.[49]

Peter's first decade of personal rule after 1689 largely repudiated Muscovite court practice. He downplayed ceremonial and cavalcades like the annual pilgrimage on 25 September to the Trinity Monastery, reassigning many grooms and stable boys to his play regiments.[50] The Grand Embassy introduced the young tsar to European court culture, but he also frequented an anti-court of hard-drinking male cronies, jesters and dwarves that scandalised foreign observers. Later the English envoy Whitworth explained these actions as Peter's breaking with 'formal servitude' and his desire to avoid expense and constraint in wartime.[51] Upon encountering Peter at Narva in November 1709, Danish envoy Just Juel recalled that 'the so-called princes behaved without shame or conscience: they shrieked, bellowed, guffawed, puked, spat and even dared to spit in the face of regular people.' Juel witnessed a food fight among Peter's table companions and marvelled how the tsar ignored their howling in his ear.[52] The sturdy Dane lived in horror of the drinking bouts at Petrine entertainments, noting in one case that straw several feet deep was put on the floor for a New Year's dinner for 182 persons that lasted sixteen hours and featured a fat man riding about the room firing a pistol.[53] Another time Juel had to draw a knife against courtiers forcing drink on him. Still he repeatedly insisted that nothing could be accomplished at the Russian court without alcoholic assistance. Juel also lamented the difficulties of access to Peter, his frequent travels and sudden departures, informal way of conducting business and lack of regular court personnel.[54]

By contrast, a European-type court gradually took shape around Peter's female relatives, especially Praskovia Fedorovna at Izmailovo and, gradually, around Catherine at Preobrazhenskoe. The latter entourage included Peter's sister Natalia Alekseevna (1673–1716), Anna (Anis'ia) Kirillovna Tolstaia, Menshikov's sister Maria Danilovna, and the Arsen'ev sisters, one of whom, Daria Mikhailovna, married Menshikov in August 1706.[55] In April 1708 Peter received his female relatives at St Petersburg, where they were taken by water to Kronstadt and Peterhof.[56] The visit presaged permanent transfer to Petersburg, capped by Peter's public marriage as rear-admiral (not tsar) to Catherine on 19 February 1712 in a modest secular ceremony.[57] Whitworth praised 'the famous Czarina' and 'this memorable Woman'. At a court ball her affability enchanted: 'As they began the minuet, She squeezed him by the hand, and said in a whisper, *Have you forgot little Kate?*'[58]

Catherine cultivated a European style of court life for her numerous offspring and stepchildren. Tsarevich Alexis's marriage at Torgau in October 1711 to Princess Charlotte of Brunswick-Wolfenbüttel (1694–1715) brought his new wife's German entourage back to Moscow, thereby intensifying German court influence.[59] Their daughter, Natalia Alekseevna (1714–28), and son, Peter Alekseevich, the future Peter II, personified further Europeanisation of the Romanov dynasty. All the new Europeanised court offices, which began in 1711 with the appointment of *kamergery*, were under Catherine's direct authority throughout Peter's lifetime.[60] At Riga in the spring of 1721 the Holsteiner Count Bassevich found a 'brilliant' and numerous court largely organised by the tsaritsa's taste and mostly German in culture.[61] During her own reign she instituted weekly public court-days, '*kurdakhi*' (*kurtagi*), a European custom also cultivated by Anna Ivanovna at Mitau in Courland.[62]

Tsar Peter 'prides himself in a Prussian original', Whitworth reported. 'He speaks High-Dutch pretty readily, which is now growing the Court language.'[63] This may have given rise to the myth that Peter intended to make Dutch the official language and turn Russia into Holland.[64] Certainly it hints at court society's cosmopolitanism. Even the illiterate Menshikov spoke and understood German, spent much time abroad and by 1710 'formed a Court after the fashion of the little German Princes, of chamberlains, marshals, secretaries, &c. most foreigners'.[65] And though Catherine herself could hardly read or write in any language, she 'spoke fluently in four, namely Russian, German, Swedish and Polish and to those it may be added that she understood some French'.[66] She corresponded in Russian with the other branch of the tsarist family, congratulating Praskovia Fedorovna from Riga in April 1721 upon visiting the Olonets waters, passing on news of Anna Ivanovna, and sending a maidservant to Ekaterina Ivanovna in February 1722.[67] The next year Praskovia Fedorovna thanked her for dispatching a doctor to treat her younger daughter's fever and her infant granddaughter's diarrhoea.[68] Catherine kept in touch with Anna Ivanovna, too, thanking her from Reval in May 1721 for a gift of cloth, and from Moscow in March 1722 passing on news of her mother and sisters and the death of an aunt, Tsarevna Maria Alekseevna (1660–1722), in Moscow on 9 March.[69] She brokered Anna Ivanovna's reconciliation with her mother just before Praskovia's death in 1723.[70]

The Europeanising court resulted in greater public visibility and prominent ceremonial roles for elite women. Petrine public celebrations routinely featured women, even at the launching of warships and the annual commemoration of the victories at Schlüsselburg (1702), Poltava (1709) and Hangö (1714). Gigantic masquerades also became very popular, as attested by the marathon festivities staged at the Chetyre Frigata (the Four Frigates, a coffee house near the Senate in St Petersburg) celebrating the peace of Nystad from 10 September to 4 October 1721 and again from 30 August to 6 September 1723 with fifty-eight groups of costumed revellers.[71]

On the thirty-ninth anniversary of Peter's coronation on 25 June 1721 the young Holsteiner chamberlain Frederick Wilhelm von Bergholz (1702–67) rapturously described Catherine's court at the Summer Garden:

> There, beside a beautiful fountain, sat Her Majesty the Tsaritsa in a very rich outfit. Our eyes were immediately

attracted to the older princess [Anna Petrovna], a brunette as lovely as an angel. Her facial colouring, hands and waist are marvellously fine. She greatly resembles the tsar and is rather tall for a woman. At the tsaritsa's left stood the other princess [Elizaveta Petrovna], fair skinned and very tender; her face, like that of the elder one, is exceptionally amiable and attractive ... The princesses' dresses were of lovely two-hued material without gold or silver, and their heads were adorned with precious stones and pearls, according to the latest French fashion and with a splendour that would have done honour to the best French hairdresser ...

Among the other ladies that were here I [Bergholz continues] especially admired Princess Cherkasskaia [1696–1747], who, I was assured, is considered the foremost beauty at court. But I counted as many as thirty lovely ladies among whom many yielded little to our [European] ladies in amiability, good manners and beauty. I confess I did not expect the local court to be so splendid. Her Majesty the Tsaritsa has four Kamer-Iunkers, all handsome and stately young men; two are Russian, Shepelev and Chevkin, and two are German, Balk and Mons (the second cousin of Lady Balk, much loved by the Tsaritsa, it is said) ... Her Majesty's pages wear green uniforms with red lapels and gold braid on all seams, like trumpeters and horn players; but lackeys and grooms, of which Her Majesty has a multitude, do not sport this braid; yet even so they are dressed beautifully. In the orchestra of the sovereign lady are many good German musicians, who are obliged to wear beautiful green coats (in general they don't like liveries). In a word, the tsaritsa's court is as fine and brilliant as almost all the German courts.[72]

Here Bergholz describes the inner core or bedchamber of Catherine's court whose servants and their salaries were enumerated at Preobrazhenskoe on 8 February 1723. The household nature of this roster shows up in informal name usages, forenames and patronymics; likely surnames have been reconstructed from later listings. The roster begins with four chamber gentlemen:

Willem Mons, Rodion Koshelev, Dmitrii Shepelev and Petr Balk @ 100 roubles per year; then chamber lady Madam Iaganna Petrovna [Karo?] @ 120 roubles; Ustin'ia Petrovna @ 90; Kozma Ivanovich [Spiridonov?] @ 60; Tat'iana Gerasimovna [Kobyliakova?] @ 50; Katerina Ivanovna @ 50 from two budgets; chamber page Gustav Golshtein @ 100; Dar'ia Gavrilovna @ 25; pages Grigor'i Kvashnin-Samarin @ 45; Petr Samorokof @ 45; Andreian Shuvalov @ 45; dwarf Moke Chelishchev @ 45; laundresses Katerina Kirilovna, Katerina Matveevna and Akulina Rodionovna @ 12; bandura player Semen [Tarabanov] @ 20; cobbler Isai Alekseev @ 21; hajduks Vasilii Grigor'ev and Aleksandr Markov @ 40; wigmaker Krest'ian Grigor'ev @ 5; blackamoor Nikolai Grigor'ev and wife Avdot'ia @ 10; protomoinitsa (special laundress) Fedor'ia Konstantinovna for 1722 @ 12; gudok player Nastas'ia Ignat'evna for 1723 @ 6; Nikita Il'in @ 21; Ivan Petukhov @ 36; guard Klim Varfolomeev with the laundresses @ 6 – a total of twenty-four persons with annual salaries of some 1200 roubles.[73]

Some almost certainly had additional income and all received grants for travel expenses.[74] Willem Mons notoriously received presents from the empress and grandees seeking access to her. Besides, salaries were a mere fraction of the 25 000 roubles for which Vasilii Olsuf'ev sought Menshikov's authorisation in October 1722 to purchase supplies for the court's return from the Persian campaign, or the 136 000 roubles budgeted for the imperial court in 1725 (an exceptional sum because of Peter's burial expenses and Anna Petrovna's marriage to Duke Karl-Friedrich of Holstein-Gottorp in Petersburg on 21 May 1725, the second time a Romanov princess had been wed in Russia).[75] All these court servitors were quite diverse in nationality, native language and religion.[76]

The Europeanising court took on a pronounced feminine appearance as 'the female revolution of Peter the Great' abolished the Muscovite women's quarter (*terem*) and rapidly embraced European modes of public sociability. Prince Shcherbatov later reflected:

> It was pleasant for the female sex, who had hitherto been almost slaves in their own homes to enjoy all the pleasures of society, to adorn themselves with clothes and fineries, which enhanced the beauty of their faces and set off their fine figures.[77]

Hence this 'sudden baring of womanly beauty' brought 'the frolicsome deity Eros flying into the Kremlin windows from Europe'.[78] The shadowy feminist commentator just quoted envisions the Petrine court hyperbolically:

> a bacchanalia of immorality with kisses on the lips of severed heads, hypersexual embraces, demons, devils, sodomites, whores, pederasts, nymphomaniacs, necrophiles – all of them dressed as bats, Dutch peasant girls, American savages, Polish noblewomen, pigs, English queens, Japanese geishas, golden asses of Apuleius and even some inanimate objects such as the notorious Volga boulder.

And Peter allegedly presided with absolute authority and without distinguishing between male and female sexual partners.[79]

Drinking and dancing became primary preoccupations of Russian elite society in the latter part of Peter's reign, with women prominently involved. Praskovia Fedorovna won renown for lavish hospitality at Izmailovo that always provided strong drink.[80] Catherine held her liquor well – an essential trait in managing her boozing husband who popularised new kinds of liquor – and she instituted an *ober-shenksha* to provide drink for her ladies.[81] Indeed, the consorts often joked about drinking or drank to drown sorrows. On 2 May 1713 Peter wrote from aboard the *Poltava*:

> Katerinushka, my friend, hello. I send you a bottle of Hungarian (and beg you, for God's sake, not to grieve: you will thereby inflict distress on me). God grant you to drink for our health. For we have drunk yours. [P.S.] Whoever does not drink today shall incur a great penalty.[82]

The grief mentioned may have been the frail health of infant daughters Natalia and Margarita who died on 27 May and 27 June 1715 at age two and ten months respectively.[83]

On a coarser note, both consorts attended the flamboyant wedding of Peter Ivanovich Buturlin (d. 1724), 'prince-pope' of the All-Drunken Assembly, on 10 September 1721 at the Chetyre Frigata, where the elderly newly-weds swilled vodka from vessels resembling *partium genitalium* – '(female for the husband, male for the wife) and rather big ones at that', remarked Bergholz – before retiring to a wooden pyramid with holes to allow observation!'[84]

Bergholz found the Moscow ladies passionate for dancing too, and recorded how they baited their Petersburg counterparts as great drunkards when the court arrived in Moscow in early 1722 to celebrate the peace of Nystad. Before Peter and Catherine left Moscow for the Olonets mineral waters he ordered the Moscow grandees to hold 'assemblies' three times a week. Although Bergholz complained that the sexes kept apart at these social functions when not dancing and did not converse, he later acknowledged that his conversational Russian improved greatly under the influence of drink.[85]

An informal hierarchy emerged among Catherine's court ladies. At the top were *stats-damy*, usually from aristocratic families. Catherine's coronation train was carried by five great ladies: Princess Daria Mikhailovna Menshikova, Countess Ekaterina Ivanovna Golovkina (1702–91), Countess Maria Andreevna Brius (Bruce) neé Margarita Manteufel, Anna Semenovna Buturlina and Princess Anna L'vovna Trubetskaia neé Naryshkina (1704–76). They were followed by six more of Catherine's own ladies: Anna Ivanovna Olsuf'eva, Elizaveta Ivanovna Vil'bua (Villebois, daughter of Pastor Glück), Baroness Kampengauzen – born von Leschut and wife of a Swedish soldier, Johann Balthasar (Ivan Ivanovich, 1689–1758) who later became a baron in Russian service – Princess Varvara Mikhailovna Volkonskaia and her sister Naryshkina.[86] These were followed by the other ladies of Catherine's suite, thirteen married and twelve unmarried (not named, unfortunately).[87] Certainly they included Matrena Balk (to be profiled below), Baroness Marfa Ivanovna Osterman (born Streshneva), Anna Golovkina (daughter of Chancellor Golovkin), Anna Ivanovna Kramer (1694–1770; daughter of a Narva merchant, Russian prisoner of war, later in service to General Balk, and *gofmeisterina* for Natalia Alekseevna), Baroness Maria Iakovlevna Stroganova (born Novosil'tseva), Princess Anastasia Petrovna Golitsyna (1655–1729), Evdokia Kosheleva, Varvara Mikhailovna Arsen'eva (Menshikov's sister-in-law), Countess Anna Gavrilovna Iaguzhinskaia (daughter of Chancellor Golovkin, she died in exile in 1749), and Anna Kirilovna Tolstaia.[88] Several of these ladies were foreign born and most had lived in St Petersburg's multilingual cosmopolitan society for a decade or more.

The Romanov court became legendary for splendid ceremonies, a trend culminating in Catherine's coronation at Moscow on 7 May 1724.[89] An elaborate description of the largely secular event was published in Russian, the first time that such a ceremony had been celebrated in print.

Planning took almost six months, necessitating several postponements, particularly so that the ladies could obtain the necessary finery; Matrena Balk informed Bergholz on 10 April that the ceremony would not happen for two weeks. Though Peter had wished it a week earlier, on the Duke of Holstein's birthday, Catherine's ladies needed at least two weeks, notably the twenty-four ladies including herself slated to wear special gowns. Only Catherine wore all gold; the others had to make do with silver and gold fabrics. At the end of April the date was still uncertain. Only on 4 May did chamber page Gustav Gol'shtein tell Bergholz that it would definitely be on Thursday, 7 May.[90]

The coronation festivities are detailed in Wortman's recent treatment.[91] In a brief oration Feofan Prokopovich compared the empress to Semiramis and Penthesileia of the Amazons and other notable women rulers. But Philip Longworth demurs: 'behind the glittering regalia, Catherine still looked for all the world like Peter's mistress: a short, corpulent woman with large feet and blackened hair.'[92] The festivities ended three days later with a gigantic firework display which lasted more than two hours. Bergholz expostulated:

> I don't think there have been many like it in the world. Looking back on the coronation that had been completed, one could not but be amazed at Providence that had raised up an

empress from the humble estate in which she had been born and had existed before, to the apogee of earthly honour.[93]

COURTIERS

By the 1720s the Petrine-Catherinian court comprised several hundred servitors of varied types. Aside from exceptional cases like the ill-fated Willem Mons (1688–1724) and Maria Hamilton (beheaded on 14 March 1719 for abortion and infanticide), most courtiers and court ladies of the era are faint figures.[94] Prominent among Catherine's ladies was Matrena Ivanovna Balk, the elder sister of Anna Mons (d. 1714), Peter's mistress from about 1692 to 1703. Born in Minden on the Weser and daughters of a German wine merchant in Moscow, the Mons sisters both married, the elder's union with Fedor Nikitich Balk (1670–1739) in 1699 supposedly arranged by the tsar himself. Balksha, as she became known in Russian, suffered house arrest for several years after 1703 when Anna Mons was found to have 'betrayed' the tsar. Balksha eventually rejoined her husband, brigadier from 1705 and general-major from 1716, so she was often called 'general'sha Balksha' while he was Russian vice-governor of Riga in 1710 and then governor of occupied Elbing from 1710 to 1714. Through Catherine's good offices she became *gofmeisterina* for Ekaterina Ivanovna, the newly married Duchess of Mecklenburg. With the duchess and her daughter Balksha returned to Russia in 1722. As *gofmeisterina* and *stats-dama* to Catherine she functioned as a power in court society until arrested in November 1724 with her brother, Willem (Villim Ivanovich Mons in Russian guise), *kamer-iunker* to Catherine from 1714 and chamberlain from 1724. Her eminence also passed on to a beautiful and outspoken daughter, Natalia Fedorovna (1699–1763), whose marriage at age seventeen to the young future chamberlain and later vice-admiral Stepan Vasil'evich Lopukhin was brokered by Peter himself.[95] Lopukhina was named *stats-dama* to Empress Anna Ivanovna in 1730, carried on an extended affair with Count Löwenwolde and later suffered disgrace, torture and exile under Elizabeth.[96] Willem Mons' household grew in size to employ nineteen persons including a major domo from 1707 and later one dwarf and two Kalmyks.[97] Found guilty of extortion, Balksha was condemned to eleven lashes of the knout and perpetual exile, a sentence lessened by Catherine's intervention to five lashes. Her sons – Pavel (Iakov before conversion to Orthodoxy) Fedorovich Balk, who later became Balk-Polev (1699–1743) after marrying Maria Fedorovna Poleva, the last of her kin, and Peter Fedorovich Balk (1710–62) – were posted to occupied Persian territory, but Catherine pardoned them and their mother soon after Peter I's death. The sons enjoyed successful careers in service: Pavel was a chamberlain under Peter II in 1727 and his three daughters married into aristocratic clans: Shcherbatov, Naryshkin and Saltykov. Peter served as general-adjutant. Although Balksha herself died soon after returning to Moscow, her husband's subsequent career apparently continued without incident and a daughter or daughter-in-law, Sofia Balk, was employed at court as mistress of the wardrobe (*kastaliansha*) from 1727 until at least 1740.[98] The Mons-Balk family's career in court service thus exhibited immense social success and staying power, scarcely interrupted by the catastrophe of Peter's final months.

Of obscure background, the brothers Matvei Dmitrievich (d. 1743) and Vasilii Dmitrievich Olsuf'ev (d. 1723) – also spelled Alsuf'ev – both entered state service around 1700 and eventually became fixtures at court for more than twenty years each.[99] Literate and well brought up, although no specifics are known about their parentage and education, they served Peter as *marshalki* (wee marshals). Matvei ostensibly waited upon Peter, who on 3 December 1709 in Petersburg ordered medical assistance for his trusted subordinate from Dr Blumentrost and a good surgeon; whereas Vasilii mainly attended Catherine, but their jurisdictions overlapped in practice.[100] They fulfilled varied duties, Matvei delivering Peter's letters to Moscow officials in October 1710 and assisting in the lengthy search for Catherine's relatives.[101] The brothers corresponded regularly with Menshikov and kept him informed of Peter's movements and moods.[102] Both travelled with the consorts, but only Matvei went on the Persian campaign when he was named *obergofmeister* in Astrakhan on Peter's nameday, 29 June 1722, whereas Vasilii stayed in Moscow, perhaps from illness that led to his death in December 1723.

After two marriages left Matvei widowed, in 1711 he married *freilina* Anna Ivanovna Seniavina (daughter of Admiral Ivan Seniavin), who became a *stats-dama*. They parented four sons and four daughters.[103] Vasilii Olsuf'ev was one of only a few new Russian aristocrats to marry a foreigner – the Dane or Swede Evva Hollander – by whom he had a son, Count Adam Vasil'evich Olsuf'ev, an eminent official and courtier.[104] Evva enjoyed high favour – Peter himself named Adam to complement her forename – and she contributed a tooth to his collection. However, while she was in late pregnancy in November 1721 the tsar refused, despite Catherine's intercession, to exempt Olsuf'eva from a penalty drink for missing a victory masquerade. She supposedly sent the tiny corpse of her still-born child preserved in alcohol to court.[105] Whatever the truth of Bergholz' lurid tale, both consorts attended Vasilii's elaborate funeral in Petersburg on 12 December 1723. Bergholz also attended and disdained the Russian custom of kissing the corpse however putrid, and noted how moved many onlookers were by the widow's wailing. Young Adam served the guests at the funeral meal.[106] On 9 December 1726 Olsuf'eva petitioned Catherine to forgive her late husband's diversion of 1800 roubles from her revenues.[107] She soon remarried a Colonel Wensel, who helped enrol young Adam in the newly established Noble Cadet Corps.[108] Matvei Olsuf'ev continued in service to the widowed Catherine, who stood godmother to his son Iakov on 5 November 1725, and he was still at Peter II's court in early 1728 with a substantial salary of 1396 roubles per year. But he retired soon and had his estate confiscated in 1732 (no particulars known), further undercutting the family as a whole.[109] As compared to the Mons-Balk family, then, the Olsuf'ev brothers laboured to maintain their newly exalted status although at least one son retained eminence.

As an individual Catherine I left an ambiguous legacy. As the heart and soul of the newly Europeanised imperial court and dynasty she facilitated a plethora of new opportunities for her family, her friends and her expanding realm. Her life became the stuff of legend and fairy tale.

NOTES

1 Philip Longworth, *The Three Empresses: Catherine I, Anne and Elizabeth of Russia*, New York, 1972, p. 3.
2 Kathi S. Sharp, 'Catherine I: Peter's Beloved Consort and Russia's First Empress', seminar paper, Russian and East European Studies, University of Kansas, 15 November 1995, pp. 1–2.
3 Larisa Vasil'eva, 'Zhenskaia revoliutsiia Petra Velikogo', *Nauka i religiia*, 1997, 3, pp. 13–14.
4 See Evgenii Anisimov, *Zhenshchiny na Rossiiskom prestole*, St Petersburg, 1997, pp. 7, 14–15; V.S. Beliavskii, 'Zolushka na trone Rossii', *Na Rossiskom prestole 1725–1796: Monarkhi rossiiskie posle Petra Velikogo*, Moscow, 1993, p. 14; M.I. Semevskii, 'Petr Velikii v ego snakh v 1714–1719', *Slovo i delo! 1700–1725*, repr. 2nd edn, St Petersburg, 1884, Moscow, 1991, pp. 274–6. See also Lindsey Hughes, *Russia in the Age of Peter the Great*, New Haven, CT and London, 1998, pp. 394–401.
5 F. Vil'bua, 'Rasskazy o rossiiskom dvore', trans. G.F. Zvereva, *Voprosy istorii*, 1991, 1, p. 139.
6 *Tak vot kogo liubil ia ... Zhenshchiny v zhizni velikikh liudei*, Moscow, 1996, p. 79.
7 Natalia Pushkareva, *Women in Russian History: from the Tenth to the Twentieth Century*, ed. and trans. Eve Levin, Armonk, NY, 1997, pp. 155–6, 187; Amaury de Riencourt, *Sex and Power in History*, New York, 1974, p. 238.
8 James Cracraft, *The Petrine Revolution in Russian Imagery*, Chicago, IL, 1997, pp. 187, 197–203, 209–12, 219, 258–9.
9 *For God and Peter the Great: The Works of Thomas Consett, 1723–1729*, ed. James Cracraft, Boulder, CO and New York, 1982, pp. 442–3.
10 I.B. Chizhov, *'Za liubov i otechestvo' (Ekaterina I i Elizaveta I: zhena i doch' Petra Velikogo)*, St Petersburg, 1994, pp. 5–7.
11 V.M. Nikitina, 'Orders of Knights and Their Feast Days', in A.V. Boldov, N.S. Vladimirskaia, eds, *Treasures of the Czars from the State Museums of the Moscow Kremlin*, London, 1995, pp. 208–9.
12 Gr.A.V.O., 'Brat'ia Olsuf'evy, ober-gofmeistery Petra Velikago: Perepiska ikh s kniazem A.D. Menshikovym (1715–1727)', *Russkii arkhiv*, 1883, 3, pp. 46–7.
13 Nikolai Pavlenko, *Strasti u trona: istoriia dvortsovykh perevorotov*, Moscow, 1996, pp. 7, 10.

14 Lindsey Hughes, 'A Note on the Children of Peter the Great', *Newsletter of the Study Group on Eighteenth-Century Russia*, 21, 1993, pp. 10–16.
15 *Ibid.*, pp. 10–11.
16 'Brat'ia Olsuf'evy', p. 23nl.
17 Ann M. Kleimola, ' "Good Breeding, Muscovite Style": Horse Culture in Early Modern Rus', *Forschungen zur osteuropäischen Geschichte*, Berlin, 1995, 50, p. 218.
18 A. Azov, 'Amazonki byli slaviankami', *Nauka i religiia*, 1998, 3, pp. 54–5.
19 V.V. Andreev, 'Ekaterina Pervaia', *Osmnadtsatyi vek*, Moscow, 1864, 3, pp. 18–19.
20 *Dnevnik kamer-iunkera F.V. Berkhgol'tsa, 1721–1725*, trans. I.F. Ammon, new edn in 4 parts, Moscow, 1902–03, appendices to *Russkii Arkhiv* (hereafter *Dnevnik Berkhgol'tsa*), IV, pp. 46–8, 50.
21 *Sbornik vypisok iz arkhivnykh bumag o Petre Velikom*, 2 vols, Moscow, 1872, II, p. 548.
22 Andreev, 'Ekaterina Pervaia', p. 20.
23 *Dnevnik Berkhgol'tsa*, IV, pp. 86–7; Andreev, 'Ekaterina Pervaia', pp. 25–6.
24 *Tak vot kogo liubil ia ...*, p. 83; N.A. Vasetskii, *Zhenshchina: vo vlasti i bezvlastii*, Moscow, 1997, p. 120.
25 Bernhard Stern, *The Private Life of the Romanoffs*, transl. Seth Traill, Washington, DC, 1896, pp. 97–8.
26 Sharp, 'Catherine I', pp. 27–9.
27 Pavlenko, *Strasti u trona*, pp. 17–20; Iu.F. Kozlov, *Liubov' gosudareva*, Saransk, 1996, pp. 104, 107–10, 117–18.
28 R.J.W. Evans, 'The Court: A Protean Institution and an Elusive Subject', in Ronald G. Asch, Adolf M. Birke, eds, *Princes, Patronage, and the Nobility: The Court at the Beginning of the Modern Era c. 1450–1650*, London, 1991, pp. 481–91.
29 L.E. Shepelev, 'Pridvornye chiny i zvaniia v dorevoliutsionnoi Rossii v sviazi s ikh znacheniem dlia istoricheskikh issledovanii', *Vspomogatel'nye istoricheskie distsipliny*, Leningrad, 1976, 6, p. 152.
30 *Opisanie vysochaishikh povelenii po pridvornomu vedomstvu 1723–1730*, St Petersburg, 1888, pp. 90–4.
31 For rosters of court personnel serving Peter's three daughters in 1720, see Semevskii, *Slovo i delo!*, pp. 195–7.
32 L.E. Shepelev, *Tituly, mundiry, ordena v Rossiiskoi imperii*, Leningrad, 1991, pp. 159, 162.

33 S.M. Troitskii, *Russkii absoliutizm i dvorianstvo v XVIII v.: formirovanie biurokratii*, Moscow, 1974, p. 166.
34 'Bratia Olsuf'evy', p. 8.
35 Kleimola, 'Horse Culture', pp. 209, 218, 222.
36 James Cracraft, *The Petrine Revolution in Russian Architecture*, Chicago, 1988, p. 179; I.K. Kirilov, *Tsvetushcheee sostoiane vserossiiskogo gosudarstva*, ed. B.A. Rybakov *et al.*, Moscow, 1977, pp. 35–6.
37 Richard L. Wortman, 'Moscow and Petersburg: The Problem of Political Center in Tsarist Russia, 1881–1914', in Sean Wilentz, ed., *Rites of Power: Symbolism, Ritual, and Politics Since the Middle Ages*, Philadelphia, PA, 1985, pp. 244–71.
38 E.V. Anisimov, *Gosudarstvennye preobrazovaniia i samoderzhavie Petra Velikogo v pervoi chetverti XVIII veka*, St Petersburg, 1997, pp. 144–5, 206, 214.
39 *Sbornik vypisok*, II, p. 134.
40 Troitskii, *Russkii absoliutizm*, p, 66; Shepelev, 'Pridvornye chiny i zvaniia', pp. 153–4; Shepelev, *Tituly, mundiry, ordena*, p. 176.
41 *Opisanie vysochaishikh povelenii*, pp. 87–90.
42 *Ibid.*, pp. 5–6.
43 N.E. Volkov, *Dvor russkikh imperatorov v ego proshlom i nastoiashchem*, St Petersburg, 1900, p. 5.
44 Brenda Meehan-Waters, *Autocracy and Aristocracy: The Russian Service Elite of 1730*, New Brunswick, 1982, pp. 68, 110, 188; N.I. Pavlenko, *Ptentsy gnezda Petrova*, 4th edn, Moscow, 1995, pp. 281–2, 308; Anisimov, *Gosudarstvennye preobrazovaniia*, pp. 282–8.
45 *Pis'ma russkikh gosudarei*, Moscow, 1867, p. 63.
46 *Dnevnik Berkhgol'tsa*, IV, p. 6.
47 Meehan-Waters, *Autocracy and Aristocracy*, p. 68; *Sbornik imperatorskago russkago istoricheskago obshchestva*, St Petersburg, 1889, 66, p. 13; Pavlenko, *Ptentsy gnezda Petrova*, p. 313.
48 Lindsey Hughes, *Sophia, Regent of Russia 1657–1704*, New Haven, CT and London, 1990, pp. xiii, 23, 27, 35–6, 246–7; Pushkareva, *Women in Russian History*, pp. 125–7.
49 Pushkareva, *Women in Russian History*, pp. 126, 133–4, 136–7; M.I. Semevskii, *Tsaritsa Praskov'ia 1664–1723: Ocherk iz russkoi istorii XVIII veka*, repr. 1883 edn, Leningrad, 1991, pp. 48, 52, 195–6, 212–13.
50 O.B. Melnikova, 'Costly Harness', *Treasures of the Tsars: Court Culture of Peter the Great from the Kremlin*, Museum Boyjans-van Beuningen Rotterdam, 10 December 1995 – 4 February 1996, pp. 218–19.

51 Charles Whitworth, *An Account of Russia as It Was in the Year 1710*, Strawberry Hill, 1758, pp. 51, 63.
52 E.V. Anisimov, ed., *Petr Velikii: Vospominaniia, dnevnikovye zapisi, anekdoty*, Moscow, 1993, pp. 88–90.
53 *Ibid.*, p. 102.
54 *Ibid.*, pp. 94, 104–10, 112.
55 Semevskii, *Tsaritsa Praskov'ia*, pp. 24–42; Anisimov, *Zhenshchiny na Rossiiskom prestole*, pp. 21–2; N.I. Pavlenko, *Poluderzhavnyi vlastelin*, Moscow, 1988, pp. 56–7, 75.
56 N.I. Pavlenko, *Petr Velikii*, Moscow, 1990, p. 236.
57 L.N. Semenova, *Ocherki istorii byta i kul'turnoi zhizni Rossii: pervaia polovina XVIII v.*, Leningrad, 1982, pp. 69–70.
58 Whitworth, *Account*, pp. xx–xxi.
59 Semevskii, *Slovo i delo!*, p. 197n1.
60 Volkov, *Dvor russkikh imperatorov*, p. 5.
61 Anisimov, ed., *Petr Velikii*, p. 162.
62 V.I. Buganov, 'Ekaterina I', *Voprosy istorii*, 1994, 11, p. 48; *Dnevnik Berkhgol'tsa*, IV, pp. 64–5.
63 Whitworth, *Account*, pp. 31, 60.
64 Nicholas V. Riasanovsky, *The Image of Peter the Great in Russian History and Thought*, New York, 1985, p. 4. The claim may go back to Karamzin's *Memoir on Ancient and Modern Russia*, ed. and trans. Richard Pipes, Cambridge, MA, 1959, p. 124.
65 Anisimov, ed., *Petr Velikii*, pp. 99–100; Whitworth, *Account*, p. 66.
66 Vil'bua, 'Rasskazy', p. 152. François Villebois (Russified to Nikita Petrovich Vil'bua) apparently entered Russian service in England in 1698.
67 *Pis'ma russkikh gosudarei i drugikh osob tsarskago semeistva*, Moscow, 1861, pp. 15–17.
68 *Ibid.*, pp. 34–7.
69 *Pis'ma russkikh gosudarei i drugikh osob tsarskago semeistva*, Moscow, 1867, pp. 64–5, 78–9.
70 M.M. Shcherbatov, *On the Corruption of Morals in Russia*, ed. and trans. A. Lentin, Cambridge, 1969, app. I, p. 301.
71 *Dnevnik Berkhgol'tsa*, I, pp. 115–28; III, app., pp. 188–99.
72 *Dnevnik Berkhgol'tsa*, I, pp. 177–8.
73 *Sbornik vypisok*, II, p. 149.
74 *Ibid.*, pp. 151, 159, 162, 165, 172–3.
75 'Bratia Olsuf'evy', pp. 64–5; *Dnevnik Berkhgol'tsa*, IV, app. pp. 125–35.
76 Semevskii, *Slovo i delo!*, pp. 195–7.
77 Shcherbatov, *On the Corruption of Morals in Russia*, pp. 135–7.

78 Larisa Vasil'eva, 'Zhenskaia revoliutsiia Petra Velikogo', *Nauka i religiia*, 1997,1, pp. 6–7.
79 *Ibid.*, pp. 7–8.
80 Semevskii, *Tsaritsa Praskov'ia*, p. 113.
81 Shcherbatov, *On the Corruption of Morals*, p. 141; Andreev, 'Ekaterina Pervaia', p. 13.
82 *Pis'ma i bumagi imperatora Petra Velikogo* (hereafter *PiB*), XIII, pt. 1, Moscow, 1992, p. 143.
83 Semevskii, *Tsaritsa Katerina Alekseevna*, p. 343.
84 *Dnevnik Berkhgol'tsa*, I, p. 120.
85 *Dnevnik Berkhgol'tsa*, II, p. 56, 68–71, 104; IV, pp. 8–9.
86 'Kampengauzen, Baron Ivan Ivanovich', *Russkii biograficheskii slovar"*, repr. New York, 1962, 8, p. 446; Heidi Whelan, 'Balthasar, Baron Campenhausen, and Sons: Making the Baltic Civil Servant', *Journal of Baltic Studies*, 1987, 1, pp. 45–62.
87 *Dnevnik Berkhgol'tsa*, IV, pp. 37–8.
88 Eugene Schuyler, *Peter the Great*, 2 vols, New York, 1884, II, pp. 435–6.
89 Richard S. Wortman, *Scenarios of Power: Myth and Ceremony in Russian Monarchy*, Princeton, NJ, 1995, 1, p. 69.
90 *Dnevnik Berkhgol'tsa*, IV, pp. 26–31.
91 Wortman, *Scenarios of Power*, pp. 69–74.
92 Longworth, *The Three Empresses*, p. 56.
93 *Dnevnik Berkhgol'tsa*, IV, pp. 42–3.
94 For the Maria Hamilton affair, see Semevskii, 'Freilina Gamil'ton: Istoricheskii ocherk, 1719', *Slovo i delo!*, pp. 185–268, and Dmitrii Fedosov's chapter in this volume.
95 Meehan-Waters, *Autocracy and Aristocracy*, p. 106.
96 V.R. 'Balk, Matrena Ivanovna', *Russkii biograficheskii slovar'*, St Petersburg, 1900, 2, pp. 448–9; L.A. Seriakov, *Russkie deiateli v portretakh izdannykh redaktsieiu istoricheskago zhurnala Russkaia Starina*, St Petersburg, 1886, p. 39.
97 M.I. Semevskii, *Tsaritsa Katerina Alekseevna, Anna i Villem Mons 1692–1724: Ocherk iz russkoi istorii XVIII veka*, repr. 2nd edn, Leningrad, 1990, pp. 244–246nl.
98 *Opisanie vysochaishikh povelenii*, pp. 42, 45; Semevskii, *Tsaritsa Katerina Alekseevna*, pp. 247–8; D.L. Mordovtsev, *Russkie zhenshchiny: biograficheskie ocherki iz russkoi istorii*, repr. Moscow, 1993, pp. 187–97, 241–5.
99 Meehan-Waters, *Autocracy and Aristocracy*, pp. 33, 86.
100 *PiB*, IX, pt. 1, pp. 475–6.

101 *PiB*, X, pp. 361, 364, 368, 380, 683–84.
102 Pavlenko, *Ptentsy gnezda Petrova*, p. 82.
103 *PiB*, XI, pt. 2. p. 75; P.F. Karabanov, 'Stats-damy i freiliny russkago dvora v XVIII stoletii', *Russkaia starina*, 1870, 2, p. 480.
104 Troitskii, Absoliutizm i dvorianstvo, pp. 166, 259, 291; Meehan-Waters, *Autocracy and Aristocracy*, p. 110.
105 *Dnevnik Berkhgol'tsa*, I, pp. 147–8.
106 *Dnevnik Berkhgol'tsa*, III, pp. 182–4.
107 *Opisanie vysochaishikh povelenii*, p. 27.
108 B. Alekseevskii, 'Olsuf'ev, Adam Vasil'evich', *Russkii biograficheskii slovar'*, St Petersburg, 1905; repr. New York, 1962, 12, pp. 232–5.
109 *Opisanie vysochaishikh povelenii*, p. 49; 'Kniga prikhodo-raskhodnaia komnatnykh deneg imperatritsy Ekateriny Pervoi (Za 1723–1725 gody)', *Russkii arkhiv*, 1874, 1, p. 566; E.I. Indova, 'K voprosu o dvorianskoi sobstvennosti v Rossii v pozdnii feodal'nyi period', in N.I. Pavlenko *et al.*, eds, *Dvorianstvo i krepostnoi stroi Rossii XVI–XVIII vv.*, Moscow, 1975, pp. 283, 289–90.

15 Images of Greatness: Portraits of Peter I

Lindsey Hughes

It often comes as a surprise to people more familiar with the history of Western art than Russian to learn that Peter I is the first Russian ruler of whom we possess reliable likenesses. We British know (or think we know) what Henry VIII (reigned 1509–47) and Elizabeth I (1558–1603) looked like, although their portraits were emblematic, rather than 'realistic'; for example, symbolic studies alluded to some aspect of the queen's mind or achievements in order to maintain the myth of her agelessness. The physical appearance of Charles I (1625–49), altogether a more modern image, can be plotted almost year by year from when he was eight years old until he was forty-two.[1] There is no contemporary Russian equivalent of this apparently visibly doomed and glamorous personality, for the art of secular portraiture came to Russia only in the later seventeenth century and then only in archaic forms. In the words of Alexander Vasil'chikov, the author of a pioneering study of Peter's portraits: 'The art of portraiture in the full sense of the word came to our country only in the reign of Peter the Great.'[2]

Seventeenth–century Russians, tsars included, were in a sense featureless. Soviet scholars, notably D.S. Likhachev, elaborated the formula of the 'emergence of the human personality (*lichnost'*)' to explain cultural developments in seventeenth-century Russia, detecting a growing appreciation of the worldly individual outside the religious context (with reference to a delayed 'Renaissance'), but this phenomenon was more strongly reflected in literature (for example, in the 'autohagiography' of Archpriest Avvakum and in 'democratic' tales) than in the visual arts.[3]

There are many possible explanations for Russia's deviant (by Western standards) path of artistic development, ranging from the country's physical and psychological remoteness from Classical antiquity to the 'despotic' nature of Russian government (the philosopher David Hume, it will be recalled, argued that the arts could flourish only under regimes which guaranteed the enjoyment of private property).[4] Whatever the reason, Russian imagery from the ninth century to the seventeenth, although rich and inventive, was overwhelmingly religious, focusing on the pious dead rather than the sinful living. There are no contemporary home-produced representations of Ivan the Terrible (1533–84) or his son Fedor (1584–98), of whom only notional likenesses survive in foreign engravings and posthumous iconic images. There are no surviving portraits made during the lifetime of Peter's grandfather Tsar Mikhail (1613–45), Charles I's contemporary, although numerous retrospective ones exist and there is evidence that miniatures were painted in connection with the search for a foreign bride for the tsar during the early 1620s.[5] In the reign of Peter's father Tsar Alexis (1645–76), with the arrival in Moscow of a handful of foreign painters and strong influences from Poland via Ukraine, painted portraits – known as *parsuny* – make a tentative appearance. Even then the new fashion did not extend much beyond the Kremlin and selected members of the boyar elite. The few surviving examples are stylised and stereotypical effigies rather than individual likenesses. The fact that the various surviving images of Tsar Alexis display different facial features suggest that portraiture from life had yet to gain a firm foothold, even though there is documentary evidence that the tsar sat for his portrait several times. The best-known picture of his successor Tsar Fedor (1676–82) is a posthumous effigy, executed in traditional materials and technique, probably commissioned for placing by his tomb in about 1685–86. The prototype is said to be a non-extant 1679 portrait made from life, but the focus is firmly on the departed pious tsar.[6]

The most striking of later seventeenth-century images are those of Peter's half-sister Sophia, produced while she was regent to Tsars Ivan and Peter in 1682–89. Hitherto, living royal and noble women could scarcely be depicted at all, except when represented in stylised poses of prayer and supplication or as donors in icons and frescoes, following the Byzantine tradition. The partial segregation of the sexes which was practised in elite Muscovite households seems to have extended to taboos on women exposing their faces – not to mention unclad parts of their bodies – to painters (Muscovite seventeenth-century fashions were totally concealing). The portraits of Sophia are remarkable in the Russian context, but they disappoint as images of femininity. The main emphasis is upon the unisex attributes of rulership, as represented by regalia and robes.[7] Celebrations of female beauty and sexuality (see, for example, the many revealing portraits of the mistresses of King Charles II) were as yet out of the question in Russia.

Peter was born during a period of tentative cultural change, but the very first image associated with him falls firmly into the realm of religious art. It is the patron saint's 'measuring' icon of St Peter made shortly after his birth in May 1672 to the infant's measurements, showing him to be nineteen and a quarter inches long.[8] The practice of making a measuring icon linked a child from birth with his or her patron saint, whose feast would be marked annually by special nameday (*imeniny*) celebrations. Thereafter there are relatively few depictions of the boy Peter and none, it would seem, irrefutably based upon an accurate likeness. Dmitrii Rovinskii lists just over a dozen engraved images of Peter dating from the period before the Grand Embassy.[9] The earliest belongs to a large bound collection of manuscript portraits of Russian and foreign princes known as the *Tituliarnik*, a sort of heraldic and dynastic reference work, the first part of which was made in the Kremlin Armoury workshops in 1672 for depositing in the Foreign Office (*Posol'skii prikaz*). Supplements contained pictures of all Tsar Alexis's sons, including a 1678 drawing of Peter. All the images in the *Tituliarnik* and its supplementary volumes are stereotypical, identifying individuals by inscriptions, approximate age and appropriate trappings rather than by distinctive facial features. At the same time, the subject matter demonstrated the availability in Moscow of foreign prints and engravings, from which images of foreign rulers were copied, not to mention a burgeoning interest in the outside world and increased diplomatic contacts, which were to be such a striking feature of the Petrine era.

The influence of the *Tituliarnik* is evident in an illustrated manuscript produced to mark the coronation of Peter and Ivan in 1682 (Plate 12), which in turn was perhaps the model for a little known, anonymous and undated oil painting, said to be of Peter.[10] In the same vein is a manuscript illustration celebrating Peter's ill-fated marriage to Evdokia Lopukhina in 1689, showing the tsar and his bride in coronation robes within a traditional composition indicating interaction between the heavenly and earthly sphere.[11] Rovinskii's list includes several allegorical prints (*conclusiones*) produced in Ukraine and Muscovy, which set the figures of the two tsars within a characteristic mix of Christian and Classical imagery, and some purely notional images made abroad, for example double engraved portraits of the tsars produced in connection with a Russian embassy to France in the late 1680s.[12] An engraving (post-1690) showing Tsars Peter and Ivan and Tsarevich Alexis as the three Magi visiting the infant Jesus is wholly in the Orthodox idiom.[13]

We have to wait until the Grand Embassy of 1697–98 for our first sight of the 'real' Peter, although now the waters are muddied by Peter's determination to conceal his true identity under a pseudonym. In view of this incognito, which he maintained for most of his travels, we might conclude that Peter was reluctant to show his face (there are numerous reports of his going to extreme lengths to avoid being stared at), regarding curious crowds in much the same way as some modern-day celebrities regard lurking paparazzi. But reluctance was tempered by a thirst for publicity, as long as it was of the right kind. Peter sat for his portrait several times, but the incomplete records of his travels means that we cannot be certain of all the details. There is a reference to a sitting in Königsberg in March 1697, at the court of the elector of Brandenburg, but no painting survives.[14] Many writers repeat the notion that Peter first sat for Sir Godfrey Kneller in Utrecht in September 1697, although the evidence for this sitting had recently been convincingly challenged, to confirm that the famous portrait was indeed executed by Sir Godfrey in London in January 1698.[15]

Even if we still cannot be sure that Sir Godfrey Kneller's was the first true likeness of Peter painted from life (Plate 2), it was certainly the most successful of the early images, though in West European terms it is conventional and unremarkable. Kneller used the same set formulae – armour and royal ermine, column and crown to our left, warship in the background to our right – as in his portrait of James II.[16] He probably painted only the face, which meant that Peter did not in fact sit (or stand) in the setting as depicted in the completed painting; this would have been added by assistants. Kneller's portrait was regarded as a good likeness by contemporaries who saw it and soon spread through the medium of engravings (notably the famous one by John Smith; Plate 3) and miniatures on enamel.[17] It spawned numerous direct copies (for example, one in the Hermitage in St Petersburg) and some imitations, one of which may be the canvas by the Dutch artist Jan Weenix (usually dated, surely wrongly, 1697?–98); this also features armour, baton, column and military scene in the background.[18]

For Kneller and Weenix, Peter was just another European monarch. All traces of Russian 'exoticism' were expunged, to produce a firmly Western royal image in the grand register. But there are other portraits from this period which remind us that the break with Old Russia was far from complete: Peter had alternative images, both in his own eyes and in the vision of artists, who had to cater for a public abroad which preferred its Muscovite monarchs exotic-looking. A painting by the Dutch artist Pieter van de Werff (1665–1718) shows Peter dressed in a more native style.[19] A famous print by William Faithorne also presents a thoroughly Muscovite Peter, while retrospective depictions of the siege of Azov in 1696 (see Adriaan Schoenebeck's engraving of 1699–1700, one of first Western-style battle scenes made in Russia) show Peter in a Russian hat.[20] (Azov's location far to the east of Europe encouraged the identification in the Western mind of Russian foreign policy as distinctly eastern oriented.)

Two further examples give evidence of a conflict of imagery at the turn of the century. In 1699 two experimental half-roubles were minted. The first, by Vasilii Andreev of the Armoury, shows Peter full face as in icon style, wearing the cap of Monomach. The second shows him as Roman emperor in profile, with laurel wreath and mantle, long before the official adoption of the imperial titles in 1721.[21]

Russia's entry into the Great Northern War in 1700 signalled the abandonment in official circles of the Muscovite-Byzantine image in favour of a Western-style Peter. Thereafter, not a trace remained in royal portraits of Byzanto-Slavic iconography or style.[22] In some cases, Peter's appearance was westernised beyond probability; for example in Schoenebeck's very French-looking image (1703–05), which shows him wearing a flamboyant wig, hat and French tunic rather than the 'German' or Swedish-style coat which he usually wore. (There are anecdotes about Peter grabbing a wig from the head of the person next to him when he felt cold rather than bothering to maintain his own.[23]) This foppish outfit was especially unconvincing on a picture of Peter dating from the tense early period of the war when he was racing round the Baltic and Lithuania with his troops and kept no court in the conventional sense.[24] From the same period and similarly incongruous (although, of course, perfectly conventional for its time) is the extravagantly bewigged Peter recently attributed to the Dutch artist Godfried Schalken (1643–1706), which testifies to the internationalisation of Peter's image in the early years of the Northern War.[25]

A 'true to life' image of the adult Peter is probably captured better in words than in paint. The Italian castrato singer Filippo Balatri, in Russia 1698–1700, an observant witness, wrote:

> Tsar Peter was tall, thin rather than stout; his hair was thick, short, dark brown; he had large eyes, black with long lashes, a well-shaped mouth, but the lower lip was slightly disfigured ... For his great height, his feet seemed very narrow. His head was sometimes tugged to the right by convulsions.[26]

These alarming convulsions, observed by many, have been attributed to the horrors which Peter endured in 1682 and 1689. The Duc de Saint-Simon, who met Peter in France in 1717, memorably evoked his split image: on the one hand, an appearance imbued with 'intelligence, reflectiveness and grandeur', which, however, for seconds at a time and without warning would be disfigured by muscular spasms which struck fear into the onlooker, giving Peter a 'wild and terrible air'.[27] Peter's 'terrible' aspect was increased by outbreaks of rage. In Bishop Gilbert Burnet's vivid image, he was a 'man of a very hot temper, soon inflamed and very brutal in his passion'.[28] At six foot seven inches tall and oddly proportioned, Peter was also evidently something of a freak of nature, an object of curious glances rather than aesthetic appreciation. Valentin Serov

(1865–1911), who studied Peter from an artist's point of view, came to the following conclusion:

> He was frightful: long, on weak, spindly little legs and with a head so small in relation to the rest of his body that he must have looked more like a sort of dummy with a badly stuck on head than a living person.[29]

Contemporary portraits, naturally, eschewed anything grotesque or unseemly. What we get is a well-proportioned and apparently well-co-ordinated body and a handsome visage, with perhaps just a hint of fiercely staring eyes. Likewise, there is hardly a trace in painted portraits of what Soviet historians anachronistically referred to as Peter's *demokratizm*, no official contemporary depictions of Peter in the alter-egos which he himself chose to adopt, such as that of Carpenter Tsar or simple bombardier, that 'great contemner of all pomp and ostentation about his own person'.[30] 'The tsar sets no store by rich garments, fine furniture, carriages and residences', wrote the Danish agent Georg Grund. 'Indeed, he gets most satisfaction from contact with simple people, especially since he loves such occupations as wood-turning, carpentry, clockmaking, engraving, pyrotechnics and other such.'[31] This was all part and parcel of the myth of 'modesty' which Peter himself was more than happy to encourage.

Sadly, there are no contemporary pictures of Peter in the workman's leather overall, in which another Dane, Just Juel, caught him at his lathe one day, working 'as though he had to earn his living from this particular form of labour'.[32] The few depictions of Peter during his lifetime as ship's carpenter – for example, one of him in Dutch dress and a wide brimmed hat signed by the unknown artist called Cr Reichel – were invariably produced abroad. A painting reputed to be of Peter in Dutch costume – a long-haired man wearing a conical hat with a narrow brim and a striped jacket, but with features very different from the Kneller portrait – is much reproduced, but never adequately documented.[33] Compositions featuring Peter chatting to shipwrights or working in the docks at Saandam and Deptford generally date from later periods, especially the nineteenth century when modern historical genre flourished; for example the painting of Peter at Deptford by Daniel Maclise (1857; a testament to Victorian enthusiasm for the dignity of labour; Plate 4).[34]

The Russian authorities, aided by the Church, energetically combated popular or amateur depictions of the tsar. In January 1723 a decree was issued complaining about portraits (*zhivopisnye persony*) of the emperor and empress 'painted unskilfully by ignorant persons', which were being sold on the streets of Moscow and displayed in people's homes. Ivan Zarudnii, the new inspector of icon-painting (sic!), was commanded to have the offending pictures confiscated and stored in the Holy Synod and 'to order such portraits to be painted skilfully by artists with certificates of good workmanship, with all care and fitting assiduity'.[35] Such measures recall efforts in the seventeenth century to stem the sale of crudely printed paper icons and religious pictures of foreign origin in Moscow and other towns. The maintenance of proper standards even in secular images was still regarded as the joint concern of State and Church. The 1723 decree did not indicate that the banned images were subversive or lewd, although it is easy to see how the notion of Peter as Antichrist could provide rich inspiration for popular art. Peter was said to be able to take the shape of an animal (his German boots were identified with the 'cow's feet' of Antichrist) or to be Simon Petrov the magician.[36] Conversely, portraits in the Classical idiom – for example of Peter with Minerva – were identified by conservatives as the 'icons' of Antichrist.[37]

In matters of fashion, as in others, Peter was a man of contrasts. At times he could appear 'so badly dressed that anyone who did not know him would never take him for the great monarch that he is'[38]; at others he displayed an unashamed taste for luxury fabrics and an eye for colour: 'send the finest calamanco cloths, cornflower blue, blue, crimson, scarlet, pink', he wrote to agent Brandt in Amsterdam.[39] He also devoted time to designing masquerade costumes, but neither these nor examples of dandyish court dress made their way into official portraits. They were limited to the 'private' sphere, while portraits belonged firmly to the public image. In official portraits Peter was depicted with the conventional attributes of successful kingship borrowed from Western art: royal ermine and warrior's armour, rearing steed, martial symbols, maps and plans of conquests, appropriate gods and goddesses and allegorical figures, and so on. In other words, the images chosen for wider circulation were images of greatness. Vasil'chikov writes: 'Wherever one conjures up this constructed image [of Peter], in the workshop or on the field of battle, at the Admiralty wharf or in the royal palace, everywhere it strikes one with its grandeur (*vezde porazhaet svoim velichiem*).'[40] In the eighteenth century court painters still adhered to the Renaissance theory, as formulated by Georgio Lomazzo, that portraits were not literal copies of nature but were infused with the Idea of Rulership: 'Emperors above all other Kings and Princes should be endowed with majesty, and have a noble and grave air which conforms to their station in life ... even though they be not naturally so in life.'[41]

Peter would not have disagreed with this principle. He was well aware of the importance of symbols and emblems – of the power of 'image' (to use the modern meaning) – and was the first Russian ruler in modern times to exploit it extensively. Fantasies were perfectly acceptable as long as they flattered: decorative armour which soldiers no longer wore, cloaks swirling in impossible folds, horses rearing in unlikely poses, the intermingling of real personages with allegorical figures. A painting done by Jan Kupetsky in Carlsbad in 1711 (Plate 13), much reproduced in engravings, has an overload of such imagery: armour, commander's baton, cannon, wild animal skin, turbulent sky.[42] There are numerous depictions of Peter at the battle of Poltava (27 June 1709), when he was mentioned in dispatches for his 'bravery, fortitude and military skill', and a legend was born.[43] Examples include J.G. Dannhauer's *Peter I crowned by Victory at Poltava* (1710s; Plate 14) and Aleksei Zubov's and Pieter Picart's engraved battle panorama (1715).[44] The equestrian image was also used on engravings marking the peace of Nystad in 1721 and Peter's adoption of the title *imperator*. Although by 1721 Peter had not fought the Swedes on horseback for a good many years, the conventional equestrian motif served to remind viewers of the crucial victories which had created Russia's ascendancy over once great Sweden. Later, under the chisel of Etienne Falconet and the pen of Alexander Pushkin, the horseman was to become the most enduring of all Petrine images.

Naval images, too, followed Western conventions, alluding to the tsar's victories over his enemies at sea rather than to his prowess as a shipwright or a navigator. These include a full length painting in the Admiralty Office, showing Peter pointing with a baton to a map of the Caspian sea (an allusion to the campaign of 1722–23) with anchors, cable and military insignia at his feet and ships in the background[45]; and a painting of the tsar in armour against the background of a naval battle, tentatively dated 1715.[46] Grigorii Musikiiskii's 1723 enamel miniature shows Peter against a background of wharves.[47] If these images fail to convey the full extent of Peter's passion for ships, it is probably because no European monarchs in recent history had had such practical, hands-on involvement in naval affairs as had Peter and there were few ready-made images beyond the allegorical and the symbolic. The naval theme appears more frequently on medals, notably one struck in 1716 to commemorate Peter's command of four fleets – Danish, Dutch, British and Russian – off Copenhagen; this medal features Neptune riding the waves on sea horses.[48]

Other portrait types suggest the statesman and even the philosopher as well as the soldier and sailor. Peter's favourite portrait of himself is said to be the half-length image painted by Karl Moor in Amsterdam in 1717.[49] Much uncertainty surrounds its history; the extant painting is sometimes said to have been copied in Antwerp (in 1724–25) by the Russian trainee artist Andrei Matveev from Moor's lost original, which is best known from Jacobus Houbraken's engraving. But the engraving shows Peter in armour, which the Moor/Matveev portrait does not.[50] At the joint Russia–Netherlands exhibition 'Peter the Great and Holland', held in St Petersburg and then in Amsterdam in 1996–97, two portraits were displayed, one by Matveev (described as a copy of Moor) and another tentatively identified as Moor's original.[51] These uncertainties underline the fact that hardly any positively authenticated originals with a proper provenance survive from Peter's time; indeed, Vasil'chikov wrote that the Kneller's was the only painting of which one could be certain.[52] We know from documentary evidence that several portraits were painted while Peter was abroad in 1716–17, but matching this evidence with surviving works is problematical; for example, a famous portrait attributed to the Dutch artist Aert de Gelder may have been the work of a foreign painter in St Petersburg.[53] An original painting done by the artist Hyacinthe Rigaud in Paris in 1717 apparently disappeared, while the much reproduced painting attributed to Jean Marc Nattier (also Paris 1717) is of disputed provenance.[54] Another image later favoured by engravers was said to have been painted by a French artist called Leroi in 1717, but no artist of that name has been traced.[55]

Similar mysteries surround the work of the only Russian artist who contributed significantly to Peter's image during the tsar's lifetime, Ivan Nikitin (ca. 1680 – after 1742), the so-called 'founder of Russian portraiture'.[56] Peter sponsored Nikitin's studies in Italy in 1716–20 with the express purpose of having a fully qualified Russian painter at court, but the scarcity of works bearing Nikitin's signature (only two signed canvases survive, neither of them of Peter) means that the identification of the artists' handiwork remains problematical. Sergei Androsov's recent study includes just six portraits of Peter in the catalogue of paintings which have been or still are attributed to Nikitin. There is documentary evidence that he painted Peter at least three times from life, in 1715, 1720 and 1721 (when the court journal records that 'on Kotlin island before mass the painter Ivan Nikitin painted his majesty's portrait (*personu*) and then his majesty attended mass'[57]). The first of these works has been tentatively identified as a study of Peter in armour against the background of a sea battle, possibly Hangö (1714),[58] the last as the so-called 'round' portrait (Plate 15), which together with the famous 'oval' portrait, is undoubtedly among the most striking of all the surviving contemporary images. Both show Peter head and shoulders, but by eliminating all extraneous details about the person – such as regalia or orders – and setting the figure against dark, neutral backgrounds, they concentrate more than any other known portraits on the tsar's face. Much has been read into them; for example, a Soviet analysis of the round portrait claimed that the artist expressed the 'tragic loneliness' of Peter's last years, when he lacked support, saw corruption all around and so on. It was the 'portrait of an epoch'.[59] In Androsov's view, it could only have been painted by someone who knew the tsar well and sympathised with him; in other words it could only have been painted by a 'Russian person, patriot and citizen'.[60]

It is this intimate quality, rather than compelling scientific evidence, which seems to have led to the attribution of the best portraits to Nikitin, on the grounds that foreign painters could not truly capture Peter's essence. (See, for example, the assertion in the authoritiative Soviet *History of Russian Art* that the German Johann Dannhauer was 'incapable of conveying all the complexity of Peter's image [in his portraits], something which was achieved only by Ivan Nikitin'.[61]) The attribution of the oval portrait to Louis Caravaque and the round portrait to an unknown artist on the basis of 'technological' studies made in the Russian Museum, has not, it seems, been widely accepted.[62]

In fact, in the absence of sufficient Russian artists proficient in Western techniques, Peter had no choice but to rely on foreign painters to produce portraits in the required quantity. In this he was in step with Western rulers of his era; for example, up to the mid-eighteenth century the leading portraitists working in Britain were nearly all foreigners. Art was international business. His first and longest-serving court painter was the German Johann Gottfried Dannhauer (Tannhauer, 1680–1733/37), who worked in St Petersburg for twenty-six years from 1710. He probably acted as tutor to Ivan Nikitin, painting portraits of members of the royal family and their circle. Dannhauer's best-known works are Peter at Poltava with trumpeting Victory and a profile portrait, made in the 1710s, the background of stormy sky suggestive of Peter's dynamism and the constant tribulations of rulership.[63] The Frenchman Louis Caravaque (1684–1754) was hired in 1716 and spent the rest of his life in St Petersburg.[64] His grandest historical composition, painted in 1718 for the palace at Peterhof, was the battle of Poltava, with Peter on horseback in the right foreground pointing to a scene of fleeing Swedes.[65] This image was reproduced on a tapestry, one of the first made in St Petersburg (1722).[66] A half-length portrait by Caravaque, now lost, forms the basis for engravings by S.M. Korovin (1723) and many subsequent copies.[67] One of the most prolific foreigners was the little-known Johann Heinrich Wedekind (1674–1736), who started work for the Russian court after the capture of Reval (Tallinn) in 1710 and 'filled almost all the walls in St Petersburg homes with his copies of portraits of the imperial family and distinguished persons'.[68]

Despite such evidence of the painting of family portraits, group studies of Peter *en famille* are a rarity. The exception are miniatures by Grigorii Musikiiskii, several painted in 1716–17 on Menshikov's orders as gifts for Peter on his return from abroad.[69] A number of engraved family groups date from this tense period when questions of succession were much on Peter's mind and the trial of Tsarevich Alexis Petrovich was pending. I.F. Zubov's allegorical engraving made for Catherine's coronation as Peter's consort in 1724, which depicts Catherine in her coronation gown and the tsar pointing to a globe, is another rare depiction of husband and wife together (Plate 11).[70]

Peter was certainly the first Russian ruler whose image was produced in three dimensions. (The art of carving human figures in marble and casting them in metal was unknown in Muscovite Russia.) The best-known of Peter's sculptors and creator of some of the most memorable images of the tsar was Carlo Bartolomeo Rastrelli (1675?–1744), father of the famous architect. He met Peter in Königsberg in February 1716, came to Russia and immediately set to work on an equestrian statue of the tsar, based on the monument to Marcus Aurelius on the Capitol in Rome.[71] It is one of the most menacing images of Peter the warrior. Rastrelli's masterpiece is considered to be the bronze bust of Peter in armour (1723–30), which with its flowing metal draperies and swirling lines succeeds in capturing something of Peter's dynamism and stern determination.[72] A panel on the armour shows Peter as Pygmalion, putting the finishing touches to a statue of New Russia – a crowned woman in armour bearing orb and sceptre – a striking metaphor for Peter's role in refashioning his country as from a raw block of stone.[73]

Rastrelli also made wax models, a speciality of Florence, his home town. His portrait bust of 1719, taken from a wax mask, found its way to Italy (in return for the Tauride Venus) and was returned to Russia in 1861.[74] Most famous of all is his full figure model, based on a death mask and casts of hands and feet taken on the night of Peter's death. The wooden body was made to Peter's measurements and dressed in the clothes which he wore at Catherine's coronation in 1724. The model wore a wig of the tsar's own hair, cut in 1722 during the Persian campaign. Eyes were cut by the master enameller Andrei Ovsov.[75] Today the model excites curiosity; in the past it must have evoked something approaching awe. There were stories about the model being fitted with a mechanism which allowed it stand up to its full height, but these have been discounted.[76]

Sculpture in stone or metal in the round was new to Russia, but in the matter of imagery Peter perhaps broke with Muscovite conventions even more spectacularly when he was painted shortly after his death. Nikitin and Dannhauer both did death-bed studies although, as with much else, attributions remain controversial. Nikitin's version (Plate 16), the better known of the two, is far from being a clinical study: the face is in repose (there is no trace of the horrible agonies which we know Peter suffered, although the impression of rest after a long struggle provides a metaphor for the struggle of Peter's life to drag Russia into the modern world) and the ermine drape reminds the viewer of the corpse's regal status. The lighting effects on the bedclothes suggest the flickering of candles, although there is no explicit religious imagery.[77] Dannhauer's study was taken from the tsar's right side, showing a less tranquil image in profile.[78] In Soviet works the existence of 'rival' works by a Russian and a German artist provoked nationalist sentiments. T.A. Lebedeva considered that Nikitin's portrait displays a 'patriotic, purely Russian understanding of the image, a grief of loss which could be conveyed only by a Russian artist'[79]; Dannhauer, on the other hand, lacked 'personal feeling': it was a straight-forward 'imitation of nature'.[80] V.G. Andreeva suggested that contemporaries gave priority to the native-born artist, claiming that first Nikitin painted his picture and only then was Dannhauer admitted to paint his, although there is no direct evidence of either man being in the room at all.[81]

Whatever the precise circumstances of their creation, these pictures, unprecedented in Russian history, owe much to the modern clinical approach to the human body which Peter himself adopted; this approach makes it plausible that he left orders for a visual record to be kept of his own corpse. Peter loved to perform autopsies. There are numerous incidents of his delaying funerals, either to prepare fitting solemnities or in order for post mortems to be carried out. In France in 1717 he bought the Dutch anatomist Ruysch's secret recipe for preserving corpses, refusing to reveal it to French anatomists who were working on models of human organs.[82] It is not known whether this recipe was used on Peter himself, although something of the kind must have been needed as Peter lay in state in an open coffin for more than a month after his death, another break with Muscovite tradition, when royal funerals were carried out within forty-eight hours and embalming was not employed. Engravings survive of the foreign-inspired hall of mourning (*castrum doloris*), replete with Classical statues, the last glimpse of Peter before he was entombed in the Peter–Paul fortress.[83]

Since the work of Vasil'chikov and Rovinskii (the 1889 edition of the latter's dictionary of Russian engraved portraits listed 778 items devoted to Peter, with numerous subdivisions) no systematic study has been made of Peter in the visual arts. In a recent article the Russian art historian Sergei Androsov calls for a new study of the iconography of portraits of Peter, arranged in chronological order and with appropriate commentaries.[84] This short survey has indicated just a few of the many gaps and uncertainties which remain in our knowledge even of contemporary portraits. The after–life of Peter's portraits is even richer than the imagery produced during his lifetime. His remains the most frequently reproduced of all Russian royal images to the present day, in numerous oil paintings, prints and engravings, book illustrations, statues (especially in 1872 to mark the bicentenary of Peter's birth). The image was reworked in the popular imagination, although a number of the folk print (*lubok)* subjects identified with Peter have been shown to be based on associations made after his death, (for example 'The Mice Bury the Cat', known already in the seventeenth century) or associated with his reforms rather than his person (for example 'The Barber shaving the Old Believer's Beard'). In Russia today Peter's image has been harnessed for advertising purposes (Petrovskoe beer, Menatap bank, Tsar Peter cigarettes) and new portraits continue to be created; for example, two controversial statues, which draw respectively on the unofficial and official spheres: Mikhail Shemiakhin's grotesque seated statue in St Petersburg, which exploits Peter's peculiar physical characteristics and makes reference to Rastrelli's wax model,[85] and Zurab Tsereteli's gigantic monument in Moscow to the tsar hero and pioneer astride his ship, which exaggerates even Peter's heroic proportions. These two conflicting images sum up for modern viewers the continuing controversy about the man and his meaning for Russia.

NOTES

1 There is a rich literature on the subject, which I shall not attempt to list here. See D. Piper's useful survey *The English Face*, London, 1978.
2 A.A. Vasil'chikov, *O portretakh Petra Velikogo,* Moscow, 1872, p. 10. This book, the first work of its kind, was an attempt to list paintings of Peter done during his lifetime. It was written to accompany a portrait exhibition in Moscow, one of many activities to mark the bicentenary of Peter's birth, and dedicated to the memory of Prince A.Ia. Lobanov-Rostovskii, a keen collector of royal portraits. Unfortunately, it contains no illustrations. On the visual arts in Peter's reign, see J. Cracraft, *The Petrine Revolution in Russian Imagery,* Chicago, IL, 1997; L. Hughes, *Russia in the Age of Peter the Great*, New Haven, CT, London, 1998, pp. 203–46.
3 For example, D.S. Likhachev, *Chelovek v literature drevnei Rusi,* Moscow, 1970.
4 See L. Hughes, 'Images of the Elite: a Reconsideration of the Portrait in Seventeenth-Century Russia', in *Forschungen zur Osteuropäischen Geschichte*, 56, forthcoming.
5 See B.N. Floria, 'Nekotorye dannye o nachale svetskogo portreta v Rossii', *Arkhiv russkoi istorii,* vyp. 1, Moscow, 1992, pp. 137–9. They were closely guarded, apparently for fear of the evil eye being transmitted to the original.
6 E.S. Ovchinnikova, *Portret v russkom iskusstve XVII veka,* Moscow, 1955, pp. 47–8, 51–3. In 1678 Ivan Bezmin went to the palace to paint Tsar Fedor: 'pisal gosudarskuiu personu u gosudiaria na domu [painted the sovereign's portrait in the sovereign's chambers]'. See A. Viktorov, *Opisanie zapisynkh knig i bumag starinnykh dvortsovykh prikazov,* 2 vols, Moscow, 1883, II, p. 446.
7 See L. Hughes, *Sophia Regent of Russia,* New Haven, CT, 1990, pp. 139–44.
8 *Sbornik vypisok iz arkhivnykh bumag o Petre Velikom,* 2 vols, Moscow, 1872, I, p. 1.
9 D.A. Rovinskii, *Podrobnyi slovar' russkikh gravirovannykh portretov,* 2 vols, St Petersburg, 1889, II, p. 1288.
10 *Chin venchaniia na tsarstvo,* in Ovchinnikova, *Portret,* plate V. See also Cracraft, *Petrine Revolution,* p. 192; *Treasures of the Czars from the State Museums of the Moscow Kremlin,* London, 1995, p. 60. Vasil'chikov, *O portretakh,* p. 40, describes the painting as a crude work, identified as Peter only by repute.

11 See L. Hughes, 'Peter the Great's Two Weddings: Changing Images of Women in a Transitional Age', in *Women in Russia and Ukraine*, ed. R. Marsh, Cambridge, 1996, pp. 31–44.
12 See Cracraft, *Petrine Revolution,* p. 162; Rovinskii, 1289–90.
13 Frank Kämpfer, *Das russische Herrscherbild von den Anfängen bis zu Peter dem Großen: Studien zur Entwicklung politischer Ikonographie im byzantinischen Kulturkreis*, Recklinghausen, 1978, ill. 157, p. 250.
14 Letter to Leibniz, in Cracraft, *Petrine Revolution,* p. 194.
15 A.G. Cross, 'Did Peter Sit for Kneller at Utrecht in 1697?', *Study Group on Eighteenth-Century Russia Newsletter*, XXVI, 1998, pp. 32–42.
16 1683–84. National Portrait Gallery, London.
17 M.M. Bogoslovskii, quoted in Cracraft, *Petrine Revolution*, pp. 132, 135–6.
18 Original in the Hermitage. See N.V. Kaliazina, *et al.*, *Dvorets Menshikova*, Moscow, 1986, p. 88. *Petr I i Gollandiia. Russko-gollandskie khudozhestvennyie i nauchnye sviazi*, St Petersburg, 1997, plate 89. Both date it 1697–98, without any evidence given for the earlier date. Vasil'chikov, p. 53, points out that Weenix was famous for studies of *nature morte*.
19 Vasil'chikov, *O portretakh,* pp. 43–52, thinks it more like Peter than the 'idealised' portrait by Kneller, who, he supposes, was used to 'flattering lords and ladies'. See also *idem*, 'O novom portrete Petra Velikogo', *Drevniaia i novaia Rossiia*, 3, 1877, 325–6. Cracraft, *Petrine Revolution*, p. 139. He is clad in even more Muscovite-looking dress in an anonymous portrait now in the Rijksmuseum, Amsterdam.
20 M.A. Alekseeva, *Graviura petrovskogo vremeni*, Leningrad, 1990, pp. 23–5.
21 I.G. Spasskii, E. Shchukina, *Medals and Coins of the Age of Peter the Great,* Leningrad, 1974, ills 5, 6.
22 Kämpfer, *Das russische Herrscherbild*, p. 250.
23 For example, J. Stählin, *Podlinnye anekdoty o Petre Velikom*, Leningrad, 1990, p. 37–9.
24 Alekseeva, *Graviura*, p. 42.
25 In the State History Museum, Moscow. L. Rudneva, 'O portrete Petra I raboty Godfrida Skhalkena', in E. Waegemans, ed., *Russia and the Low Countries in the Eighteenth Century*, Groningen, 1998, pp. 172–9, points out that the wig served to 'disguise' the source for the face and armour, that is Kneller.
26 F. Balatri, quoted in Iu. Gerasimova, 'Aria dlia Petra Velikogo', *Nedelia*, 1966, 16.

27 Duc de Saint-Simon, *Memoirs of Louis XIV and the Regency*, quoted in M. Raeff, ed., *Peter the Great Changes Russia*, Lexington, MA, 1972, p. 20.
28 *Bishop Burnet's History of His Own Time*, 4 vols, 2nd edn, Oxford, 1833, IV, p. 407.
29 From I. Grabar', *V.A. Serov. Zhizn' i tvorchestvo*, Moscow, 1913, pp. 248–9. Quoted in S.F. Platonov, *Petr Velikii. Lichnost' i deiatel'nost'*, Paris, 1927, pp. 126–7.
30 J.-G. Korb, *Diary of an Austrian Secretary of Legation at the Court of Czar Peter the Great*, ed. and trans. Count Mac Donnell, 2 vols, London 1863/1968, II, p. 155. See also F.C. Weber, *The Present State of Russia*, 2 vols, London, 1722–23, I, p. 210: 'the Czar himself loves a plain Dress and a small Retinue.'
31 G. Grund, *Bericht über Rußland in den Jahren 1705–1710 (Doklad o Rossii v 1705–1710 gg.)* ed. and trans. Iu.N. Bespiatykh, St Petersburg, 1992, p. 126.
32 Just Juel, 'Iz zapisok datskogo poslannika Iusta Iulia', *Russkii arkhiv*, 1892, 3, pp. 45–6.
33 See, for example, Gregory Freeze, ed., *Russia: A History*, Oxford, 1997. A caption reads: '[it] reveals his impressive physique, European style (no beard and simple clothing) and democratic or plebeian aspect' (p. 79). The description of the Reichel portrait in G.K. Frideburg, *Portrety i drugie izobrazheniia Petra Velikogo: Pamiati 30 maia 1872 goda*, St Petersburg, 1872, pp. 7–8, mentions a wide-brimmed hat and red tie, right hand on hip, the left resting on a cane.
34 Vasil'chikov, *O portretakh*, p. 114; Frideburg, *Portrety*, pp. 7–8; Rovinskii included a large section on historical prints, see nos 471–90.
35 *Polnoe Sobranie Zakonov Rossiiskoi Imperii*, St Petersburg, 1830, VII, 4148, pp. 16–17.
36 See N.B. Golikova, *Politicheskie protsessy pri Petre I*, Moscow, 1957, pp. 145–6; G.V. Esipov, *Raskol'nichi dela XVIII stoletiia*, 2 vols, St Petersburg, 1861, II, p. 64.
37 See E. Shmurlo, *Petr Velikii v otsenke sovremennikov i potomstva*, St Petersburg, 1912, for this and other examples.
38 *Exacter Relation von der ... neu erbauten Festung und Stadt St Petersburg ... von H.G.*, Leipzig, 1713, pp. 66–7.
39 Letter of 11 February, 1724. The cloth was to be packed with young trees ordered for Peterhof and two elephant tusks (Sankt Peterburgskii Filial Instituta Rossiiskoi Istorii, f. 270, d. 106, l. 426).
40 Vasil'chikov, *O portretakh*, p. 96.

41 G.P. Lomazzo, *Trattato dell'arte della pittura* (1598), quoted in Piper *English Face*, p. 33.
42 See Vasil'chikov, *O portretakh*, p. 25. Did the painting survive? It was reproduced in the book *Kniga Marsova ili Voinskikh del* in 1712.
43 See *Kniga Marsova* (1713/1766), p. 71.
44 Alekseeva, *Graviura*, pp. 140–1.
45 Frideburg, *Portrety*, p. 14. See I.D. Chechot, 'Korabl' i flot v portretakh Petra I. Ritoricheskaia kul'tura i osobennosti estetiki russkogo korablia pervoi chetverti XVIII veka', *Otechestvennoe i zarubezhnoe iskusstvo XVIII veka*, Leningrad, 1986, pp. 54–82.
46 T.A. Lebedeva, *Ivan Nikitin*, Moscow, 1975, p. 37, but also attributed to Dannhauer or Caravaque.
47 N.V. Kaliazina, G.N. Komelova, *Russkoe iskusstvo Petrovskoi epokhi*, Leningrad, 1990 (hereafter Kaliazina), ills 134, 136.
48 See 'Sobstvennoruchnyi imp. Petra zhurnal v kalendare 1716 g.', diary of naval manouevres in July–August 1716 (Sankt Peterburgskii Filial Instituta Rossiiskoi Istorii, f. 270, d. 81. ll. 661–76).
49 E. Schuyler, *Peter the Great*, 2 vols, New York, 1984, I, p. vii.
50 Cracraft, *Petrine Revolution*, pp. 197–9; *Portretnaia zhivopis' v Rossii XVIII veka iz sobraniia Ermitazha: Katalog vystavki*, Leningrad, 1987, plate 31; Kaliazina, ill. 111, suggests unconvincingly that Matveev painted 'from memory of a meeting with the emperor'.
51 *Peter I i Gollandiia: Russko-gollandskie khudozhestvennye i nauchnye sviazi*, (exhibition catalogue), St Petersburg, 1996, ills 98 and 101. *Peter de Grote en Holland* (exhibition catalogue), Amsterdam, 1996, no. 236.
52 Vasil'chikov, *O portretakh*, p. 34.
53 Cracraft, *Petrine Revolution*, p. 197; Frideburg, *Portrety*, p. 18.
54 Vasil'chikov, *O portretakh*, pp. 30, 69–74.
55 Frideburg, *Portrety*, pp. 21–2.
56 For a new study, see S.O Androsov, *Zhivopisets Ivan Nikitin*, St Petersburg, 1998. Also, Lebedeva, *Ivan Nikitin*.
57 *Pokhodnyi zhurnal za 1721*, St Petersburg, 1855, p. 73 (3 September).
58 See I.M. Zharkova, in *'Kogda Rossiia molodaia muzhala s geniem Petra': Vserossiiskaia konferentsiia posviashchennaia 300-letnemu iubileiu otechestvennogo flota. Tezisy dokladov*, Pereslavl'-Zalesskii, 1992, p. 76; however, S.O. Androsov, 'O portrete Petra I raboty Ivana Nikitina iz Ekaterininskogo dvortsa-muzeia', *Kuchumovskie chteniia*, St Petersburg-Pavlovsk, 1996, pp. 9–14, and *Zhivopisets*, p. 30, believe that the sea battle portrait was commissioned in 1716 by Menshikov.
59 N.P. Sharandak, *Russkaia portretnaia zhivopis' petrovskogo vremeni*, Leningrad, 1987, p. 65. It is probably this painting which Vasil'chikov, *O*

portretakh, p. 107, described (without reference to Nikitin) as an image of Peter 'close to death'. Androsov, *Zhivopisets*, pp. 77-8, 173-4, retains the traditional attribution, although he does not agree that this was the portrait for which Peter sat in 1721.
60 Androsov, *Zhivopisets*, p. 78.
61 *Istoriia russkogo iskusstva*, ed. I.E. Grabar', 12 vols, Moscow, 1961, VI, p. 304.
62 See S.V. Rimskaia-Korsakova, 'Attributsiia riada portretov Petrovskogo vremeni', *Kul'tura i iskusstvo petrovskogo vremeni*, Leningrad, 1977, pp. 191-9. Sharandak, pp. 60-3, accepts the attribution of the oval portrait, as, tentatively, does Androsov, *Zhivopisets*, pp. 79, 181-2.
63 Kaliazina, ill. 89. Sharandak, p. 59. L. Hughes, 'German Specialists in Petrine Russia', in *The German Lands and Eastern Europe: Essays in Historical, Political and Cultural Relations*, ed. R. Bartlett and K. Schönwälder, Basingstoke, London, 1998, pp. 72-90.
64 *Sbornik*, II, p. 112.
65 Kaliazina, ill. 118.
66 Kaliazina, ill. 217.
67 Kaliazina, ill. 174
68 I.M. Zharkova, 'Zhivopisets petrovskogo vremeni Iogann Genrikh Vedekind', *Soobshcheniia Gosudarstvennoi Tret'iakovskoi Galerei: Drevnerusskoe iskusstvo: Iskusstvo XVIII – pervoi poloviny XIX veka*, Moscow, 1995, pp. 64-78, also quoting *Zapiski Iakoba Shtelina ob iziashchnykh iskusstvakh v Rossii*, Moscow, 1991, I, p. 53.
69 Kaliazina, ills 134, 136. On the popularity of enamels, see Cracraft, *Petrine Revolution*, pp. 219-20.
70 Alekseeva, *Graviura*, pp. 95-7. Another is Fedor Zubov's engraving of their wedding in 1712, in which the consorts sit separately, presiding over separate male and female tables.
71 Kaliazina, pp. 94-5. It was also reminiscent of statues of Louis XIV (by Francois Girardin, which Peter saw in 1717, in the Place Vendôme) and the Great Elector Friedrich Wilhelm in Berlin by Andreas Schlüter. The bronze was not actually cast until the 1740s. Today it stands in front of the Mikhailovskii fortress in St Petersburg.
72 Kaliazina, ill. 75.
73 E. Mozgovaia, 'Obraz Petra I v tvorchestve Karlo Bartolomeo Rastrelii', *Problemy razvitiia russkogo iskusstva*, XVIII, Leningrad, 1985, p. 33; N.I. Arkhipov, A.G. Raskin, *Bartolomeo Karlo Rastrelli*, Leningrad-Moscow, 1964; V.Iu. Matveev, E.A. Tarasova, *Bartolomeo Karlo Rastrelli (1675-1744): K 300 letiiu s dnia rozhdeniia: Katalog*

vremennoi vystavki, Leningrad, 1975. There was also the bust of the tsar 'as was made in ancient times for the Roman emperor' (1724), an iron casting of which was sent as a gift to Frederick IV of Denmark.

74 Kaliazina, ill. 78.

75 N.M. Sharaia, *Voskovaia persona,* Leningrad, 1963.

76 The Soviet writer Iurii Tynianov based the story 'Voskovaia persona' (1929) around this idea, in which the model comes to life amidst the other freakish exhibits in the *Kunstkamera* (Chamber of Curiosities). Oleg Beliaev, who reverentially guarded the figure when it was still kept in the *Kunstkamera* along with other relics of the tsar and his era, pronounced the image to be 'lifelike', except for the fact that the cheeks were slightly sunken, 'because a dead body had no elasticity'. O. Beliaev, *Kabinet Petra Velikogo*, 4 vols, St Petersburg, 1800, I, p. 4. See Friedburg, *Portrety*, p. 29, who states that the model did once have a mechanism which allowed it to stand up and bow.

77 See Kaliazina, ill. 100. For a summary on attribution, Androsov, *Zhivopisets*, pp. 83–4. Vasil'chikov (pp. 97–8) thought it was by Nikitin, but Frideburg (p. 28) declared it anonymous. See also Sharandak, pp. 66–8. The painting was presented to the Russian Academy of Arts by Catherine II in 1762.

78 llustrated in *Portretnaia zhivopis'*, 49.

79 Lebedeva, *Ivan Nikitin*, p. 88.

80 Androsov, *Zhivopisets*, p. 83.

81 See *Pervye khudozhniki Peterburga*, Leningrad, 1984, p. 215.

82 E.A. Kniazhetskaia, 'Nauchnye sviazi Rossii i Frantsii pri Petre I', *Voprosy istorii*, 1981, 5, p. 93.

83 See ills in Alekseeva, *Graviura,* pp. 164–5, by A.I. Rostovtsev and S.M. Korovin.

84 S. Androsov, 'Painting and Sculpture in the Petrine era', in A.G. Cross, ed., *Russia in the Reign of Peter the Great: Old and New Perspectives*, Cambridge, 1998, p. 165. Rudneva, p. 176, mentions over 60 copies of Peter portraits in the Historical Musuem alone, most not on show.

85 See J. Alexander, 'Comparing Two Greats: Peter I and Catherine I', in M. di Salvo, L. Hughes, eds, *A Window on Russia: Papers from the V International Conference of the Study Group on Eighteenth-Century Russia, Gargnano, 1994*, Rome, 1996, p. 44.

Index

Academy of Arts, 270
Academy, Naval, xviii, 96, 121, 146, 148
Academy of Sciences (Russian), 95, 123
Admiralty (St Petersburg), 15, 16, 97, 121–3, 148
Ajbar, 45
Åland islands, 94, 177, 183
Alekseev, M.P., 6, 13
Alexander the Great, xxi, 200
Alexander I, Emperor, 152
Alexander II, Emperor, 31
Alexander Nevskii, Order of, 97
Alexis (Aleksei Alekseevich), Tsarevich, 183
Alexis (Aleksei Mikhailovich), Tsar, 89–90, 131, 143, 232, 251, 252
Alexis (Aleksei Petrovich), Tsarevich, 21, 207, 221, 234, 253, 261
Allan, William, 17
Amsterdam, 8, 96, 113, 211, 257, 259
Anderson, M.S., 177
Andreev, Vasilii, 254
Andreeva, V.G., 263
Andrew, St, Order of, xviii, 98–9
Androsov, S.O., 260, 264
Anisimov, E.V., 130
Anna Ivanovna, Tsarevna, Empress, 43, 148, 181–2, 232, 233, 235, 241
Anna Leopoldovna, Duchess of Mecklenburg, 233
Anna Petrovna, Tsarevna, 181, 227, 235–6, 237
Anne, Queen of Great Britain, 10–11, 41, 74, 109
Apprentices, xix, 71–85, 112
Apraksin, Count Fedor Matveevich, 108, 194, 211, 221

Apraksin, Peter Matveevich, 174
Archangel, 59, 81, 96, 99, 108, 110, 111–13, 133, 142, 166, 191, 194, 197–8, 210, 215–16
Arsen'eva, Varvara Mikhailovna, 240
Ataturk, Kemal, 38, 46
Augustus II (the Strong), King of Poland, 65, 92, 180, 183, 186
Austria, 40, 130, 170, 178, 182
Autocracy, 34, 37
Avvakum, Archpriest, 250
Azov, xxi, 131, 164, 181, 191–3, 194; 1695 war, 167–9; 1696 war, xx, 17, 53, 62, 91, 169–71, 254

Bagger, Hans, 185
Balatri, Filippo, 255
Balk, Fedor Nikitich, 241
Balk, Matrena Ivanovna, 239, 240, 241
Balk, Pavel Fedorovich (Polev), 242
Balk, Peter Fedorovich, 236, 237, 242
Baltic sea, *passim*, 30, 55, 60–1, 165, 177–87, 190–1
Baranov, Antip and Boris, 79, 86
Barrow, Sir John, 14, 140
Barrymore, Ethel, 20
Bassewitz (Bassevitch), H.-F. de, 234
Bazhenin, Fedor, 139
Beale, John, 85
Benbow, Admiral, 135
Bergholz, Frederick Wilhelm von, xxii, 235–7, 239, 240, 243
Bestuzhev, M, 184
Bestuzhev, N.A., 146
Bestuzhev, resident, 81
Betterton, Thomas, 6

Bezsonov, Ivan (John Bassanoff), 77, 82, 86
Bie, Jacob de, xix, xxii, 206–22
Black sea, 16, 53, 131, 165–6, 192–3
Blathwayt, William, 133
Blumentrost, Lawrence, 95, 242
Bogoslovskii, M.M., 8, 14, 130, 135
Bolingbroke, Lord, 105–6
Bothmar, Baron Johann Casper von, 62
Bradlee, John, 146, 146
Brandenburg: see Prussia
Brandt, 257
Britain, influence on Russia, 41, 43, 45, 130–50, 149; comparisons, 125–6; Peter in (1698), xvi, xvii–xix, 3–23, 53–4, 72, 130–2, 146. See also Grand Embassy, Deptford
Bruce, James (Iakov Vilimovich Brius), xviii, 94–5, 99, 144–5, 147, 151, 156
Bruce, Maria Andreevna, 239
Bruce, Peter Henry, Captain, 95–6
Bruce, Robert (Roman Vilimovich), 93–4
Bruyn, Cornelius de, 9
Burnet, Bishop Gilbert, 12, 18, 54, 85, 255
Buturlin, Peter Ivanovich, 219, 239
Buturlina, Anna Semenovna, 239
Butyrskii regiment, 91, 92, 174
Byzantium, 45, 173

Cabinet (*kabinet*), 41
Cabinet of Curiosities (*kunstkamera*), 16, 95, 270
Caithness, William, 98
Calendar, 47, 223
Cambridge, 11, 22–3
Campbell, Colonel James, 93
Campbell, John, 63
Caravaque, Louis, 15, 260–1

Carmarthen, Peregrine Osborne, Marquess of, 54, 60, 132, 134–40, 146–7
Carteret, Lord John, xx, 56, 62–3, 65, 66
Carver, Isaac, 144
Caspian sea, 16, 95, 148, 165, 258
Catherine I (Ekaterina Alekseevna), Tsaritsa, later Empress, xxii, 20, 95, 207, 227–43, 261
Catherine II (the Great), Empress, 44, 46, 48, 197, 199, 203, 228, 270
Catherine, Order of St, 227–8
Catholics, Catholicism, 91
Chambers, John, 92
Charles I, King of England, 133, 250, 251
Charles II, King of England, 252
Charles VI, Holy Roman Emperor, 183
Charles X, King of Sweden, 143
Charles XII, King of Sweden, 19, 65, 182, 183, 184, 186, 194, 200
Charlotte of Brunswick-Wolfenbüttel, Princess, 207, 234
Charykov, N.V., 90
Chebotaev, Rodion and Vasilii, 79, 86
Cherkasskaia, Princess A.I., 236
Chicherin, B.N., 44
Chigirin, 91
China, 46, 113, 165
Christ's Hospital, 146, 156
Clarke, Christopher, 11–12
Colbert, J.-B., 124
Colleges (*kollegii*), 42, 41, 94, 124
Collier, Jeremy, 5–6
Collot, Marie, 16
Colson, John, 145, 156
Colson, Richard, 145
Consett, Thomas, 132
Constantine the Great, xxi, 45, 201
Constantinople, 172, 192–3, 200
Cossacks, 164, 166
Courland, 181–2, 218, 233

Court, Courtiers, xxii, 230ff
Cozens, Richard, 140
Cradock, Joseph, 20
Craggs, James, 65–6, 117, 141
Crevet, Andrew, 147
Crimean campaigns (1687–89), 91, 165, 168
Crimean war, 21
Cross, Letitia, 5–9, 13, 18–19
Crowne, John, 6
Cruys, Cornelius, 218
Culpeper, Edmund, 143–5, 155

Danby, Lord, 136
Dannhauer, Johann Gotfried, 258, 250–1, 262–3
Danzig, 66, 181, 206, 212
Dayrolle, James, 58
Deane, Captain John, 117, 147, 152
Deane, John, 137, 152
Deane, Sir Anthony, 135
Decembrists, 44
Deev, Ivan (John Dejaff), 77, 86
Defoe, Daniel, 4, 73
Demidov, Nikita, 120
Denmark, 40, 46, 58, 107, 110, 181–2, 184, 185, 193, 212, 218, 259
Deptford, xvi, 15, 17–18, 20, 78, 135, 256
Devis, Arthur, 73
Diest, J. van, 12
Dilworth, W.H., 19
Dmitriev-Mamonov, I.I., 233
Dolgorukii, 211, 221
Dolgorukii, Prince Iakov Fedorovich, 174
Dolgorukii, Prince Vasilii Lukich, 107, 182
Dositheus, Patriarch of Jerusalem, 167
Douglas, Gustav Otto, 93
Dress reform, 30, 47, 67
Dubois, Cardinal, 61
Dwarfs, 18, 231, 233, 237, 242

Dysart, Earl of, 80
Edwards, William, 85
Egypt, xx, 46, 47
Ehrenskjöld, Admiral, 16–17
Ekaterina Ivanovna, Tsarevna (Duchess of Mecklenburg), 181, 232, 233, 235, 241
Elbing, 206, 241
Elizabeth (Elizaveta Petrovna), Tsarevna, later Empress, 236, 241
Elizabeth I, Queen of England, 250
Ellis, John, 54, 83
Elton, Abraham, xx, 106, 111
England: see Britain
Erapkin, General P.D., 203
Erestfer, battle of (1701), 92
Erskine, Robert, 95, 97
Estonia (Estland), 179, 190
Evelyn, John, xvii, 135

Faithorne, William, 11
Falconet, Etienne, 9, 16, 258
Farquharson, Henry, xviii, 96–7, 121, 147–9, 157
Fedor Alekseevich, Tsar, 232, 251, 265
Fedor Ivanovich, Tsar, 251
Fielding, Henry, 4–5
Finch, William, 56, 66
Finland, Finnish campaign (1713–14), 109, 110, 178, 182, 184, 213
Follett, George, 134
France, 40, 45, 53, 185, 219, 221, 253, 259, 263
Frederick II, King of Prussia, 46, 48, 94
Frederick IV, King of Denmark, 269
Freeth, Samuel, 75–6
Friedrich of Hesse, 184
Friedrich Wilhelm, Duke of Courland, 181
Friedrich Wilhelm, Great Elector, 269

Gagarin, Prince Matvei Petrovich, 196
Gagarin, Prince Vasilii, 196
Gart(h)side, Samuel, 111–13
Gelder, Aert de, 259
General Regulation (1720), 122
Gent, Jan van, 220
Geography, 118–27 and *passim*
George I, King of England (on the post-1707 principle), Elector of Hanover, 62, 109, 143, 144, 182, 183, 185–6
Germany, Germans, 45, 48, 59, 231
Gierowski, Jan, 186,
Gildon, Charles, 6
Godunov, Boris, Tsar, 119
Golitsyn, Prince Vasilii Vasil'evich, 91
Golitsyna, Princess Anastasia Petrovna, 240
Golovin, Avtamon Mikhailovich, 168
Golovin, Count, 105
Golovkin, Gavrila Ivanovich, 113, 213, 214
Golovkina, Anna Gavrilovna, 239
Golovkina, Ekaterina Ivanovna, 239
Goodfellow, Charles, 108, 187
Gordon, Admiral Thomas, 92, 97, 98
Gordon, General Patrick, 91–2, 96, 151, 163, 168, 169, 171, 171, 173, 174
Gordon, Colonel James, 92, 100
Görtz, Georg Heinrich von, 54, 182–3
Gradovskii, A.D., 44
Grand Embassy (1697–98), xviii, xxi, 3–14, 48, 71, 72, 91, 96, 130–1, 162, 172, 185, 193, 233, 252–3
Grandfather of the Russian Fleet, 132
Greenwich, xvi, xvii, 135

Grey, Ian, 10, 15
Grice, Richard, xviii, 146–7
Grodno, siege of, 93
Grund, Georg, 256
Gwynn, Stephen, xviii, 146–8
Gyllenborg, Count Carl, 105–7, 109, 110

Habsburg Empire: see Austria
Haile Selassie, 47
Haldhife, Edward, 80
Hamilton clan, 89–90
Hamilton, Admiral, 111
Hamilton, Lieutenant Peter, 98
Hamilton, Mary, 99, 241
Hangö, naval battle of (1714), 16, 109, 216, 235, 260
Hanway, Captain Jonas, 105
Harley, Robert, 134
Hay, Captain William, 97
Hayes, William, 83
Hebdon, John, 133
Henry VII, King of England (on the post-1707 principle), 250
Hill, Aaron, 20
Hogarth, William, 80
Holden, Samuel, 82
Holland, 41, 55, 58, 59, 96, 108, 110, 114, 130–1, 134–5, 138–9, 170, 178, 206–22, 259
Holloway, Thomas, 17
Holowczyn, battle of (1708), 100
Holstein-Gottorp, 181–4, 207
Holy League, 162
Holy Synod, 122, 257
Houbraken, Jacobus, 259
Hulst, Hendrik van der, 206
Hume, David, 251
Hume-Campbell, Alexander, 58

Iaguzhinskaia, Countess Anna Gavrilovna, 240
Iflant, General Nikolai, 34
Ingermanland, Ingria, 179, 190
Inglis, Colonel, 93

Index

Iran, xx, 47
Irving, Sir Henry, 20–1
Irving, Laurence, 20
Italy, Italians, 260, 262
Ivan Alekseevich (Ivan V), Tsar, 13, 233, 253
Ivan Vasil'evich (Ivan IV), the Terrible, Tsar, xvi, 89–90, 119, 177, 191, 251

Jacobites, 63–4, 70, 92, 97, 137, 140, 149
James II, King of Great Britain, 20, 137, 140, 253
Jansen, Jacob, 169, 171, 174
Japan, xx, 46, 48
Jefferyes, James, 55–6, 114, 141–2, 184,
Jerusalem, 172
Joseph II, Emperor of Austria, 46, 48
Juel, Just, xxii, 224, 233–4, 256
Julius Caesar, 4–5
Jurass(k)off, Stephen and Tichon, 77, 79, 86

Kahan, Arcadius, 189
Kampengauzen, Baroness, 239
Kalmyks, 170
Karamzin, Nikolai, 21
Karashev, Aleksei and Mikhail, 79, 86
Karelia, 28, 42, 51, 54, 56
Karl Friedrich, Duke of Holstein, 181–2, 184, 185, 237
Karlowitz, treaty of (1698), 172
Kavelin, K.D., 44
Kennedy, Luke, 96
Kenneth, Lord Duffus, 97
Kerch, 172
Kexholm, 59
Khmel'nitsky, Bogdan, 166
Kikin, Alexander Vasil'evich, 217
Kirillov, 122

Klepanitsyn, Fedor (Theodore Klepanicen), 75–6, 81
Kliuchevskii, Vasilii, 164
Kneller, Sir Godfrey, xvii, xxi, 9–11, 15, 18, 253–4, 256, 259, 266
Kokoshkin, F.F., 44
Kondar'ev, Semen (Simon Condratur), 77, 86
Königsberg, 206, 253, 262
Korovin, S.M., 261
Korsakov, 217
Kozmin, Andrei (Andrew Cuzmin), 77, 86
Kramer, Anna Ivanovna, 239
Krekshin, Peter, 10
Kronstadt (Kotlin Island), 16, 97, 194, 211, 234
Kunstkamera: see Cabinet of Curiosities
Kupetsky, Jan, 258
Kurakin, Prince Boris Ivanovich, 81, 107, 108, 111, 114, 116, 141, 182, 206, 221

Land tenure, 39–40
Lange, de, 219
Lebedeva, T.A., 263
Lee, Nathaniel, 7
Lefort, Franz, 12, 92, 161, 167, 168
Lely, Sir Peter, 9
Lermontov, Mikhail, 4
Leslie, Colonel, 93
Lesnaia, battle of (1708), 93, 221
Likhachev, D.S., 250
Lindsay, John, 96
Lithuania, 29, 33, 78
Little, Captain Robert, 97
Livonia (Livland, Lifliandiia), 59, 180, 191
Lobanov-Rostovskii, Prince A.Ia., 265
Loft, Matthew, 144
Lomazzo, Georgio, 258
Longworth, Philip, 240
Lopukhin, Stepan Vasil'evich, 241

Lopukhina, Evdokia, Tsaritsa, 253
Lopukhina, Natalia Fedorovna, 241
Louis XIV, King of France, 179, 185, 269
Löwenhaupt, Count Adam Ludvig, 221
Löwenwolde, Count, 241
Lubok, 264
Lups, Jan, 219–20
Luttrell, Narcissus, 6, 11, 133, 139

Macaulay, Lord, 8
Macclesfield, Lord, 79
Mackenzie, George, 110
Maclise, Daniel, xvi, 17–18, 19, 256
Magnitskii, Leontii, 157
Makarov, Aleksei Vasil'evich, 232
Malborough, Duke of, 6
Mankiev, A.I., 323
Maps, 95, 121ff, 147–8
Margarita Petrovna, Tsarevna, 239
Maria Alekseevna, Tsarevna, 235
Martynov, Fedor (Theodore Martinoff) and Aleksandr, 79, 86
Masquerades, 229, 235
Matiushkin, Mikhail, 134
Matveev, Andrei (painter), 259
Matveev, Andrei Artamonovich, 41, 89–90, 144–5, 223
Matveev, Artamon Sergeevich, 89–90
Matveeva, Evdokia, 90
Mauvillon, Eléazar, 7
Mazepa, Ivan Stepanovich, 166
Mecklenburg, 55, 181–2, 222
Mehmed II, 46
Mehmet Ali, 46
Menshikov, Alexander Danilovich, 8, 115, 144, 152, 180, 186, 205, 207–8, 214, 217, 218, 221, 227, 229, 234, 237, 242
Menshikova, Daria Mikhailovna, 234, 239
Menshikova, Maria, 234

Menzies, Paul, 90–1
Mikhail Fedorovich, Tsar, 143, 164, 251
Miliukov, Pavel, 120
Miloslavskaia, Maria, Tsaritsa, 232
Mines, mining, 150–4
Mironov, Boris, 198
Mitchell, Sir David, 96, 135, 137, 157
Modernisation, xix–xx, 30–1, 36–43, 84, 118 and *passim*
Molchanov, N.N., 130
Monasteries, Alexander Nevskii, 233; Trinity-St Sergius, 91, 233
Mons, Anna, 241
Mons, Willem (William), 229, 236, 237, 241
Montesquieu, C.L. de Secondat, 36
Moor, Karl, 17, 227, 259
Mordvinov, Admiral, 14
Mordvintsova, A.S., 186
Morgan, Francis, 146
Morley, Robert, 105–6
Mottley, John, 7, 19
Moxon, Joseph, 144
Murav'ev, General N.E., 197
Muromtsev, S.A., 44
Musikiiskii, Grigorii, 227, 259, 261

Nantes, Edict of, 12
Nartov, Andrei, 7, 22, 144–5, 152
Narva, 67, 191, 194; siege (1700), xx, 11, 92, 167; siege (1704), 92
Naryshkina, Natalia Kirillovna, Tsaritsa, 41, 90, 232
Nasser, Gamal Abdel, 47
Natalia Alekseevna, Grand Duchess, 234
Natalia Alekseevna, Tsarevna, 240
Natalia Petrovna (2), Tsarevna, 229
Natalia Petrovna (1), 239
Nattier, Jean-Marc, 259
Naval Statute (1720), 97, 132, 152

Index

Navy, Russian, *passim.* See in particular 53–70, 96–8, 105–14, 118–27, 142, 162, 258–9
Nesvitskii, Ivan, 175
Netherlands: see Holland
Neuville, Foy de la, 90
Newton, Sir Isaac, 95, 140
Nicholas I, Emperor, 17
Nicholas II, Emperor, 44
Nikitin, Ivan Nikitich, 260, 262–3
Nix, George, 79–80
Nobles, 31–2. See also Table of Ranks
Norris, Admiral Sir John, xxi, 57, 65, 116
'Northern Crisis', 109
Novikov, Dmitrii (Metrius Navikoff), 77, 86
Noye (Nye), Joseph, 140, 147
Nyenskans, 189, 191, 194
Nystad, peace of (1721), 55, 58, 60, 61, 66, 94, 184, 194, 197, 200, 235, 239, 258

O'Keefe, John, 19
Odoevskaia, Princess Anastasia Ivanovna, 232
Ogilvie, General George, 92–3
Olsuf'ev, Adam Vasil'evich, 243
Olsuf'ev, Matvei, 231, 232, 242–3
Olsuf'ev, Vasilii, 237, 242–3
Olsuf'eva, Anna Ivanovna, 239
Olsuf'eva, Evva (Hollander), 243
Onslow, Arthur, 13
Ordin-Nashchokin, A.L., 191
Osterman, Andrei Ivanovich (Heinrich Johann Friedrich), 183, 215, 225
Osterman, Marfa Ivanovna, 239
Ovsov, Andrei, 262

Pahlavi, 47
Palestine, 25, 27
Paul, Emperor, 199
Pavel Petrovich, Tsarevich (d. 1717), 228
Pavlenko, N.I., 228 , 229
Pelham-Holles, Thomas, 66
Perry, John, 7, 8, 139, 140, 147, 172, 192, 196
Persia, 54, 113, 228–9, 242, 262
Peter Alekseevich (Peter I), the Great, Tsar and Emperor of Russia, *passim*; see also Antichrist; 257; appearance, 9–10, 255–6; character and tastes, xvii, xxi, 186; disguises and pretence, 168, 219, 253, 256; dress, 256–7; drinking, xxii, 14–15, 219–20, 238–9, 233; education, 90; funeral, 263; health, 216–17; hobbies, 155, 256; languages, 137, 224, 234; portraits of, xxi, 250–64; and St Petersburg, 180; ships and shipbuilding, xvii, 18, 131ff, 166, 212–13, 258–9; statues of, xvii, 178, 262–3, 264; titles, 175, 200. See also Britain
Peter Alekseevich, Grand Duke, (Peter II, Emperor), 232, 234, 242
Petty, Sir William, 138
Picart (Pickart), Pieter, 258
Plotnikov, Ivan, 173
Poland, Poles, 53–4, 165–6, 177, 180, 185, 186, 206, 251
Polonskii, 207
Poltava, battle of (1709), 19, 55, 90, 100, 182, 194, 212, 235, 258, 261
Pomerania, 209
Porter, Sir Robert Ker, 15–16
Postnikov, Peter, 144
Potemkin, I.S., 216
Praskovia Ivanovna, Tsarevna, 233
Preobrazhenskoe village, 193, 234, 236
Preobrazhenskii Guards, 171, 174

Prikazy, 42; Estates (*pomestnyi*), 119, 120; Foreign Office (*posol'skii*), 252
Prior, Matthew, 53
Prokopovich, Feofan, 240
Protapopov, Stepan (Stephen Protapopoff), 77, 78, 86
Prussia, 40, 62, 130, 170, 182–3, 184, 207, 218
Pruth, battle of (1711), 21, 180
Pushkin, Alexander Sergeevich, 123, 258

Quare, Daniel, 144

Raeff, Marc, 29
Raguzinski, Savva, [61, 82??] 220
Rastrelli, Carlo Bartolomeo, sculptor, 262, 264
Regulations, 42
Renne, Elizaveta, 15
Reval [Revel] (Tallinn), 67, 95, 106, 167, 194, 207, 218, 232, 235, 261
Reynolds, Sir Joshua, 18
Riga, 59, 60, 67, 110, 180, 194, 206, 207, 212, 218, 232, 235, 241
Rigaud, Hyacinthe, 259
Ripley, William, 140
Robinson, Jacob, 13
Robinson, Ralph, 105–6, 108, 111, 113, 161
Rokotov, Vasilii, 81, 86
Rome, Roman imagery, 173–4, 200–1, 254
Romodanovskii, Fedor Iur'evich, (Prince-Caesar), 219
Rondeau, 232
Rovinskii, D., 252, 263
Rowley, John, 133, 143
Royal Transport (yacht), xvii, 54, 55, 134–5, 137–40
Russia Company (Muscovy Company), 25, 60, 105–6, 111, 116, 132–3, 136

Ruysch, Frederick, 263
Ryswick, peace of (1697), 12

Saandam, 134, 256
Saint-Simon, duc de, 255
Saltykov, Fedor, 107–8
Saltykova, Praskovia Fedorovna, Tsaritsa, 232, 233, 234, 235, 238
Schalken, Godfried, 255
Scheltinga, 209
Schlüsselberg, battle of, 235
Schlüter, Andreas, 269
Schmettau, Wolfgang von, 54
Schoenebeck, Adriaan, 254
School of Mathematics and Navigation, xviii, 82, 96–7, 145, 147–9
Schumacher, J.D., 144
Scotland, Scots, xviii, 17, 89–101
Scott, Benjamin, 146
Scott, James, 62, 63
Selim III, 48
Semenovskii Guards, 92, 171
Senate, senators, 42, 43, 209, 214
Seniavin, Ivan, 243
Serfdom, xx, 31–3, 34, 44
Serov, Valentin, 255
Shafirov, Peter Pavlovich, 178, 185, 214
Shaw, George Bernard, 21–2
Shcherbatov, Prince Mikhail Mikhailovich, 237–8
Shcherbatova, Maria, 15
Shein, Aleksei Semonovich, 171, 174
Shemiakin, Mikhail, 264
Sheremetev, Boris Petrovich, 168, 209, 224
Sheremetev, Vasilii, 131, 174
Ships, Ship-building, 54, 130–58, 172
Shrewsbury, Duke of, 161
Sievers, Jakob, 204
Sisson, Jonathan, 144

Index

Smith, John, engraver, 10–11, 254
Smollett, Tobias, 4
Sophia Alekseevna, Tsarevna, 91, 251–2
Soubeyran, P., 15
South Sea Bubble, 65
Spain, Spanish Succession, War of, 130, 183, 193, 213
Speranskii, M.M., 44
St Petersburg, xx, 189–205 and *passim*. See also, as capital, 186, 209; industry, 152–3; New Rome & New Jerusalem, 173; population, 230; shipyards, 106, 114, 142; trade, 67, 110
Stalin, Joseph, xviii
Stanhope, James, 58, 64, 65–6, 117
Stanyan, Abraham, 63
Staropadsky, Ivan, Hetman of Ukraine,
Stasov, V.V., 11
Stewart, J. Douglas, 9
Stiles, Henry (Andrew), 115, 133, 144–5, 153
Stiles, Thomas, 133
Stirling, Sir Henry, 92
Stratford, Francis, 187,
Strel'tsy, 46, 168, 172; 1698 revolt, 91, 162, 173
Stroganov, 120
Stroganova, Countess Maria Iakovlevna, 232, 240
Struense, 46
Struve, P.B., 44
Sweden, Swedes, 67, 92–3, 94, 97, 108, 162, 177ff, 185–6, 189, 194; influence on Russia, 40, 44, 179; navy, 59–60, 106, 109–10, 180, 255. See also Charles XII and *passim*

Table of Ranks (1722), 40–1, 42, 46, 231
Taganrog, xxi, 172, 192, 194
Tanzimat, 46

Tartars, 53, 164–8, 169
Teplov, Grigorii, 190
Terry, Ellen, 20
Thomson, James, 20, 89
Tichavsky, Tobias, 12
Tilson, George, 62, 64–5, 66
Timmerman, Franz (Ivan), 132, 143
Tobacco, 54–5, 60, 133, 139
Tolstaia, Anna Kirillovna, 234, 240
Tompion, Thomas, 144
Townshend, Charles, 56, 62, 63, 65, 110
Trade, 59–61, 110–13, 178–80, 191–2, 197–9, 207, 210–1, 214–15. See also Archangel, Russia Company, St Petersburg
Tradescant, John, 142
Tret'iakov, Andrei, 83, 86
Trubetskaia, Anna L'vovna, 239
Trubetskoi, Prince, 219
Trumbull, William, 54, 133
Tsaritsyn, 168, 169
Tsereteli, Zurab, 264
Turkey, Turks, xx, xxi, 40, 46, 48–9, 53–4, 63, 130, 161–2, 164, 167, 184, 191–3
Tynianov, Iurii, 269

Ukraine, 110, 166, 251, 253
Ukraintsev, Emel'ian, 172, 202
Ul'ianov, Ivan (John Ulianoff), 77, 83, 87
Ulrika-Eleanora, Queen of Sweden, 109
Urquhart, Lieutenant Adam, 97
Usliumov, Ivan (John Uslumoff), 77, 83, 87
Ustrialov, N., 130
Utrecht, treaty of (1713), 110, 179, 213

Vaksel', Lev Savel'evich, 14
Valuev, N.A., 44
Van Dyck, Sir Anthony, 237
Vanbrugh, John, 4, 5, 6

Vasil'chikov, A., 250, 257, 259, 263
Velde, Willem van der, 9
Venice, 130, 170
Veselovskii, F.F., 76, 83
Viborg (Viipuri, Wybourg), 59, 67, 178
Vienna, 183
Villebois (Vil'bua), Elizaveta Ivanovna, 239
Vinius, Andrei Andreevich, 161, 169
Volga, river, xxi, 172, 192–3, 196, 199
Volkonskaia, Princes Varvara Mikhailovna, 239
Volkonskii, Prince G.I., 217
Voltaire, 23, 139
Voronezh (dockyards), 120, 121, 131, 169–70, 192, 194
Vyshnii Volochok canal, xxi, 196–7

Wager, Sir Charles, 67
Walker, Anthony, 15
Walker, George, 96
Walpole, Horace, 9
Walpole, Sir Robert, 4, 66, 70
Warren, George, 83
Weber, Friedrich Christian, xxii
Wedekind, Johann Heinrich, 261
Weenix, Jan, 254

Weide, Adam, 134–5, 152
Werff, Pieter van de, 254
Whithead, Richard, 144
Whitworth, Charles, 57–8, 59, 60, 63–4, 66, 82, 113, 163, 170, 171, 174, 178, 179, 206, 233, 234
William III, of Orange, King of England, xvi, xvii, 6, 12–13, 18, 133–4, 137, 161
Witsen, Nicolas, 12, 161
Witte, S.Iu., 44
Wittfogel, 36
Wolfe, Sir John, 151
Women, 96, 237–8, 251–2
Woolfe, Sir Joseph, 147
Wren, Sir Christopher, xvii
Wyndham, Willliam, 106
Wynne, Henry, 155

Yeltsin, Boris, xix

Zakharov 15
Zarudnii, Ivan, 257
Zherebtsov, Nikita (Nick Goribsoff), 77, 87
Zotov, Konon Nikitich, 223
Zotov, Nikita Moiseevich ('Prince-Pope'), 218–19, 223
Zubov, Aleksei, 258, 261